THE
LIFE-GIVING MYTH

By the Same Author

KINGSHIP (*Oxford* 1927)

THE LAU ISLANDS OF FIJI
  (*Honolulu* 1929)

THE TEMPLE OF THE TOOTH IN KANDY
  (*London* 1931)

THE PROGRESS OF MAN
  (*London* 1933)

KINGS AND COUNCILLORS
  (*Cairo* 1936)

CASTE, A COMPARATIVE STUDY
  (*London* 1950)

THE NORTHERN STATES OF FIJI
  (*London* 1952)

THE
LIFE-GIVING MYTH
and other essays

A. M. HOCART

Edited with an Introduction by
LORD RAGLAN

Second Impression edited with a Foreword by
RODNEY NEEDHAM

Tavistock Publications Limited
in association with
METHUEN & CO LTD

First published in 1952
Reprinted 1970

Foreword to the Second Impression
© Rodney Needham 1969

Printed in Great Britain by
Butler & Tanner Ltd, Frome and London

SBN 416 50110 9

First published as a Social Science Paperback
in 1973

SBN 422 75580 X

Distributed in U.S.A.
by Harper & Row Publishers, Inc.
Barnes & Noble Import Division

CONTENTS

CHAPTER		PAGE
	FOREWORD TO THE SECOND IMPRESSION	vi
	INTRODUCTION	xi
I.	THE LIFE-GIVING MYTH [1935]	9
II.	FLYING THROUGH THE AIR [1923]	28
III.	TURNING INTO STONE [1948]	33
IV.	THE COMMON SENSE OF MYTH [1916]	39
V.	THE PURPOSE OF RITUAL [1935]	46
VI.	RITUAL AND EMOTION [1939]	53
VII.	THE ORIGIN OF MONOTHEISM [1922]	66
VIII.	THE DIVINITY OF THE GUEST [1927]	78
IX.	YAKSHAS AND VÄDDAS [1931]	87
X.	MONEY [1925]	97
XI.	MODERN CRITIQUE [1929]	105
XII.	IN THE GRIP OF TRADITION [1938]	117
XIII.	SNOBBERY [1936]	129
XIV.	CHASTITY [1939]	139
XV.	SAVIOURS [1935]	143
XVI.	THE AGE-LIMIT [1937]	149
XVII.	CHILDHOOD CEREMONIES [1935]	153
XVIII.	BAPTISM BY FIRE [1937]	156
XIX.	INITIATION AND MANHOOD [1935]	160
XX.	INITIATION AND HEALING [1937]	164
XXI.	TATTOOING AND HEALING [1937]	169
XXII.	KINSHIP SYSTEMS [1937]	173
XXIII.	BLOOD-BROTHERHOOD [1935]	185
XXIV.	COVENANTS [1935]	190
XXV.	THE UTERINE NEPHEW [1923]	195
XXVI.	WHY STUDY SAVAGES?	199
XXVII.	ARE SAVAGES CUSTOM-BOUND? [1927]	205
XXVIII.	FROM ANCIENT TO MODERN EGYPT [1942]	208
XXIX.	INDIA AND THE PACIFIC [1925]	234
XXX.	DECADENCE IN INDIA [1934]	240
	ACKNOWLEDGEMENTS	249
	INDEX	251

FOREWORD TO THE SECOND IMPRESSION

"How can we make any progress in the understanding of cultures, ancient or modern, if we persist in dividing what the people join and in joining what they keep apart?"[1]

The query is typical of Hocart. He had an unorthodox and often unpredictable mind, and his writings were correspondingly unconventional; but all of his work shows this intense concern for the integrity of the evidence, and a clear-eyed scepticism about received ideas. He distrusted the generalisations of anthropology, which he considered ill-founded and prejudicial, and he thought that "endless classifications, definitions and distinctions" had been "the curse of human studies".[2] What counted first of all, in the study of historical materials or in ethnographical enquiry, was to give the point of view of the people under study in their own words, and "not romance about what is going on inside their minds".[3] There is no method for this, but only a resolute habit of "taking nothing for granted".[4] It is largely this attitude which gives the present collection of essays their distinctive and continuing value. They do not teach techniques of analysis or methods of research, and they do not propound empirical generalisations or ambitious theoretical constructs. They are exercises in how to think about social facts and collective representations, examples of a style of thought.

The man whose lucid talents of intellect and imagination are illustrated in these papers had a rather unusual and unfulfilled life. Of French extraction, he was born in Brussels in 1883 and was educated on Guernsey, in the Channel Islands, and at the University of Oxford. After a degree in classics he did ethnographical research with Rivers

[1] Below, p. 23. [2] p. 156. [3] p. 184 [4] p. 28.

in the Solomon Islands, became headmaster of a Fijian school, lectured for a time at Oxford, and then fought as an infantry captain in France in the first world war. After the war he was appointed Archaeological Commissioner for Ceylon, in which country he spent over eight hard years of registration and conservation before he was retired, in 1929, because of ill health. For a few years he worked at University College London, in association with Elliot Smith and Perry, until in 1934 he was elected to the chair of sociology, his only academic appointment, at Cairo. He contracted an infection while doing research in upper Egypt and died in 1939.[1]

In his lamentably curtailed career Hocart had written five books and nearly two hundred minor items, and these made up a substantial testimony to his gifts.[2] But the articles, notes, and letters were dispersed among twenty-five journals and other organs, and this must have much reduced their impact, as it probably contributed also to the neglect of Hocart by the anthropological profession. It was therefore a great benefit to his reputation, and a convenience to the student of culture, that the late Lord Raglan should have brought together into one volume, first published in 1952, the essays which are now reissued. It was fitting that he should have done so, for he and Hocart were men of a very similar turn of mind, bold, curious, and unconventional; and it may prove an incidental advantage if the reader is encouraged by these qualities, as displayed in this book, to make a new appreciation of Lord Raglan's writings as well.[3]

[1] A fuller account of his life, together with an extended estimation of his work, will be found in the introduction to the reissue of Hocart's *Kings and Councillors* (1st ed., Cairo, 1936), edited by Rodney Needham (Chicago: University of Chicago Press, 1970).

[2] See *A Bibliography of Arthur Maurice Hocart* (Oxford: Blackwell, 1967), by the present editor. Additional items are reported in a letter headed "Hocart Bibliography" in *Man* (N.S.), IV (1969), 292.

[3] His works languish at present very much out of academic fashion, and there exists no consolidated listing of them, but it is much to

The present essays, which Lord Raglan so judiciously collected, are still the best introduction to Hocart's thought, and they have proved to possess a marked appeal to students of social anthropology in particular.   One attraction is that a number of the papers deal with matters that students can at once recognise and which they can easily regard as having some humane importance.   Instead of Omaha terminologies, elementary structures, or transformation rules, Hocart's investigations are concerned with topics such as emotion, snobbery, chastity, and money.   More generally, too, they are "always well and simply written and often state useful and important ideas".[1]   Some of the ideas may, it is true, seem pretty wild at first, but this is often because they are formulated in unusual terms, and this in turn is because they were conceived by an unusual mind.   For the most part they are well worth taking seriously, and if to do so demands a special conceptual effort the reason is likely to be that the real worth of conventional notions is being subjected to an acute and uncomfortable scrutiny.

Hocart's radical approach is well typified, also, by the kind of question that he asks.   For example, on cultural change: "When we come to think of it why should a custom develop in any direction at all?   Why should it not stay as it is?"[2]   Or, on the origin of monotheism: "Once man has come to believe in gods, why should he ever cut their number down to one?"[3]   There is a view, of course, which declares that these are not proper questions for a social anthropologist, and that to trace "the development of human institutions", which is Hocart's main intention, is an outmoded antiquarianism that can never be of scientific value.   Radcliffe-Brown's opinion, which still has its pro-

---

be hoped that they will be made the subject of a serious account in the future.
  [1] George Caspar Homans, review of *The Life-giving Myth*, in the *American Anthropologist*, LV (1953), 747.
  [2] p. 140.   [3] p. 71.

ponents, was indeed that speculative enquiries of the kind were pseudo-history and as such "not merely useless but worse than useless".[1] This crude form of positivism, however, is itself invalidated by a narrow definition of evidence, according to which only direct testimony counts, and by a scientistic conception of the means, namely sociological laws, by which social phenomena are to be explained. At any rate, the ideal of a natural science of society has not been substantiated by empirical work rigorously done, least of all by Radcliffe-Brown himself, and the case against conjecture (an odd interdiction, after all, in an academic discipline) rests today on little more than textbook pronouncements, and the authority of these is readily enough gauged.

An essential point is that problems of historical reconstruction such as Hocart deals with are of quite inescapable interest, and if they are abjured by social anthropologists they will not thereby lose their intriguing appeal to intellectual curiosity or their claims to scholarly attention. They are certainly significant, and in principle they are open to circumstantial resolution. The real question, therefore, is how they should be tackled, and it may then be asked whether there could well be any precept more sane and practical (not to say "scientific") than this: to formulate "a theory that will explain all the variations in the simplest possible way without invoking any processes that have not been observed".[2] At very least, the search for origins and past developments may restore a sense of reality to minds deluded by the empty forms of structuralism, and an intelligent speculation about hidden connexions can revive imaginations dulled by the banalities of latter-day functionalism. Hocart's own investigations, as represented here, are admittedly summary, and they are couched in plain and

[1] A. R. Radcliffe-Brown, *Structure and Function in Primitive Society* (London: Cohen and West, 1952), p. 3; cf. John Beattie, *Other Cultures: Aims, Methods and Achievements in Social Anthropology* (London: Cohen and West, 1964), p. 8.

[2] p. 170.

unpretentious words; but it is not only scholars who may profit from the reminder that "important results are sometimes achieved by simple means, and . . . the production of an encyclopaedia is not necessarily the prelude to far-reaching conclusions".[1]

The Life-giving Myth has been out of print and unavailable for some years, but an increasing attention to Hocart's work has provided the occasion for a new impression. In particular, the masterly essay on kinship systems (Ch. XXII), one of the most incisive and cogent ever written on the topic, would alone have justified a reissue; and it is to be expected that many who have been impressed by that paper[2] will be pleased to be given the opportunity to become better acquainted with the mind of its author.

This impression reproduces the text of the first, the only changes made being the correction of misprints and other minor points. The single change of sense is on page 234, where the meaningless "Southerns" has been amended to "South Indians". The chief editorial improvement has been the addition, at pages 249–50, of a bibliographical list of the places of first publication instead of the undated indications originally given.[3] The dates which are provided here make it more plain, moreover, that the papers span a period of twenty-one years, from 1916 until 1939, the year of Hocart's death. The reader will thus be able to place them in relation to the currents of anthropological thought, and should better appreciate their connexions with each other.

R. N.

University of Oxford

---

[1] p. 66.
[2] It has been reprinted in *Readings in Anthropology*, ed. by E. Adamson Hoebel *et al.* (New York: McGraw-Hill, 1955), pp. 189–93, and in *Kinship and Social Organization*, ed. by Paul Bohannan and John Middleton (Garden City, N.Y.: Natural History Press, 1968), pp. 29–38.
[3] The source of one paper, Ch. XXVI, has not been traced.

INTRODUCTION

A GLANCE at the chapter-headings might suggest that the subjects of these essays are largely unconnected, but this is not so; there are themes which run through nearly all of them.

Of these the most important is that myth, ritual and social organisation are inseparably connected and cannot profitably be studied apart.

Myth, owing chiefly to the use made by the Latin poets of the Greek myths, most of which had become function-less survivals, has persuaded scholars that myths are merely a strange kind of fiction, but for all illiterate peoples, and many that are not illiterate, myths form the most important part of their traditions, not merely justifying and sanctifying all their rites and customs, but being regarded as in themselves a source of life.

Whether myth is older than ritual we cannot say, but ritual as we know it everywhere depends on myth. The myth purports to tell how the ritual originated, and a knowledge of it is necessary to enable the officiant to perform the ritual correctly and thereby obtain the life which the ritual, if correctly performed, confers.

Social organisation is, in its origins, organisation for the performance of ritual, and it too depends on the myth, which purports to tell how the kingship, classes, castes, clans and so on came to be instituted, and thereby explains and justifies the part which they play in the life of the community. The two most important institutions are, or were, the divine kingship and the dual organisation. The worship of the divine king is the earliest religion of which we have any certain knowledge. It is still wide-spread to-day, and beliefs and customs derived from it are almost universal. In the dual organisation a community is divided into two groups; members of one group initiate, marry and bury members of the other group, and are, as the Fijians say "gods to one another". This idea will seem strange to those who regard gods only as remote and awe-inspiring beings, but to savages, as to the ancients, a god is any person or thing with power to confer life. The dual organisation has left in Europe but a few traces, such as team games, and is found in full operation only among savages. This might suggest that it is older than the divine kingship, but this need not be so. Unlike the divine kingship, it can hardly flourish except in communities so small that everyone can stand in some sort of relationship to everyone else.

The second thesis which runs through these essays, or many of them, is that all ritual consists in investing some person or thing with power, in order that he or it may be able to confer life, and by life is meant health, wealth and fertility. This is done by performing certain acts and at the same time reciting the myth, which tells what the originator of the rite is supposed to have done. No person or thing has any power to confer life until they have been invested with it in this way. There is no such thing as "nature-worship". Nobody ever worshipped the sun simply as the sun; it is worshipped only when it is deified, that is to say when a god has been put into it. The same applies to idols of all kinds, including stones and trees, and to human beings. Those who speak of nature-worship are ignorant of the theory and practice of ritual, which are everywhere the same.

In his *Kingship* Hocart showed that the ritual of the divine kingship, in whatever part of the world it is performed, is not merely similar, but is the same ritual. He reverts to this fact here and also shows that the ritual of initiation is the same in North America and Central Australia, that the sister's son has the same strange ritual functions in South Africa as in Fiji, and that there are many curious resemblances between the customs of the Hindus and those of the Melanesians. Since none of these rites and customs can reasonably be supposed to arise naturally in the human mind, their distribution must be due to historical causes.

The last essay is on a different subject. It is a contribution to the study of the causes of decadence. We do not know why civilisations decline, but we do know that it cannot be because nations grow old. Nations are not organisms, and civilisations are sometimes rejuvenated, as individuals never are. Hocart studies the problem in so far as it is concerned with India and Ceylon.

In conclusion I should add that Hocart contemplated a book of this kind and there is a draft list of essays among his papers. Some of these, however, I have been unable to identify and this book contains many which he did not mention. These have been obtained through references in his writings, and searches in likely periodicals. I should like to acknowledge the help which I have received in the latter task from Miss B. J. Kirkpatrick, Librarian to the Royal Anthropological Institute. I have omitted many papers which seemed to me too long or too technical, and have made cuts in some of the papers which I have included.

RAGLAN

CHAPTER I

The Life-giving Myth

THE Renaissance was an age of discovery: it discovered not only America, not only the course of the earth round the sun; it discovered Greek art and literature, and with them the Greek myth. It first discovered the myth, however, in the pages of Ovid, Virgil, Horace, and other late authors who had long since ceased to believe in their myths; who looked upon them merely as stories which it is good form not to question, or still more as good themes for literature, mines of plots and poetic ornaments. Far from bearing any relation to real life, those myths were rather a welcome escape from reality. The poet, jaded by the bustle and drabness of the city, found an idyllic retreat in the company of nymphs and dryads, ranging the sylvan wildness of his fantasy.

In the course of their explorations, the scholars of the Renaissance came upon Sophocles and Æschylus, but they interpreted the drama of those times as they interpreted their own stage—that is, as literature enacted. They failed to realise that the early Greek drama, literary as it might be, was still something more than mere theatricals, that it was still part of the national ritual, and that the myths were enacted not merely to amuse, but because the religion demanded it. This connection of drama with religion is now generally known, but it is doubtful if it is generally realised—to most scholars the Greek drama remains literature pure and simple.

The Renaissance scholars learned from Homer, the greatest of all mythologists. He was still earlier than Æschylus, nearer to the supposed age of myth. Homer's legends, however, are not Greek but Achæan. They

were traditions passed on to the Greeks by their predecessors, just as the Arthurian Cycle was inherited by
the English from a pre-Roman civilisation. The *Iliad*
and the *Odyssey* are as Greek as the *Morte d'Arthur* is
English. It is as vain to look to Homer for the primitive
significance of the myth as it would be to seek it in
Malory.

Thus everything conspired to persuade classical scholars
that the myth is nothing but the creation of fancy, a
kind of Midsummer Night's Dream. Several centuries
of purely literary studies have allowed this conception of
the myth to drive in its roots so deeply that it cannot be
uprooted in a day. These roots have now spread beyond
the Græco-Roman world into the East.

When the nineteenth century extended the sphere of
discovery to Biblical lands and beyond, scholars naturally
approached the myths of Egypt, Babylonia, and India in
the spirit they had imbibed from their classical studies.
They picked out the myths from the texts in which they
were embedded, arranged them into neat systems of
mythology after the fashion of the Hellenistic mythologists, and threw the rest of the text on the rubbish-heap.

In India they had this excuse, that they first became
acquainted with its literary language, Sanskrit, in its late
form, which is known as classical Sanskrit, and with
works belonging to the centuries after Christ, contemporary
with the break-up of the Roman Empire or even later.
This classical form was a dead language carried on from
a bygone civilisation, just as the Middle Ages continued
to write Latin after the fall of Rome. With this dead
language the Hindus inherited a store of dead myths.
Some of these made good copy, so they were worked into
epics such as the *Ramayana* and the *Puranas*. These
epics did not assume their present form till long after
Alexander had opened the gates of India to Hellenistic
influence—not till that influence had had time to permeate

Indian art, as it began to do in the first century of our era. It is difficult to believe that Indian literature escaped an influence which affected Indian art, and that the Indian epic owes nothing to Greek models.

If we want to study the real myth, not the literary exercise; if we want to know what the myth meant for mankind at large, not merely for poets, we shall no more look to the *Ramayana* or the *Vishnu Purana* than we should to Milton's *Paradise Lost* or Morris's *Earthly Paradise*. We shall turn rather from the Sanskrit which was a dead language to that Sanskrit which was still a living language about 800 B.C., a thousand or more years earlier. That Sanskrit, known as the Vedic, has a very different character from the classical. Instead of being florid, ingenious, subtle, unreal, it is simple and direct, because it wants to convey information and not to display literary skill. It is concerned not to amuse or astonish, but to impart that knowledge which is necessary for the welfare of the community.

What really mattered to the ancient Brahman, as it does to us and to everyone, was life; not merely keeping alive, but living well, enjoying bodily vigour for the full span allotted to man. To have life it is necessary to have food, to escape sickness and the wiles of enemies, and to have stalwart sons. The Brahmans' quest, in the words of the first hymn of the *Rigveda*, is "wealth day by day, prosperity, glorious and abounding in heroes". They pray to Soma to save them from disease, to prolong their years as the sun the days of spring, not to abandon them according to the desire of their foe, to save them from disease.

Life depends on many things—on food, and food on rain and sun; on victory, and victory on skill and strength; on unity, and unity on wise rules and obedience. An elaborate ritual grew up designed to secure all these good things, all that contributed to the full life. This ritual

became so elaborate that its accurate transmission became
more and more difficult. One or two recitals were not
enough; it had to be committed to memory, and its
meaning and its reasons had to be expounded in lesson
after lesson. Schools were formed, and from those
schools issued the voluminous literature which is known
as the *Brahmanas*.

The ritual was then, as it is now, based on precedent.
If we have a king to crown, our experts search the old
records to find out exactly what was done at previous
coronations so that it may be done again. So the ancient
Indians had their precedents. The sacrificer—that is,
the man who presided over the ritual and was consecrated
by it—acted strictly according to precedent; his actions
merely repeated the actions of other sacrificers before
him.

Thus one of the highest sacraments consists in setting
up a mound, or altar, which represents the world. The
sacrificer by the ritual recreates the earth, but he recreates
it by the same methods as were used by the original
creator. That original creation is first recalled in a myth,
which tells how the creator brought forth foam from the
waters, earth from the foam, and gradually built up this
world. Then the sacrificer proceeds to imitate the
creator by dissolving clay in water and producing foam
from it, and then moulding the clay into a pan of which
the bottom is the earth, the lower part of the sides the air,
and the upper part the sky.

The relation of myth to ritual is best illustrated in the
words of the Indian ritualist himself. He discusses the
rite of carrying round Soma, the plant from which the
sacrificial beverage is made. Soma is a god and a king,
as well as a plant and a drink. He is carried round the
way of a clock, or of port after dinner. Our authority
states the precedent on which the rite is based in these
words: "The gods and Titans strove together for these

worlds. They strove for this eastern quarter. The Titans beat them thence. They strove for the southern quarter. The Titans beat them thence ". And so they went fighting round the compass until "They strove for the north-eastern quarter: they were not beaten thence. This quarter is the unconquerable . . . the gods said, 'Through our lack of a king they beat us: let us make a king'. They made Soma king. With Soma as king they conquered all the quarters. He who sacrifices has Soma as king. They place Soma on the cart as it stands facing east: he conquers the east. They carry him round by the south: thereby he conquers the southern quarter," and so on round the compass. The conclusion is : "By Soma, the king, he conquers all the quarters who knows this." The text, like most of these texts, is not easy to understand. It is tempting to put the blame on the writer, or rather the lecturer (for there were no written records in those days); but we must remember that he was addressing his own people in his own time and not record-ing the facts for the scholars of a foreign race centuries later. He could assume in his hearers a knowledge which we lack, a knowledge of the ritual, the social organisation, the nature of the gods. He had only to expound the points which were not known to his pupils. The general outlook he could take for granted, but unfortunately we do not possess that outlook; we must reconstruct the principles from the applications which follow one another with deadly monotony.

We gradually come to realise that the sacrificer's object is to get control of the whole world—not temporal but ritual control; that is, he seeks to bend the forces of Nature to his will, so that they may produce plenty for him. The world consists of four quarters, and whoever secures the parts secures the whole. So the sacrificer proceeds to the supernatural conquest of the parts in a fixed order, that in which the sun goes round the earth.

To succeed, however, a divine king must lead them. That king is the plant and god Soma, under whose leadership they take one quarter after another. That is the proper way to proceed, because once upon a time the gods under the leadership of Soma recovered one by one the quarters which they had lost to their rivals, the Titans, in the ritual struggle for power over the world. As the gods did, so must the sacrificer, for the sacrificer and his acolytes represent the gods. It is necessary that he should know the myth which describes how the gods succeeded.

The slaying of the serpent Vritra by Indra is the chief myth in Vedic mythology, as is the slaying of the monster Tiamat by Marduk in Babylonia. It is the theme of hymn after hymn to the glory of Indra, the wielder of the thunderbolt. "He slew the serpent; he released the water; he split open the bellies of the mountains. He slew the serpent lying in the mountains. Tvashitri fashioned his whizzing thunderbolt. . . . His missile the Bountiful One (Indra) grasped, and smote that first-born of serpents. When, Indra, that smotest the first-born of serpents, thou didst set at naught the enchantments of the enchanters; then bringing forth the sky, dawn, at that time thou foundest no enemy at all. Indra slew Vritra . . . with his thunderbolt, that great weapon of death. . . . Indra, the lightning armed, is the king of him that goes and him that rests and of tame cattle; yea, he rules over busy men as felly encloses the spokes." Such is the myth as told, or rather alluded to, in the *Rigveda*. One incident is omitted in this hymn but is referred to in others. All the gods deserted Indra except the Maruts, a troop of gods who are the gods of the commons, as Indra is the kingly god. This episode is thus commented on by the teacher: "Indra, being about to slay Vritra, addressed all the deities 'Do you support me, call to me.'—'So be it' they said. They ran forward with intent to slay him (Vritra). He realised: 'They are running to slay me.

Come, let me terrify them.' He snorted at them. At his snorting all the gods ran away in haste. The Maruts did not foresake him, saying: 'Smite, Blessed One, strike, put forth thy might.' Speaking these words they supported him. . . . He realised: 'These are indeed my friends; they showed me love. Well, let me give them a share in this litany.' He gave them a share in this litany. Up to that time both litanies were entirely his." Such is the myth which explains why in the time of the lecturer the officiating priest "draws a draught of Soma for the Maruts, sings an introductory stanza for the Maruts, sings a hymn for the Maruts". The reason is "wherever with them he (Indra) conquered, wherever he showed strength, by mentioning that also, he (the sacrificer) makes them fellow-drinkers of Soma with Indra". It comes to this, that in the course of the ritual of which Indra is the central figure an offering is made to the Maruts, a cup of Soma is drawn for them, a hymn sung, and a formula recited, of which the verses are still preserved for us in *Rigveda*, iii, 47, 4. The reason for this practice is given in the myth, that whereas all the other gods deserted Indra in his fight with the Serpent, the Maruts stood by him. It was apparently not a physical struggle, and the Maruts did not support him by force of arms, but by calling out to him, by uttering a formula which strengthened Indra. Therefore, the Maruts have a share in Indra's ritual. Now, as we are told over and over again, the sacrificer impersonates Indra. He has therefore to act exactly as Indra acted. He re-enacts the myth, even to giving the Maruts a share in the libations and the litanies.

In other words, the myth is the precedent. It is not a tale told to while away an idle moment, nor is it a deep and purely inquisitive speculation about the phenomena of nature. Nothing could be less entertaining than these myths, and nothing could shed less light on the sun, the moon, and the beginning of the world. A collection of these myths would, as the reader can see from these specimens, be dreary in the extreme; that is why they do not figure in the handbooks of Indian mythology, or only in a readable abstract. The handbooks confine themselves to those myths which approximate to the Greek standard, such as make good stories and have artistic possibilities. The rest is swept into the dustbin as so much nonsense spun by the subtle brains of priests. Such is the artistic tyranny of Greece, that scholars reject what is dull because it is real, because it pursues the prosaic needs of food, health and progeny, while they write volumes on gorgeous but unreal fantasies.

Let us stick to the real myth, the myth which has some relation to the serious business of life. It is a precedent, but it is more than that. Knowledge is essential for the success of the ritual. "He who knows this," ends our first myth, "conquers all the quarters." That is the conclusion which winds up myth after myth. The myth itself confers, or helps to confer, the object of men's desire—life.

The myth is necessary because it gives the ritual its intention. Thus if the Maruts are to have a share in the sacrifice along with Indra, it is necessary that the sacrificer should know the myth which relates how they earned that share. "Thus by mentioning that also," says the text, "he makes them share in the Soma drink with Indra."

It must be remembered that the sacrificer impersonates Indra; he is Indra; but only because he has been made so. His consecration has made him Indra. The myth reciting the exploits of Indra has to be recited in order that his action may be identified with the actions of Indra in the past. It is not sufficient just to carry Soma round the compass. The myth has to make it plain what the intention of this circumnambulation is; just as it is not sufficient for a Christian pilgrim to walk round the church; he must have the intention of repeating the stations of the cross. The mere sightseer gains no religious merit.

Knowledge is essential; it bestows life. The following passage will illustrate this. "For this death is the same as the year. For he destroys by nights and days the life of mortals; so they die. Therefore he is death. He who knows this death to be a year, death does not destroy his life by days and nights before old age. He attains the fullness of life." Thus he who knows the nature of death, that it is the same as the year which by the passage of time wears out our lives that man holds the secret of a long life. This knowledge protects him from an untimely death. This teaching is turning towards the mystical, but there is no doubt that it goes back to the old idea of Nature's dying with the year. When the attention of a leading Assyriologist was drawn to this passage from the *Satapatha Brahmana* he at once remarked, "Why, that is the Babylonian conception of the dying year".

The increasing mysticism of the later ritual books lays increasing stress on knowledge. Towards the end of that period we are told, "Here there is this verse, 'By knowledge they ascend where desires are vanished: thither sacrificial gifts go not, nor ascetics without knowledge;' for indeed he who does not know this does not attain to that world either by sacrificial gifts or by austerities; but to them who know this does that world belong." In the end knowledge alone is necessary. But knowledge without works cannot long survive; cut off from the realities of the world it pines away and degenerates. The myth was doomed once it became divorced from action. About 500 B.C. movements took place which broke away from the old mythology. Of these movements Buddhism is the most famous. It taught salvation by knowledge, but not by knowledge of the myth: it was knowledge of psychological causes. Like our modern psychological schools, it taught that one can escape pain and sorrow by tracing them to their source. It substituted scientific knowledge for the traditional knowledge which had lost contact with reality.

At first sight it looks as if Buddhism had killed the myth. It has its legends, but they are scarcely alluded to in the ritual, nor are they represented as necessary to a higher life. On the contrary, knowledge of causes is constantly insisted upon as the only way. But tradition is stronger than consistency, and survives underground when it is driven from the surface. If we look beneath the surface we find that the myth is not dead after all. When the writer was following the services at the Temple of the Tooth in Kandy the officiating priest volunteered the information that the service was repeating the daily attendance on the Buddha while he was alive. Thus the Buddhist ritual is really re-enacting the life of the Master. It is the Buddhist legend enacted for the welfare of the people.

Such is the Indian point of view. That point of view is regarded by those bred in Hellenic traditions as being merely a priestly view. The fantastic story, it is argued, is the original myth, the myth of the people, and the ritual myth is a distortion of it by priests obsessed by ritual. The priests, we are told, appropriate everything. They pluck the fresh blossoms from the free-growing fancy of the people, to wither in the musty atmosphere of their pedantry. We may ask how it is, then, that in India the ritual myth antedates the epic myth by many centuries. But the way of chronology is long and full of pitfalls, so we will leave it and go to the people to find out what is their conception of myth.

In Malaysia we are still in the Indian world. The Malay may be nominally a Mohammedan, but his culture is basically Hindu. "In all his undertakings—marriage, cultivation, hunting, or whatever they may be—he seeks success with the aid of charms. A striking feature of these charms is that they involve the recitation of, or at least allusion to, a myth. Whatever he is dealing with, the Malay has to recall its mythical origin. Thus in mining tin, when a tin-bearing stratum is reached, the ore is addressed in these words:—

> "Peace be with you O Tin-Ore,
> At the first it was dew that turned into water,
> And water that turned into foam,
> And foam that turned into rock,
> And rock that turned into tin-ore, . . ." [1]

and so on. You will recognise at once the Indian creation myth as it was told and enacted some 800 years B.C. But the Malay miner is not renovating the whole earth; he is only preparing tin-ore for extraction, so he is content to trace the genealogy, the ritual genealogy, of tin only; to affiliate it to the earth, and thereby derive the efficacy of his rite from that of the all-embracing ritual of creation. He is tracing but one line of the ritual pedigree, leaving the wider issue of general prosperity to the priest.

Such spells of origin, as we may call them, abound in the Finnish epic of the *Kalevala*. They are also used in Assyrian medicine, as is shown by the following incantation for toothache:—

"After Anu made the heavens, the heavens made the earth, the earth made the rivers, the rivers made the canals, the canals made the marsh, the marsh made the Worm. The Worm came weeping unto Samas, unto Ea, her tears flowing: 'What wilt thou give me for my food, and what wilt thou give me to destroy?'. 'I will give the dried figs and apricots.' 'Forsooth what are these dried figs to me or apricots? Set me amid the teeth and let me dwell in the gums, that I may destroy the blood of the teeth, and of the gums chew their marrow. So

---

[1] W. Skeat, *Malay Magic*, p. 265.

shall I hold the latch of the door.' 'Since thou has said this, O Worm, may Ea smite thee with his mighty fist.'" [1]

This spell also harks back to the creation, and tacks a particular disease on to it. The trouble can be controlled if you know its pedigree.

The same intimate relation between the myth and the affairs of everyday life is to be seen in Fiji, far from India and from the region of professional priests. There we find the striking fact that almost every myth is told in connection with some custom still observed. A myth may be told to explain why two tribes behave towards one another with insolent familiarity, call each other names, play tricks on one another, and even take each other's property. Thus two clans belonging to two different tribes in the North-east behave in this manner on account of their gods Wandamu and Vanda. "Wandamu went to beg for wild yams to plant. Vanda baked them, wrapped them up, and gave them to Wandamu. When Wandamu unwrapped the yams they were already cooked. Vanda came to beg for bananas; so the god of Nandaranga (Wandamu) brought in suckers of wild bananas from the jungle (not true bananas). Vanda planted them, and when they grew he found that they were not true bananas." To this day if the descendants of Wandamu go over to visit those of Vanda they are feasted on the very kind of yam over which Vanda tricked his friend.

Why do the people of Tunuloa and Nanggelelevu hoax one another? Because "Nggala, the god of Tunuloa, went to climb a palm stealthily. But Matawalu, the god of Nanngelelevu, had eight eyes, and saw him, and was angry, and drove him away, throwing after him coconut husks which became reefs between Nanngelelevu and Tunuloa. This is the cause: they are cousins because they abused one another and stole."

At bottom the idea is the same as in India; the living

[1] R. Campbell Thomson, *Proc. Roy. Soc. Medicine*, xix, p. 59.

behave as the ancestors did. The gods cheated and abused one another, and therefore their descendants must do the same. This behaviour is not so obviously connected with life as it is in India, yet the connection is indicated. The plundering of one clan by another is done under divine sanction. The guests on arrival must make an offering to the chief of the village, the representative of the gods, before they can exercise their right to kill the fowls and pigs of their hosts. If they neglect to do this, the ancestor-god makes them ill, as he does any one of the hosts who resents being plundered. The whole procedure is of a ritual nature.

Custom and myth are as inseparable in Fiji as in early Brahmanic India, though the myth does not play quite as important a part in Fiji as in India. This is not because they have no priests, for we find the ritual myth in full vigour in Australia.

In his manner of making a livelihood the Australian Black has not progressed beyond Palæolithic man. He does not sow, nor spin, nor make pots, and lives from hand to mouth by hunting or digging up anything which can be eaten. The struggle for life admits of no specialisation, and no one is released from the quest of food in order to devote himself to study and speculation. There are no priests.

Let us take, for example, a tribe exposed to the most rigorous conditions in the arid central lands. The Aranda have their myths. What do these myths tell us? Not the doughty deeds of heroes, nor the movements of sun and stars. They are content to tell how the divine ancestors went about performing ceremonies, which they taught, and which are still performed. These myths are inexpressibly dull to us; there is none of that free flight of fancy which is supposed to be characteristic of myths. It takes some determination to wade through Strehlow's collection of myths. But that is not, of course, how the

Aranda approaches his myths; he does not collect them, but learns them in connection with the ceremonies to which they relate, exactly as did the Brahman's pupil. They have for him a practical value which makes them interesting; they show him what to do and explain to him why. They contain the precedents for the ceremonies which help him to live.

These ceremonies take up a great part of his time. We wonder how he can spare so much from the struggle for existence to spend on mere ceremonies, but he does so precisely because existence is so uncertain; the ritual aims at abolishing that uncertainty. There are years when kangaroos, snakes, grubs, yams are scarce, when pools dry up. The ritual is designed to ensure a supply. For every species of food there is a ceremony which causes its increase. That ceremony's performance by an ancestor is recorded in the myth. The performers of to-day reproduce the ancestor's actions and like him, identify themselves with the animal or plant to be increased. The myth is not merely a record of the precedent, but has to be chanted in the course of the dance to make it effective. On the other hand, the complete myth, as told to candidates for admission to the ritual, includes a detailed account of the ritual. Thus the myth is part of the ritual, and the ritual part of the myth. The myth describes the ritual, and the ritual enacts the myth. However much the Aranda myth may differ from the Brahmanic in detail, the principle is the same: the myth completes the desired identification of man and god for the attainment of plenty. It is not then the barren pedantry of the Brahmans which created the ritual myth, since it is found where there are no priests.

Aranda myth and ritual are so closely interwoven that it would seem impossible to separate them. But our chief authority, Strehlow, had, like all of us, been brought up on Greek and Roman mythologies. In order to conform to the traditions of the schools he cut all the descriptions of ritual out of the myths, and inflicted on his reader a wearisome succession of meaningless tales. We should never have known how closely the two were associated had he not in the course of one myth remarked: "Here follows a detailed account of the ritual which I shall reproduce elsewhere."[1] How can we make any progress in the understanding of cultures, ancient or modern, if we persist in dividing what the people join and in joining what they keep apart?

The connection between myth and life is even more apparent in North America. Each Winnebago clan has its own myth of origin, and if a man wants to know the myth he asks "about the origin of life". He is not told it without more ado, as one might be told a tale, but has to give gifts or make offerings. It is not that the teller is rapacious, for he will not tell it even to his own children without a fee. "It is really essential", a Winnebago told Mr P. Radin, "to make a gift". The applicant is told the myth not publicly but alone. "Then", says an informant, "the old man who had the right to tell the origin myth would announce subsequently at a feast that he had told So-and-so the story of the origin of the clan, and that if any one wished to be told of the same he should, in the future, when he himself had died, go to this young man and ask him in the proper way. Remember . . . that before everything else it is the duty of an individual to try and learn the origin of his clan." We may ask why it should be anyone's duty to learn a story. Because it is not a mere story, but a thing of power that affects the fortunes of the individual and of the clan. "My son", said an old man to an applicant, "he who makes the most gifts obtains life therewith." Then again, when the gifts are complete, "My son, you have done well—very well indeed—for the life that I am to give you is holy; and as

[1] C. Strehlow, *Die Aranda etc.*, I, i, 20.

you know, even if one was loved very much, they would not tell him this merely because they loved him, as it is holy". The origin myth cannot be told at a public feast "because it is sacred and it must not be told without proper ceremony, for the telling of it would injure the individual". [1] Thus the myth itself confers life, but it cannot be recited without ritual; the two are inseparable.

Nowhere is the oneness of myth and ritual more evident than it is among the Yuma of California. Professor Daryll Forde tells us that "The mourning ceremony of the Yuma is intended to perpetuate a ritual taught by the first men after the death of the creator Kukumat. . . . Informants constantly tend to refer to the activities of the existing rites in terms of the original. The Yuma, in other words, does not clearly distinguish between the mythological foundation and the existing ceremonial; and it was at first a matter of some difficulty to analyse and compare the two". [2] The Yuma funeral then is enacted myth, the myth a description of an ancient funeral. The Yuma myth is not a fable; it is a record which claims to be true, a claim which there is not the slightest reason to question. If the Yuma now perform certain funeral rites, why should not their forefathers have done so? If the present rites agreed in every detail, we might suspect that the myth was merely modern practice ascribed to the past, but there are slight differences. The only possible explanation is that the rites have changed since the time to which the myth refers.

The word "myth" has unfortunately become synonymous in our language with fiction. That is merely because it has become associated with a certain set of traditions in which we do not believe. It is necessary to go back to

[1] P. Radin, 37th Rept. Bureau of Amer. Ethnology, pp. 226 ff.
[2] C. D. Forde, *Univ. Cal. Publ. in Archæology and Ethnology*, vol. xxviii, p. 214.

the original meaning—a sacred story; a story which purports to be true, and which research shows more and more to be true in essentials, however much the details may become distorted. It is a true record of ritual.

This ritual myth is not the result of perversion by that bugbear of scholars, an all-grasping priesthood. It flourishes most where there is no professional priesthood, because there it remains in contact with reality. The myth detached from reality can continue to exist only in a society which is itself divorced from reality, one which has such a reserve of wealth that it can afford to maintain an intelligentsia exempt from the pursuit of bare life, and free to devote all its energies to intellectual play, to poetry, and to romance. Such a society was the Hellenic, which had so far freed itself from mere labour that it had come to despise it. For Aristotle leisure, not work, was the end of a gentleman's life. The myth fell in with this conception of life; it was no longer required to give bare life, but to adorn it with the elegancies of fancy.

When a myth has reached that stage it is doomed. Myths, like limbs, atrophy and perish when they no longer work. The allegories of Plato were really an attempt to save the myth by giving it something to do. They were put to the task of educating the mind and improving morals. But allegories did not save the Greek myths; they went down before the impact of new myths which came out of the East and promised life to the believer.

To understand the animus of the early Christians against the pagan myths, which seem to us so beautiful and harmless, we must put ourselves in their position. The Roman peace had made daily bread secure, but it had raised mental problems such as always arise where there is idleness and luxury. The old myths and traditions had become the playthings of dilettantes, and the contemporaries of St Paul, like the contemporaries of the Buddha five hundred years earlier, found no help in them. They turned to those Eastern myths which offered them not health of the body, as their own myths had once done, but health of the soul. The Christian myth offers quite a different life from that conferred by the earlier myths. A Christian may be lusty and strong yet, in the words of Malory, "dead of sin"; he may be sickly, like St Paul, yet living in faith.

Here is a mighty revolution in mythology, but it was not accomplished in a day. We are all familiar with the story that Constantine, the night before the battle with Maxentius, "was admonished in a dream to inscribe the shields of his soldiers with the *celestial* sign of God, the sacred monogram of the name of Christ; that he executed the commands of heaven; and that his valour and obedience were rewarded by the decisive victory of the Milvian Bridge". "There is still extant a medal of the Emperor Constantius where the standard of the labarum is accompanied by these memorable words, BY THIS SIGN THOU SHALT CONQUER." [1] This is a standpoint little removed from that of the Vedic kings, or the Fijian chief who turned Christian because the missionary succeeded in healing his daughter.

Such a conception of the myth was still very strong in the Middle Ages side by side with the Pauline. We read in the *Morte d'Arthur* of how King Evelake was about to do battle with the Saracens, but was told by Joseph son of Joseph of Aramathea that he would be defeated and slain unless he accepted the new law. "And then he showed him the right belief of the Holy Trinity, to the which he agreed with all his heart; and there this shield was made for King Evelake, in the name of him that died upon the Cross. And then through his good belief he had the better of King Tolleme."

The Christian conception of life as a better life, and of the myth as bestower of that better life, is not as anciently

[1] Gibbon's *Decline and Fall*, ii, 30.

established among us as we may be inclined to imagine. We need not go many centuries back to find our fore-fathers still clinging to a myth not very different in intention from that of the Vedic Indians and Winnebagoes, the myth which confers health, wealth and victory over one's enemies. Perhaps if we look up from our books and glance round we may find that myth still flourishing. Many years ago the writer obtained in Heidelberg a "Powerful prayer whereby one can protect and preserve oneself from bullet and dagger, from visible and invisible enemies, as well as from all possible Evil". This preamble is followed by the myth: "Count Philip of Flanders had a man who had forfeited his life, and as the executioner (tried) to execute him, no sword could cut him. Then the Count was astonished and spoke, 'How am I to understand this? Show me the thing and I will grant thee thy life.' Then he showed him the letter, and copied it out (for him) together with all his servants." There follows an enumeration of all the evils against which this letter is a protection: law suits, loss of master's favour, childbirth, nose-bleeding and so on. The charm itself is full of allusions to the Christian myth: "Make their weapons as weak as the blood which Jesus Christ shed on Mount Olive" and so on. Every effect of the charm is linked up with some episode in the Christian story, which is made to confer not spiritual benefits or a mystical life, but life as the Winnebagoes, the Fijians and the rest understand it.

Thus we have gone round the world in search of the true myth, the myth that is bound up with life. We have found it in India, beneath the Southern Cross, in the plains of North America. We have come home to find it at our door.

3

CHAPTER II

Flying Through the Air

THE commonest miracle in Buddhist literature consists in flying through the air, so much so that the Pali title *arahat* (saint) has given rise to the Sinhalese verb *rahatve*, which means to disappear, or pass instantaneously from one point to another. In fact, flying through the air has become the test of *arahatship*.

In Sanskrit literature standing in mid-air is a sign by which one can tell a god from a man. A passage in the story of Nala, familiar to Sanskrit readers, tells how Damayanti, at a loss to distinguish her lover from the four gods who have assumed his form, in her distress prays to them to reveal their divinity. They do so by appearing "sweatless, unwinking, crowned with fresh and dustless garlands, and not touching the ground".

This is an instance of how saints have assumed the attributes of gods, or rather, perhaps, how both derive their attributes from a common source.

But why this insistence on the power to float in the air? Why is it made a test of divinity or sainthood? It has been taken for granted that if there are supernatural beings, they must move in the regions of the air instead of treading the earth. This idea may seem natural because we are used to it, but when we come to think about it there is no reason why they should not walk as we do, swim in the sea, or burrow in the earth. If we are to explain customs and beliefs we must begin by taking nothing for granted, and must seek to explain not by vague phrases such as "poetic fancy" or "primitive thought", but from precise causes from which the custom or belief derives by logical necessity.

In this case I use as my basis the fact that over a large part of the world kings are divine; they are impersonations of gods, and as such have all the attributes of godhead, so that what is true of the god is true of the king and *vice versa*. I have no hesitation in believing that all the varieties of this doctrine, wherever they occur, are derived from the same original source, since the area which they cover is continuous from West Africa to Peru, and, even if it were not continuous, the doctrine itself is sufficiently strange and elaborate to warrant us in denying that it could have sprung up independently in various parts of the world.

Now in some of the countries where the kings are divine it is the rule that the king must never touch the ground. Instances are cited by Sir James Frazer from Uganda, Persia, Siam, Japan and Mexico.[1] The case which gives us most support comes from Tahiti, and I will therefore quote Ellis's account in full: "Whether, like the sovereigns of the Sandwich Islands, they were supposed to derive their origin by lineal descent from the gods, or not, their persons were regarded as scarcely less sacred than the personification of the deities. . . . The sovereign and his consort always appeared in public on men's shoulders, and travelled in this manner wherever they journeyed by land. . . . on these occasions (changes of mounts) their majesties never suffered their feet to touch the ground. . . . The inauguration ceremony, answering to coronation among other nations, consisted in girding the king with the *maro ura*, or sacred girdle, of red feathers, which not only raised him to the highest earthly station, but identified him with their gods. . . . This idea pervaded the terms used with reference to his whole establishment. His houses were called clouds of heaven, the glare of torches in his dwelling was denominated lightning, and when people saw them in the evening as they passed near his

[1] *Golden Bough*, x, pp. 2–4.

abode, instead of saying the torches were buring in the palace, they would observe that the lightning was flashing in the clouds of heaven. When he passed from one district to another on the shoulders of his bearers, instead of speaking of his travelling from one place to another they always used the word *mahuta*, which signifies to fly; and hence described his journey by saying, that the king was flying from one district of the island to another." [1]

In Tahiti, then, it was literally true that gods were distinguished from ordinary men in that they never touched the ground, but that they flew where others walked. But the reason why the king-god did so was not the reason given by the people themselves; they said that if he touched the ground the spot would become sacred and could never more be used for profane purposes. This may have been a good reason for keeping up the practice, but the other observances I have cited leave no doubt that its true origin was that the king of Tahiti, like the kings of Egypt, of the Hittites, of Ceylon, of various parts of India, and of Japan, to name a few among many, was the sun-god, or the son of the sun-god, and as such lived in clouds, flashed lightning, and moved above the earth. The king of Tahiti, like other Polynesian kings, was called Heaven, and at death, or transference of a king's temporal power, it is said, "The sun has set". The king was called "the man who holds the sun" or the "Sun-eater".

"You have produced evidence", some will object, "from Mexico, from Tahiti, from Uganda, from everywhere except India, from which the argument set out. You have not attempted to show us in existence in India the custom which is supposed to explain the miracle of flying through the air." But if my suggestion is right, we ought not to find the custom practised in India at the time and in the place where the Nala episode or any

[1] W. Ellis, *Polynesian Researches*, ii, pp. 348 ff.

writing containing the same belief was written; for as long as the gods are to be seen being carried about so that their feet may not touch the ground, this mark of kingship or divinity cannot be regarded as a miracle. But when the custom has been forgotten, the perfectly true statement that gods used to move above the earth can be interpreted only in the sense of a supernatural manifestation. In Sanskrit and Pali literature therefore we cannot expect to find more than echoes of this old custom, indications that it once existed. We seem to have such an echo in the history of Sona as related by Spence Hardy.[1] From his childhood Sona never put his foot to the ground, because he had a circle of red hairs under the sole. He had only to threaten to put his foot down to bring his servants to reason, as they dreaded that so much merit should thus be lost. Now this wheel on the sole has been shown by Senart to be originally an emblem of the Sun-god.

Others better read than I may find more traces of this very ancient custom; I should just like to make one suggestion for what it is worth. Both Egypt and Polynesia have a story that heaven and earth were in close embrace until a hero came and parted them by lifting up the heavens. May not the custom of not allowing the solar king to touch the earth have some connection with this myth?

Let us leave that aside, however, and return to the other attributes attributed to gods by the *Mahabharata*: "sweatless, unwinking, crowned with fresh and dustless garlands". If we explain one attribute by the theory of divine kingship, we must explain the others in the same way, but I confess that these puzzled me until I happened to read in the *Golden Bough*[2] the following passage taken from Kaempfer's *History of Japan*: "In ancient times,

[1] *Manual of Buddhism*, p. 254.
[2] *Golden Bough*, iii, p. 3.

he (the Mikado) was obliged to sit on the throne for some hours every morning, with the imperial crown on his head, but to sit altogether like a statue, without stirring either hands or feet, head or eyes, nor indeed any part of his body, because, by this means, it was thought that he could preserve peace and tranquillity in his empire". I mentioned at the outset the parallelism which exists between kings and saints, but we should hardly have expected that it would extend even to the contemplative exercises of Indian ascetics.

Our enquiry, then, has had results which bear out the opinion which I have often expressed before, that myths and miracles are reliable history, not of events but of customs. No one will be surprised at this who has busied himself with collecting oral tradition and knows how anxious the average man is to get his tradition faultlessly accurate. If he goes wrong, it is not that he alters what he has heard, but that he misconceives its meaning because the custom which was the clue to that meaning is lost.

CHAPTER III

Turning Into Stone

COUNTLESS are the legends which end in someone's being turned into stone. Familiar examples are Niobe in Greece, and Lot's wife in Palestine, and such stories are told in many other parts of the world, including Britain. The motive is known as far afield as Fiji, where it is said that a man and woman taken in guilty intercourse were turned into stone.

And not only men but things can be turned into stone. On the south-eastern coast of Ceylon are two long rocks, exactly similar, and shaped like inverted canoes. They are said to be the canoe in which the god of Kataragam came to Ceylon; a Vedda tried to chop it up, but it turned into stone. There is a parallel case in Fiji where two small long rocks are said to be a mythical canoe.

Ceylon and Fiji have another close parallel. Not far from Galle there is a rock said to be the lace pillow of a demoness, and in Lakemba I have seen a rock called the Beating-board of the Two Ladies, who are dreaded goddesses or demonesses. It is not definitely stated that the pillow and beating-board were turned to stone, but it must be inferred.

How are we to explain these legends? Are we to be forever content with mere words? I fail to understand what satisfaction anyone can find in labelling a legend "ætiological". Newton's theory of gravitation is ætiological, and so is this essay, but does it help us to tell us so? No; neither would it help us to understand the origin of these myths, even if they were ætiological. What we want are the mental mechanism which has come into play and the antecedents on which it has worked.

Perhaps we may find a clue in the legend of the Jetavana-rama in Ceylon.

The Jetavanarama is one of the colossal topes of Anuradhapura built in the fourth century of our era. Popular tradition has interchanged it with another colossal tope built earlier and lying to the north of the city. The southern entrance is flanked on either side by a guardstone consisting of an upright slab on which is carved the image of a guardian deity. The images are those of pot-bellied dwarfs, such as are in great favour with Buddhist artists. They probably date from the tenth century.

The following legend is told about these two stones. "When King Muhasena was depositing the hair relic of the Buddha, the body relic, together with a portion of the girdle relic four fingers long, brought by Sakra, King of the Gods, the fact was reported to the two great Bhairava who kept guard at the door of the Jetavanarama in India. Those two came and asked 'Who has the power to establish in Ceylon a Jetavanarama called after that in India?' They were brought into the presence of King Muhasena by his attendants. When the king had seen them, the anger that was in the minds of the two Bhairava passed away, and they made obeisance to the king. Then, on the king's asking them why they had come, they told him the whole affair, concealing nothing. Thereupon the two Bhairava were told by the king that in the same manner as they mounted guard at the Indian Jetavanarama, so they ought to mount guard at this Jetavanarama, till the end of the Buddhist religion. Receiving his commands, they carved two stone images in likeness of themselves, fixed them by the south porch, and departed to India after promising, 'In our absence, whoever unfolds his troubles in presence of our statues, by our look those troubles will all pass away.'

"They dwell in India. Whoever explains his troubles

or any other matter in the presence of the two images that are here, by their look he will find consolation. The Bhairava, when they come to Ceylon, stay near the images."

The relation between the spirits and the stones is so vague that when I first heard the legend mentioned in conversation through an interpreter, I understood that the two spirits had actually been turned into stone. What happened in my office in 1928 may very well have happened elsewhere in prehistoric times. It cannot too often be insisted that it is in ourselves and our neighbours that we must study the processes which build up legends and dogmas, and not in ideal constructions such as "primitive man". Such ideal constructions may be all very well in mathematics, but in history we are dealing with actual specimens. The present instance shows that a story in which spirits are somehow attached to stones may become one in which their bodies are actually turned into stone.

It may be objected that my mind was already familiar with petrification, and thus a predisposition existed which was not present in the minds of the first men who ever conceived such a process. The objection, though not fatal, is quite a proper one, and I set myself to find out whether the less theologically-minded among the people might not misconceive as I had. From my cleaner, who reads a great deal, I got the following version. Muhasena was preparing to build the Jetavanarama. As the building went on, they came at night and broke it up. When the king was informed, he went armed with a sword. He went and seized them both and bound them on the berm (not with ropes, he explains, but "by word"). Having bound them he gave them work to do. From the time he seated them until now, he made them stay there at the door. The Bhairava deities have become like those images. They are a guard for the Jevatanarama. Now they are even as stones. They have been cut out of stone and placed there. The two Bhairava deities are indeed those stones.

As the narrative stands, anyone might be excused if he believed these stones to be the deities. The narrator actually says that they are. Yet he certainly does not believe the Bhairava to have been turned into stone, but that they have been attached to the stones in some manner which he, like my other informants, could not define. The connection is such that the images are spoken of as if they were identical with the deities, and they are treated as if they were.

Between identity and equivalence a very fine line is drawn, so fine that at times it is invisible. The Hebrew prophets and the Puritans could not see it. They accused idolators of worshipping stocks and stones. It is, however, very doubtful whether idolators, when they think out their actions, ever address their worship to stones, but rather to something that resides in the stones. They have only themselves to blame, however, if their subtle distinctions escape observers. If Isaiah and Milton could imagine that the senseless stone was itself the god, others may have imagined the same thing long before.

It is quite possible, then, that legends of turning into stone have arisen out of the belief that the double or the powers of a person can be fixed in some material object, and out of the custom of acting on that belief. We know that statues can be cut out of stone and become not merely symbols of the god but actual receptacles of divinity. Before the invention of sculpture, rude stones were used. They are still used by Indian coolies and villagers in Ceylon. Sometimes the rude stones have figures drawn on them in line to show what god they stand for. Some people, like the Fijians, have never known anything but natural rocks, and idols of natural rock are common throughout the world.

It should be remembered that a statue is not *ipso facto*

a god; a ceremony is required to make it divine. In Ceylon it is the ceremony of putting in the eyes. As regards natural stones I have no evidence, but since the villagers of Ceylon set up stones for worship, it is clear that these stones become representative of the god, and have not always been so. I have no instance from Fiji of a stone's being installed as an idol. All the stones were traditional and seemed to represent an earlier stratum of gods, the land gods as opposed to the later war gods. The worship of stones had thus ceased to be a living force, and was merely a survival. Ancient stone gods continued to be worshipped, but no new ones were created, just as in France the old titles of nobility continue to be used, but no new ones are awarded.

There are thus stones reputed to be gods. They were once made into gods by a ceremony of consecration. That ceremony has fallen into disuse, and the only fact remembered is that a certain god who did certain things was fixed in a certain stone, and the god is now represented by the stone; in fact, he is known only as the stone. It might well be inferred that somebody changed the god into a stone.

In the case of sculpture such an inference is excluded by the knowledge of sculpture. In parts of Ceylon the art of sculpture is still practised, and those familiar with the art know that a statue was not originally a god. But were the art of sculpture lost, as it has been over most of Ceylon, the belief might well arise that a statue was a person turned into stone, or that a god had made the statue to represent some person. We are not very far from such a belief when we find a dam of the tenth century ascribed to demons, and irrigation channels said to be the work of giants. There can be no knowledge of the construction of natural features such as rocks, and there is nothing to prevent their being regarded as the petrified bodies of remote personages.

Legends of petrifaction can thus ultimately be traced to a rite which has played a great part in human history, the rite of consecration. The idea at the bottom of this rite is that by the performance of certain acts and the utterance of certain words, a man or a thing can be made into the receptacle of certain intangible entities the original nature of which is still obscure, but which at one stage take shape as spirits. By consecrating a man you make him the vessel of a god; you can make him for all practical purposes equivalent to a god. You can do the same with a tree or a bird, a statue or a boulder. Why should stones have been particularly used for this purpose? The one constant obsession that runs through all the ceremonies of divinisation is the desire for immortality, and stones are of all possible receptacles the least likely to decay.

I hope that this essay may convince folklorists of the futility of mere collections of legends and tales. Either the stories must be accompanied by a commentary by the narrators themselves, or we must have sufficient knowledge of their theology to understand what they have in mind. For the narrator is accustomed to addressing his own people, and they can fill in the gaps and so grasp his meaning.

CHAPTER IV

The Common Sense of Myth

WE shall not quarrel with anyone for postulating a mythopeic man, with a mind differently constituted from ours, if firstly he remembers that it is a hypothesis to be proved, and secondly if he shows that some such hypothesis is required.

The first condition has not been observed; mythopeic man was no sooner imagined than his existence became a dogma. We are assured that such a man did exist (exactly when and where is not specified), and mythologists tell us of all his habits and ways of thought as if they had met him. They state that he was addicted to composing poetry about the sun, the moon and the dawn; that he had a curious twist for hiding the most common-place facts under piles of metaphor; that to him the sky was "not an airy, infinite, radiant vault, but a person, and most likely a savage person", and so on. So completely is the hypothetical nature of all this lost sight of, that the mythologist never looks for proof, but accepts it as fact.

In the second place, does this hypothesis explain anything? You cannot explain psychological, any more than physical, phenomena unless there are unvarying laws. To deduce the peculiarities of myths from the minds of their makers, or the mind of the myth-maker from the myth, we must agree that his mind worked according to such laws. But then we are no better off than we were before, because mythopeic man was invented precisely to account for the apparent absurdities and vagaries of myths. They were all put down to minds dominated by an incalculable element called fancy. This is to give up all explanation; it is to strike at the root of science by admitting chance or caprice.

We cannot hope for success unless we are ready to abandon guesswork and brace ourselves for patient research. But patient research alone will not suffice if the point of view is too narrow. So long as an anthropologist confines himself to myth or religion his material will be a useless congeries of facts, because the key to nine-tenths of it will be outside his province, but if we cast our net wide enough to embrace the whole culture, the clues required to explain a myth are unlikely to escape us.

A common type of myth in Fiji explains the name or features of an island or piece of land by a story telling how a god or divine ancestor brought it from somewhere else. Here is a specimen.

The island of Kambara is little more than a rocky plateau; there is one small area of good soil where all the cultivation is done, but the island abounds in a species of tree called *vesi* which is highly prized as timber. These features are accounted for in the following myth: "There was a spirit called Mberewalaki, the god of Kambara. He went to Oloi, a village of Viti Levu, to beg for soil to bring to his own island. He got soil and besides a *vesi* tree, which he intended to use as a digging-stick when he began to plant in the soil he was taking home. He brought these home, and returned to Oloi for a second lot. As he was approaching Kambara on his way back, he found that the people were baking the soil he had brought on his first journey. He was standing on the reef when he saw the smoke go up. He flew into a passion and hurled the soil at Kambara so that it fell anyhow, all in a heap, instead of being properly laid out."

The mythologist as a rule dismisses such a myth with the remark that it is ætiological. If he means by that that it is *used* to explain why Kambara has little good soil but many *vesi* trees, the myth is ætiological; but that does not explain its origin. If by ætiological he means that it was *invented* to explain these facts, we demur. If a theory purports to explain certain facts it does not follow that it was invented to explain them. It is quite possible that the theory existed before and was merely applied to new facts, or facts that had not attracted attention. This is an everyday occurrence in science; new phenomena are brought into relation with old theories, and if the theories do not fit they are slightly modified. We have no reason to think that other races proceed otherwise, and until it has been proved that their ways of thought are entirely different from ours, we must assume that they are not. What should we do if we wished to account for the geology of Kambara? Should we simply sit down and let our fancy play about the subject, and dream out some theory? If we were to do that there would be no end to the theories we might think of. We might imagine that the soil had been let down from heaven, as the Rotumans believe of a certain rock on their island; it might be the decayed body of some monstrous animal; or a great tidal wave might have washed the soil away except at one spot; or that soil might be a certain kind of rock decomposed, and so on. We should have a large number of possible explanations, and no means of deciding which was the right one. That is not what we do; we assume existing geological theories to be true, and approach the island of Kambara with them in mind. Straightway all these fanciful explanations are rejected, and we are left with a small number which a careful examination reduces to one. In explaining things then we are driven to certain conclusions by our preconceptions and the facts we perceive in their light.

If the Fijians think as we do, what will they do when they begin to take an interest in the physical peculiarities of their island? They will approach the problem from

the point of view of their preconceptions, and since these
are different from ours the result will be different. They
take little interest in matters purely physical; their
physics reduces itself to a few theories about the action of
heat and cold on yams, and some weather lore. These
can throw no light on the geology of Kambara. Their
culture consists almost entirely of what we should call
the humanities, and it is therefore to human agency that
they will most readily look to explain why there is so little
good soil in Kambara and so many *vesi* trees. We must
turn to their customs and beliefs if we are to understand
the myth.

There is no word in Fijian meaning "to create". The
nearest equivalent is *mbuli*, which means to form, shape,
fashion, or make into a heap. The noun *veimbuli* is used
for the installation of a chief. Each tribe inland in Viti
Levu has a tradition of an original installation that took
place at a certain spot; at this ceremony they piled up
earth to make the sacred foundation of the tribe—that is,
the foundation of the chief's or the god's house. A kava
ceremony was held, the effect of which appears to have
been to install the chief as representative of the god.
When the chief died he was buried in the foundation.
When the people migrated they dug up some of this soil
and took it with them to their new home, where they
proceeded to shape it (*mbulia*) into mounds. They also
carried their tribal tree to plant in the new home. These
ancient and sacred customs underlie the description of
how the divine ancestor formed Kambara. The tendency
to explain the topography, fauna and flora of a place by
the action of a divine ancestor, however, did not originate
in Fiji, for it is found all over the Pacific. It is therefore
evident that it was brought into the Pacific from outside,
and there received numerous local applications. Here is
another myth of the same type.

The Rotumans relate that Raho embarked with his

people in Samoa, taking with him two basketfuls of sand. They sailed westward till it seemed good to them to stop. They then began strewing the sand to make an island, but, reflecting that they were too near the setting sun where cannibals live, they moved eastward leaving an unfinished island, the present reef of Vaimoan. The second time they made Rotuma, but as some of the sand had been wasted at Vaimoan they had enough for only a small island.

If this is an ætiological myth it is a bad one, for Rotuma is not at all sandy; it has beautiful black soil. But if we examine the myth in the light of the installation ceremonies, this detail becomes intelligible. We saw that in Fiji the sacred land was the burial-place of chiefs. There they bury in earth, but in Rotuma they bury in sand, and one objection a Rotuman has to dying abroad is that he would be buried in dirty earth. It is quite consistent therefore that they should carry sand, not earth, about as the sacred soil. This interpretation of the myth is confirmed by two memorials: one is a large rock on the beach on which Raho and his people are said to have made kava when they first landed (we saw that kava was a part of the installation ceremonies); the second is a circular foundation close by, which is said to have been erected by them and which is sacred (we saw that sacred foundations were made at installations). We are further told that they appointed a Lord of Rotuma. Putting all this together we may conclude that this is another case of "shaping the land"—that is, of explaining topography in terms of ceremonies.

To us Europeans, who have our heads full of geological and biological preconceptions, it may seem impossible that rational beings could hold such theories as that islands were fished up from the bottom of the sea, as in Polynesia, or brought in baskets. We are so used to our preconceptions that we think them self-evident and do not realise what centuries of tradition they represent. Banish these traditions from our minds, and there is nothing impossible in a divine ancestor's carrying tons of earth across the sea. If a chief is endowed, like Fijian and Polynesian chiefs, with miraculous power—*mana*—there is no limit to what he can do. Personal agency is still a favourite mode of explanation in Fiji; it is still suggested at times that the gods or the ancestors caused this or that feature of the land. But these suggestions are advanced as cautiously as an unsupported hypothesis by a modern scientist; their author is fully aware that there is no evidence for them, and they die without passing into tradition because myth gives no warrant for them.

Another class of legends is common in Fiji and the neighbouring islands. It tells of great competitions between the natives of some place and a party of visitors. These competitions always include an eating contest; each side is obliged to eat all that the other provides and leave nothing over under forfeit of life. "That is a common motive in fairy tales", you may say: "It is just the kind of thing a story-teller would imagine to amuse his hearers." But that explains nothing, and I was puzzled till I came across the following. Before quoting the writer, a Fijian, I must explain the custom of *vei-tambani*. The word means "related as one half to the other", and is applied to intermarrying tribes or clans. *Veitambani* may abuse and plunder one another and there are some other features. "*Veitambani*", says our writer, "are lands that vie with one another; it is a disgrace for them that the report should go about that they are weak in war, or have been overwhelmed in exchanges, or in eating or in drinking. It is better that they should die in battle than run away; it is better that they should be poor than that their contribution to the exchange should be small; it is better that their bellies should burst than that food and water should be left; all must be eaten up."

One of these tales is about ten brothers who go to Tonga to marry ten sisters; they and the Tongans with whom they hold a contest become *Veitambani*.

We are all familiar with the fairy tales in which a king's daughter will not laugh, so her father promises great rewards to whosoever makes her laugh. The Alaskan Eskimo, we are told, hold comic dances on the first day of their inviting-in feast, and if during the day's dances the home tribe can make the visitors laugh, they can ask of them anything they wish. I do not wish to argue that the fairy tales referred to above are derived from this Eskimo feast; it is a long way from Alaska to Europe. It is possible that the custom and the tales have a common origin, but we have no connecting links. The custom, however, seems to be fairly widespread; in Rotuma at the making of a state mat the women seize men as prisoners and keep them till they are ransomed, but if one can make them laugh he must be set free. Of course they try not to laugh. This custom may have some connection with the Eskimoan, but again we lack evidence.

A notable example of a custom explaining a myth is the killing of the divine king. It is all the more notable because the custom was postulated to explain the myth, and was afterwards found to be a fact. We cannot therefore be far wrong if we follow a clue which in one case has given such brilliant results and has achieved the highest ambition of science, which is prediction. I have no wish, however, to add another hasty generalisation to the swarms that infest anthropology. My object is to show that if, instead of running through a myth and then guessing its origin, we make a systematic cultural study of the region in which a myth is found, it will explain itself.

CHAPTER V

The Purpose of Ritual

THE one man who is never consulted as to the theory of ritual is the one who performs that ritual. Is he not likely to know better what he intends than the man who has never carried it out, and who probably scorns it in his heart?

"That is all very well", I may be told, "but if you ask a savage why he baptises or is baptised, marries or is married, buries or is buried, he will either be completely nonplussed or else give you some rationalisation which is quite worthless." I leave aside the question whether any rationalisation is worthless. I think most psychologists would be very careful to note rationalisations as clues to the motive which is rationalised. But let that be. What I object to is the suggestion that the savage (if there is such a thing) stands quite apart in his inability to answer a difficult question fired at him without warning, or in his tendency to invent an explanation when he has not got one on the tip of his tongue. Put the same sort of question to any intelligent European, ask him why he goes to church, why he had his children christened, and he will either have no answer, or else invent some reason which we can show is not the right one.

Before going and observing strange peoples let us try our hand at home. Ask an English mother why her children have been christened, and, taken by surprise, she will have no answer; she may even be annoyed at the suggestion that a holy rite might be dispensed with. It is almost blasphemous to require a reason, for it is the command of God. If you have patience, however, some day when talking of family matters she may tell you how her baby was not at first baptised, how it was always ailing, how the grandmother insisted that an unbaptised child never thrives, how eventually the child was baptised, and has thriven ever since. She has unwittingly given away the fact that she believes baptism to promote life. Yet if you ask her the direct question the very next day she may be just as unable to answer as before.

We can reach our goal more quickly and more certainly if instead of questioning the million we go straight to the expert. He has been trained to answer such direct questions. He will tell you that baptism confers "supernatural life". Ask him about the last sacrament and he will answer that it "helps to restore the health of the body, if it be profitable for the salvation of the soul".[1] In other words, it gives supernatural life for a certainty, and bodily life perhaps. Another mine of theory lies in the ritual texts, the hymns, prayers, and sacred books. If we hunt among baptismal hymns, for instance, we shall find requests for the gift of "undying life". We shall not be content with texts, we shall go and see and listen. Let us go to Albert Hall on an Easter Monday and see the crowds surging to seek life, bodily and spiritual; let us listen to the preacher explaining how that life is to be gained.

We may extend our experience by travelling in the spirit, if we cannot in the body. We can look up our classics. Why does the Homeric singer compose hymns to his gods? He reveals his purpose at the end: "Graciously bestow satisfying sustenance"; or, "Grant that we rejoicing may attain to further seasons, and from seasons to abundance of years." [2]

Having thus prepared ourselves by practical exercises on our own people we can now proceed to tackle men whose beliefs are remote from our own and expressed in

---

[1] *The Catholic Faith*, p. 100.
[2] Homeric Hymns, xxxi: xxvi.

a strange and difficult language. We shall not expect much from a direct question, though it is worth trying, just to see what happens. We shall expect much more from a careful study of the structure, from a careful record of all the formulæ, and from comments made upon all that takes place or is said.

The Fijian gives away very clearly what he expects from those ceremonies that make a man into a chief: he expects prosperity. I have dealt with these ceremonies so fully elsewhere that I need not recapitulate the evidence, but will turn to funerals, weddings, ceremonial receptions. If you ask the direct question you will get the usual answer: "That is the Fijian way"; yet the words he uses in the course of the ritual show that he has definite results in view. However much the words may differ, the burden is always the same: "Let us live, let the land prosper, may concord reign", and so on.

Whether the Eddystone Islander treats a man for illness, makes a burnt-offering to the dead, or consecrates a priest or a new skull-house, the request is always, "Let us not be ill; let us live".

From the South Seas let us jump to Africa. The following Igbo prayer will suffice: "I want child; I want yam; I want koko yam. Permit not trouble, permit not misfortune. Life for men, life for women. Life for children; life for child in belly." [1]

Let your witnesses talk freely, as the psychologist allows his patients to do; let them ramble on. When thus given a free rein, no one perhaps will state what he intends by the ritual more explicitly than the Red Indian. The word life is written large over his ritual. There is perhaps not a page of Miss Fletcher's magnificent monograph on the Hako Ceremony which does not contain the word. She chose the greatest expert on that ritual, and got his comments on every action and every word. Endless

[1] From Dr M. D. W. Jeffreys.

repetition is the consequence, for the ritual is at bottom very simple, and is merely one long series of variation on the theme of life. The wind is called in to give life; the sun is a life-giver, and so it goes on. The whole objective is summed up in these words: "The ceremony of the Hako is a prayer for children, in order that the tribe may increase and be strong; and also that the people may have long life, enjoy plenty, and be happy and at peace." [1]

If you want to know why the Medicine Dance was instituted don't ask a Winnebago; ask his myths. They put into the mouth of the man in the East the following words: "We are to teach the meaning of life, so that they may hand it down from one generation to the other. . . . Life (all that life consists of—wealth, honour, and happiness) they shall have from now on." [2] In the clan war-bundle feast, tobacco is poured into the fire with these words: "I am using the tobacco as a means of obtaining life for myself and my relations." [2]

I shall give most prominence in my illustrations to the death ritual, because it would seem the very last occasion on which to seek life. So much so that our theorists have found every kind of reason for funerals except life.

What has the Winnebago got to say on the subject? Addressing the dead an orator says: "Do you see to it that all those things that belonged to you and that you would have enjoyed had you lived longer—such as victories on the war-path, earthly possessions, life—that all these you leave behind for us to enjoy." [3] The dead man is instructed to say to the old woman in the Underworld: "I have made all my relatives lonesome, my parents, my brothers, and all the others. I would therefore like to have them obtain victory in war and honours. . . . I would that they could have all that life which I left behind me on earth." [3]

[1] *Hako*, p. 26.   [2] Radin, *The Winnebago Tribe*, pp. 358, 453.
[3] *Ibid.*, pp. 142, 143.

The Inca view was that if they venerated the bodies of their sovereigns "the generation would be multiplied by their bodies being conserved and respected." [1]

The composers of the *Rigveda* agree in substance, as can be gathered from the funeral hymns of book X. The fourteenth hymn seeks life for both deceased and survivors: "Give him welfare and freedom from disease" (v. 11). Then (v. 12): "May these two messengers of Yama give us back here to-day auspicious life that we may see the sun." Or take xvi., 5: "Clothing himself with a full life let him attain to posterity; let him unite with a body." In other words, let him be reborn in a descendant with a full life. In xviii., 5, the officiant prays on behalf of the survivors: "As days are in sequence, as seasons go with seasons in the right way, as one does not leave the other, even so, creator, complete the lives of these." Then turning to them he says: "Attain to full life, choosing old age."

The worship of the Buddha is the worship of one who has passed away. His relics are worshipped even as are the relics of saints, the mummies of pharaohs, the skulls of New Georgian dead. The tooth in particular is the object of a daily cult in Kandy. It is spiritual welfare which is sought, because the ritual has been overhauled by philosophers who look upon mere life as an evil thing to escape from. But all the philosophers in the world cannot abolish the desire for life. The service concludes with the prayer: "Let the god rain in due time who promotes the welfare of the crops; and let the world rejoice and let the king be just."

The desire for life is just as strong in the Arctic as it is in the Tropics. The Koryaks have a whale ceremony the purpose of which is to ensure a supply of whales during the coming year; but the prayers also include petitions to avert sickness and evil spirits during the coming winter.

[1] Karsten, *The Civilization of the South American Indians*, p. 352.

The ceremony has, then, both a narrow specific object, whales, and a wide general one, health. The connection is obvious: Health depends on a good supply of food.

There are numerous rituals in which only the narrow specific end is expressed. Thus the Eddystonians, besides ceremonies that promote life in general, have others which concentrate on one staff of life, such as bonito. In their structure these rituals are exactly like the others, but their application is highly specialised. Such are also the charms, numerous everywhere, which limit themselves to one particular form of ill-health. Such also are those ceremonies of the Australian aborigines which cause a particular species to multiply. These can be very highly specialised; for instance among the Aranda, who have ceremonies directed not to food, or animal food, or even to kangaroos, but to brown kangaroos, grey kangaroos, and so on. Now the biologist regards specialisation as a sure sign that a type is not primitive. By his standards, then, these specific ceremonies of the Arandas are anything but primitive, for they are as highly specialised as they could be. We shall have to look among the more generalised forms for primitive ritual, and life on its widest sense—you may call it weal, if you like—is what the ritual aims at.

After all, man's chief pre-occupation is to keep alive. Is it surprising, then, that ritual should pervade human society as it does? A friend of mine thinks I hang too much on the peg of ritual. When you see a man reducing many things to one, it is natural to get alarmed, to think he has a bee in his bonnet; but my friend forgets we all have one great bee in our bonnets and that is Life—life for ourselves, life for our progeny, as much life as is possible with as great a margin as possible over bare existence. When we want a thing we devise means to obtain it. One technique for securing life we call ritual. The term is not too fortunate: it has become too specialised, too much associated with all kinds of local prejudices and sectarian animosities. If we call the theory that underlies that technique the science of life, and that technique itself the applied science of life, then we shall feel less alarmed for the reason of our friends if they trace discovery after discovery to this theory of life, discoveries in the life-giving properties of foods, of minerals, of heat and of light, discoveries even in social organisation. For man is a social animal and can only live by being social. This science of life must consequently be essentially social in its application. You can kill a deer all by yourself. You can all by yourself manufacture a spear to kill that deer. But you cannot perform all by yourself a ritual, because life requires at least a pair to propagate itself, and that pair engenders further living forms which depend on the first. "This is a pairing", is the comment of an ancient Indian text on a rite, "even by pairing he procreates him thus with offspring, with cattle for generation." This science being essentially social requires a social organisation in order to be applied.

St Chrysostom was then merely stating a fundamental condition of ritual when he prayed: "Almighty God, who hast given us grace with one accord to make our common supplications unto Thee, and dost promise that when two or three are gathered together in Thy name Thou wilt grant their requests. . . ." The Winnebago expresses the same idea somewhat differently: "Cry that you may obtain life, even as the host and his people have done. Act thus that you may be of help to one another even as our ancestors of old were. If people act together they will accomplish their purpose" (Radin, p. 515).

Ritual is not merely a quest of life, it is a social quest.

CHAPTER VI

Ritual and Emotion

I

THE bulk of our convictions is taken over lock, stock, and barrel from our predecessors. We have no time to overhaul any but a very small proportion: the rest is taken for granted. It is, however, necessary to keep re-examining a few, so far as our short lives allow, in order that our culture may be kept fluid and adaptable.

The conviction I have selected for revision is the very general one that ritual is essentially emotional, is in fact the child of emotion. This opinion has seldom, if ever, been challenged during the last hundred years or so. The only difference of opinion has turned on the particular emotion that has given birth to ritual, whether fear, or sex, or conflict, or whatever the fashion of the times might, suggest.

Undeterred by this unanimity, let us go straight to the facts. They are not difficult to find, especially on Sundays.

It is at once obvious that the series of actions which we call ritual is accompanied by emotion. But so is everything we do. Scientific work is the very type of intellectual activity; yet it is accompanied and sustained by emotion. It cannot flourish without enthusiasm. One of the greatest scientists of the last century, Pasteur, was continually talking of the sacred flame, and thus giving away the source of his energy. The fact is that no one could face the intellectual drudgery of science without the support of emotion. Emotion furnishes the driving power for science, but it is not science. So ritual may may be tinged with emotion; but it is not on that account made of emotion.

If ritual proceeded from emotion, then we should expect that the greater the ritual the greater the emotion. That is not the case. The most complete and elaborate rituals in this island of ours are the Anglican and the Roman. They are also the earliest, as we know from documents. Now the striking fact about these rituals is that they have a consistent and detailed structure which results from working out logically a central idea. They are worked out with consistency and such attention to detail that emotion can never really let itself go. That is precisely the reproach which the anti-ritualists make against ritual, that it is cold and freezes the emotions. They want freedom and spontaneity, so that emotion can flow where it will. That is their great argument in favour of extemporised prayer. They, accordingly, break up the ritual pattern in order to free the emotions.

If we compare the degree of emotion in the various cults of our own country we find that, contrary to received opinion, the greater the emotion the less the ritual. The emotionalists, those who want worship to be an emotional exercise, not a creative act, are invariably anti-ritualists. The final break-up of the ritual is reached in those revivalist movements where emotion works itself up to hysteria. They retain nothing but fragments of the pattern—namely, the hymns, the prayers, and the sermon. They retain them as stimulants of the emotions, not as parts of a well-ordered sequence of episodes developing one out of another. If we know that they once formed part of such a sequence it is only that we have documents to prove it.

Even these fragments may disappear, and the ritual may cease to be a ritual at all. Such are the meetings of the Society of Friends. They may be a model of placidity now, but it must be remembered that originally inspiration took such a violent form that the Friends were nicknamed Quakers.

Our rituals have set hard; they are no longer in the plastic state of a new cult. We can, therefore, observe only the spirit in which they are performed, not that in which they are built up. There are parts, however, in which the spirit of the designers pierces through very clearly. Some of them, notably the creeds, sound more like legal documents than like emotional outbursts. If we had no history of the councils we could still guess that they were the work of committees met to explore every avenue of reconciliation, to find a formula which would unite a majority in damning the exotics.

II

We can still, to some extent, watch how a ritual is built up if we turn to the old Brahmanical books. The ideas at the back of the sacrifice were then still just alive enough to work out points of detail. These are worked out in a manner more akin to Euclid than to the mystics. The teacher had as definite an end in view as a modern agricultural expert: he wanted to insure prosperity, largely in the shape of cattle, crops, or sons; and he reasoned out the means from first principles mainly by a series of equations.

This period was the culmination of ritual complexity. Intellectualism is generally followed by an emotional reaction. It happened in this instance. Emotionalism began to corrode the ritual in the Upanishads; and in the shape of Buddhism to destroy it. This religion addressed itself to those who suffered from world-weariness, and from what Dr H. G. Baynes calls desirousness, a condition of chronic desire, which cannot be allayed by attaining its ostensible object, because that object is not the cause, but the excuse. Buddhism sets out to treat these emotional disturbances, and so discards a ritual which has been worked out for external purposes.

The usual thing happened. Ritual cast out at the door came in again in disguise. It clothed itself in the healing phraseology of Buddhism. The final result is far from being emotional. There is as logical a structure as in our Mass. The central idea is different: there it was the king suffering, here it is the king triumphant. We are present at the daily repetition of his consecration. He is bathed, robed, invested, and finally presented with a collation. The procedure is rigidly fixed, and nothing can be more uninspired than the stanzas that accompany it, because the author was not so much venting his emotions, as bringing the act into harmony with the doctrine. On the other hand, there is a dignity about it that belongs to all well-ordered, well-thought-out ceremonies, in which the emotions are kept in their places.

In this respect the official Buddhist ritual contrasts with the popular cults of the gods. These gods have only saved themselves by becoming good Buddhists. At Gammadupitiya, for instance, the centre of the holy ground is occupied by a tree dedicated to the Buddha; the four gods face him at the four quarters. The cult begins in an orderly manner with texts borrowed from Buddhism; then, having affirmed its orthodoxy, it breaks out into a wild orgy of possession, into a go-as-you-please in which there is little structure to be seen.

The same contrast is to be observed in Fiji. The main ritual there, as elsewhere, is the king's ritual, only not a departed spiritual king as in Ceylon, but a present one. From beginning to end it forms an ordered sequence in which all emotional display would be considered bad form. Of course, there is emotion, but it does not break through as it does in the spiritualistic cult of "The Children of Water". This cult has copied its opening forms from the royal kava, and so it begins with the same chain of actions slightly altered; but this is merely a formal introduction to a formless proceeding. When the kava has been drunk the initiates become possessed, and from that moment order is abandoned for a competition in quakings and ejaculations. The weaker spirits are bullied into being possessed, just as in our own revivals.

This exhibitionism and this bullying are characteristic of emotional cults. They appear again in the very careful observations Professor E. E. Evans-Pritchard has given us of the Azande witch ceremonies.[1] The witch proceeds to work himself up to a frenzy, the details of which depend on the individual temperament. "I have seen men", Evans-Pritchard says, "in a wild state of excitement, drunk with the intoxicating music of drums and gong, bells and rattles, throw back their heads and gash their chests with knives till the blood poured out in streams down their bodies." We look in vain for an orderly progress from preparation to climax and close, or for an expression of the underlying ideas. Since there is little thinking there is little speech: "It is not the magic words, or ritual sequences which are stressed". If the witch has to speak it is only to render oracles. His replies "are not concise and straightforward, but long-winded, rambling, broken discourses", full of repetition after the manner of such performances. They lack structure. The witches often adopt a bullying tone. Since the object of all this class of rituals is emotion, all present have to share in it, and the laggards are bullied into the proper state of excitement.

Nowhere has emotion simplified ritual more than in Egypt. There, as everywhere, there exist beneath the official cult popular varieties which appeal to the mass because they let loose the emotions. For that very reason they are condemned by the intellectuals as being

[1] E. E. Evans-Pritchard, *Witchcraft, Oracles, and Magic among the Azande* (Oxford, 1937), pp. 155 ff.

against the doctrine, for the intellectuals dislike all violent emotional display. Nevertheless, these cults shelter under that doctrine.

There is, for instance, in Cairo a saint's tomb where assemblies are held every Friday afternoon. The audience is so keyed up that ecstatic swayings break out sporadically even before worship has begun. At first loyalty to the doctrine is expressed by repeating the Creed; but this is done with rhythmic swayings. Short as is the Creed, it seems too long for the growing excitement, and the assembly soon plunges into the indefinite repetition of the two syllables that form the name of God.

The *zikr* that is often to be seen at the festivals of saints carries simplification even further. The ritual has there been boiled down to violent rhythmic swaying to the right and left, sometimes punctuated with humphs that represent the name of God. Intense emotion becomes inarticulate, as we can often observe on the golf course. Therefore emotional cults always tend to stagnant repetition; this dwindles into ejaculations, which in extreme cases become mere grunts.

III

To return to our own country, we have been able to observe with our own eyes the gradual emotional reduction of another class of ritual, the funeral ceremonies. Note that it is the most sensitive that are most inclined to cut down all the traditional observances, the flowers, the elaborate processions, the collations, and the other funeral episodes that are so well preserved as parts of a definite structure in countries where people take death more as a matter of course. The intensity of grief cannot endure this cold elaboration; it is continually revolting against public opinion which demands the traditional observances. Just now it has been so successful that even signs of mourning have almost disappeared. If any vestige is retained it is not as an expression of grief, but as a warning to others to avoid stirring up that grief.

We must note that here we have to do with a different type of emotionalism. The emotion may be keen, but it is all driven inwards, whereas in the hysterical cults it finds boisterous expression. We are not, however, concerned here with the different types; if I draw attention to them, it is to point out that they make no difference to the rule that, whether emotion breaks out, or whether it withdraws into its shell, the moment it becomes the chief consideration the structure which logic has built up shrivels away.

If emotion dissolves the ritual structure, absence of emotion complicates it. There are dry minds for whom ritual is nothing but an arena for intellectual gymnastics. They produce not ritual, but ritualism. The purpose is lost sight of, and deduction is pursued for deduction's sake. The old ritual books of India are interminable in their refinements, because common sense is not there to keep the teachers within the bounds of the essential; for there is no emotion there, and common sense is nothing but healthy emotion keeping thought along the lines that are worth while.

IV

Ritual is a social activity, and so requires an organisation, and organisation means hierarchy. Emotion breaks up the organisation as it breaks up the performance. Emotional cults are at once individualistic and gregarious, individualistic in so far as each man follows his whim, gregarious in so far as all the actors do it together, and their whims are monotonously alike. They need company in order to work themselves up, but they work themselves up each for himself. There is little teamwork. Emotional rituals are democratic, and so therefore are emotional sects.

5

It is not an accident that our most elaborate rituals are in the keeping of the most elaborate and hierarchical sects, while the most emotional sects are the most amorphous, kept together, not by a cadre of officers, but by sharing a common emotional display.

In India, too, an elaborate ritual goes hand in hand with a complex social structure in which each one has his place appointed by descent.

Fijian society is as much a church as a state, since the whole organisation is worked out for the king's service, and the king is a present god. It has a symmetry which might be described as crystalline, though simpler than the caste system of India, even as the ritual is simpler.

At the other extreme lies the Egyptian mass which might be compared to a colloid, a crowd with little structure. One single fact will perhaps serve to illustrate this characteristic: no one is appointed to serve a saint; his priest is anyone who "has succeeded in imposing himself by busying himself with the tomb actively and assiduously".[1] That might be said, with the necessary adaptations, of many emotional sects in our country, but more especially in America; it cannot be said of the Church of England, or the Indian caste system, or the Fijian king's court. And yet Egypt did once possess an elaborate hierarchy which also had the king or the god as its centre, and the people as its periphery. If we are to judge the spirit of Ancient Egypt by its art, then we must conclude that at the times when that organisation was most settled, the spirit of the times was most serene.

Evidently we are here in the presence of an interesting social phenomenon, the dissolution of a structure, leaving in the end an amorphous, but none the less cohesive community. I can do no more here than draw attention to the phenomenon, and pass on to the Azande.

[1] Mohammed Jalal, *Essai d'observations sur les rites funéraires en Égypte, Études Islamiques* (1937), p. 216.

We are told that their witches' seances are popular, and repugnant to the aristocracy; for an aristocracy needs dignity, and dignity involves control over the emotions. "Consequently", says Dr Evans-Pritchard, "the political pattern of Zande social life has left no imprint upon the institution of their witch-doctors, for had princes entered into the corporation they must necessarily have done so as leaders."[1] The Azande witch-doctor, like the Fijian leader of the Children of Water, is not appointed, but simply practices in virtue of his knowledge of plants. His staff of drummers is often the result of a scramble to get possession of the drums. He is backed by a fortuitous crowd of small boys.

V

Ritual is not the only intellectual construction that is liable to be broken up by emotion. Science can be disintegrated in the same manner. A man like Pasteur may be encouraged in his work by hopes of great benefits to be conferred upon mankind by his discoveries; but that is secondary: his real interest is in hypothesis and proof, and so he never lets his heart run away with his head, but pursues his experiments with implacable logic. There are others, however, with no more heart but considerably less head, for whom the vision of mankind delivered of all suffering is primary. Intellectual constructions, so far from pleasing them, cause resentment, because they shackle the emotions which are straining after quick results. Quick results are not to be achieved by wishing; but it is possible to imagine results, in order to keep up the ecstasy. From applied science, as from emotional ritual, it is a fatally easy step to self-deception and quackery.[2]

Whatever is human lies closer to the emotions than carbon or hydrogen; so it is in the science of man that

---

[1] Evans-Pritchard, *op. cit.*
[2] *Cf.* C. A. Flexner, *Universities* (Oxford, 1930).

emotion most readily attacks the structure of thought. A distinguished professor of one of the branches of this science once complained to me that all his pupils who came to his subject directly were suffering from an emotional upset, and it took him two years to teach them how to think. My experience confirms his. Logical constructions give way to emotional appeals. Emotion is assisted by the repetition of words that have acquired a strong emotional colouring, and this colouring again is intensified by repetition. The word *man* does not so much describe a featherless biped as suggest universal love. In a world of ruthless individualism the word *social* expresses unsatisfied yearnings, and the idea of the *family* becomes an emotional substitute for a fading reality. The phrase "culture contact" has become limited entirely to contact of dominant and dominated; it comes thus to evoke sympathy for the underdog, and is turning into a thin disguise for welfare work *in partibus*.

It is power which the soul seeks in ecstasy, power to fly, to prophesy, to heal body or soul, or to cure social ills. The word *power* belongs to everyday speech; *dynamis*, being Greek, is more imposing, and the termination *ism* has become associated with powers, capitalism, communism, militarism, and the rest, which push mankind this way and that like the gods of old. *Dynamism* is not an explanation, but a confession of faith; faith is the attainment of power. Where there is love of power bullying readily appears, and this is not unknown among professors of the sciences that deal with man.

VI

If science is considered the type of intellectual activity, art is generally considered to be essentially a vehicle of emotion; yet it has its logic too. "Logic, the science of reasoning", an architect has recently told us, "is the basis of all artistic processes, and in architecture is the basis of the art itself." And he proceeds to show the logic being broken up by the emotional pursuit of the useful; functionalism, I believe it is called in architecture: "In the kind of slang architecture", he says, "aptly described as modernistic, you will find that logic has been put on afterwards, just as style used to be. The architect has felt like a balcony in one place, and a patch of glass bricks in another, and only at the last moment has contrived for them some apparent reasons for existence." These disconnected features correspond to the ejaculations of emotional rituals and the slogans of emotional science. There is something aggressive about them, something bullying.

This slang architecture is an emotional revolt against what a friend of mine calls the copybook style. This is the architectural equivalent of ritualism. It is the combining of traditional motives, not in subordination to an end, but for the sake of virtuosity. For the copybook architect, "a gable", as our critic puts it, "is a gable and not the natural end of a necessary roof, and a buttress is a convenient means of distracting attention from a soil pipe".

We do not condemn all architecture because there are architects who lose sight of the purpose in the elaboration of details. There is an unfortunate tendency to spurn all ritual, because there are ritualists who weave wearisome subtleties. Even if it were a disease of religion, as some would have us believe, it would require to be studied: disease is a suitable object of study, and our great medical schools were built up on the study of disease.

VII

As a matter of fact, ritual is not a disease, though it may become diseased just like science or art. The trouble is that we talk of ritual very much as if it were a thing in itself, an unchanging entity which can be defined like mass or elements. In reality, the word merely describes chains of action which can vary infinitely. They are in a perpetual state of flux, so that, as we have seen, ritual may become the negation of ritual.

We cannot define what is always changing, because we can never find a formula that will express all the varieties, and include even opposites. It takes some analysis to discover something in common between the Brahmanical ritual and our Mass; it takes a great deal to find anything in common between a Fijian consecration and the Mass; no amount of analysis will find a common denominator between a Quaker meeting and a Fijian medical charm.

Then by what right do we classify them together under the heading ritual? It is not by reason of their emotional colouring. What emotion is shared by a medical charm and vespers? by an Egyptian *zār* and a Unitarian service? Some rituals are joyful, others sad; some are all dignity, others sheer buffoonery. It cannot be by reason of function, for the function of a *zār* is to cure disease, of a coronation to install the head of the state.

Then what right have we, I ask again, to place all these incommensurables under one common heading—ritual? The same as we have for classifying elephants and herrings as vertebrates. They have little enough in common, and if there were no other animals in the world anyone who classified them together would very properly be laughed at. There are, however, many other animals which can be arranged in a more or less complete series, and then we look round for fossils to fill up the gaps, and we find them. In the same way it may seem ridiculous at first sight to talk of our coronation ceremony and a Fijian medical charm in the same breath, but we can link up the Fijian charm with the consecration of a Fijian chief, and this with consecrations further west. Working from the other end, we can join up with India, and so gradually weave two chains that meet in the middle into one single one that cannot be broken at any point. If there are gaps, our fossils from Ancient Egypt or Mesopotamia may fill them. The extreme members may appear totally unrelated, but each one is obviously related to its neighbour, and this to the next one, and so on.

Let us then cease to define ritual and make generalisations about an abstract concept, such as that it is coloured by fear, or sex, or conflict; let us rather concentrate on the task of describing its forms minutely so that we can put them in their proper relations. Then we can see the transformations they undergo. The next step is to discover the causes of those transformations.

I have tried to indicate one cause, the paralysing effect of strong emotion upon thought.

Every scientific problem solved merely leads to another. Science has no end. The solution I have offered merely raises the further question, why should the degree of emotion which attaches to all rituals, as to all intellectual activities, vary at all? And especially why should it vary in different strata of a society, or at different periods of its history? We have seen that it is chiefly in the lower classes that emotion lets itself go, and breaks up the structure. We have also had reason to believe that these popular movements can spread through a society and simplify the whole religion.

We here find ourselves in presence of a very big problem, how are cultures built up and dissolved? It is a problem we are constantly coming up against, and which we shall have to tackle soon if we are not to come to a stale end. The problem is too big for a short paper; I shall be content if I have succeeded in drawing attention to its fundamental importance.

CHAPTER VII

The Origin of Monotheism

To trace the origin of monotheism may seem a presumptuous undertaking, but it is perhaps less presumptuous than may appear at first sight. Scholars often forget that important results are sometimes achieved by simple means, and that the production of an encyclopædia is not necessarily the prelude to far-reaching conclusions. They assume that the preparations must be as great as the subject, but it requires neither genius nor learning to discover a law so important as that the rise of nations is followed by their fall. On the other hand, it is only a profound and accurate scholarship which can discuss such a minor problem as the composition of the *Æneid*. It may require more abundant or remoter facts to find the origin of monotheism than to trace the phases of a nation's rise and fall, but perhaps we have gathered enough facts of late to make at least a guess at this origin. If I can suggest a theory which is simple, which is reasonable, and which does not invoke a single process that cannot be shown actually to occur, I shall have achieved at least something.

THE EARLIEST KNOWN RELIGION

We must take our start from the fact that the earliest known religion is a belief in the divinity of kings. I do not say that it is the most primitive. Some will say that animism is the most primitive; others that magic is. Let them prove it; so far these are mere surmises, unsupported by any evidence which a historian would accept. Here we are dealing only with facts, and the facts are that our earliest records show us man worshipping gods, and their earthly representatives—namely kings. We have no right, in the present state of our knowledge, to assert that the worship of gods preceded that of kings. Perhaps there never were gods without kings, or kings without gods. When we have discovered the origin of divine kingship we shall know, but at present we know only that when history begins there are kings, the representatives of gods.

In Egypt "as far back as we can go", says Foucart, "we find ourselves in the presence of a conception of monarchy based solely upon the assimilation of the king to the gods". The king was the embodiment of "that particular soul that came to transform the young prince into a god on the day of his anointing". [1]

Langdon tells us that "before B.C. 3000 ancient Sumerian city-kings claimed to have been begotten by the gods and born of the goddesses. . . . Although the rulers of that period were not deified, and did not receive adoration and sacrifice as gods, nevertheless their inscriptions show that their subjects believed them to be divinely-sent redeemers and the vicars of the gods". Later they are worshipped, but it is most important to note that, in Sumer, kings were not deified after death, but "worship of dead kings was forbidden unless they had been deified while living. Evidently some kind of consecration of the living mortal alone gave the possession of immortality. Temples were built everywhere to these kings in Sumer". [2]

In Greece it is also the earliest religion that we can trace. The Homeric kings are called divine. This is usually taken to be merely an expression of admiration, but the same was once thought of the titles bestowed upon Egyptian kings, and these have now been proved to

[1] Hastings's *Encyclopædia of Religion and Ethics*, s.v. "King (Egyptian)".
[2] The Museum Journal, Philadelphia, 1917, p. 166.

have a literal meaning. "None of these epithets", says Foucart, "should be regarded (as they too often are) as arising from vanity or grandiloquence, for each corresponds theologically to a very precise definition of a function or force belonging to one or other of the great gods of Egypt." This warning should be remembered in dealing with Greece or any other country. The Homeric king was descended from gods (*diotrephes*); he was a priest, and a good king "caused the black earth to bring forth wheat and barley, the trees to be loaded with fruit, the flocks to multiply, and the sea to yield fish".[1] All these attributes are characteristic of divine kingship.

It is a pity that our Hebrew chronicles are coloured by late theology, but nevertheless we can find in them traces of divine kingship, or shall we say chieftainship? The Judges were certainly vicars of God or gods; they were not hereditary, but heredity, though a usual, is not a necessary feature of this institution. It is quite possible that in its earlier form it was hereditary. The phrase "And the Spirit of the Lord came upon him", which is used of Othniel, Jephthan and Samson, ought, I think, to be taken quite literally. The story of Samson suggests that he was thought to have been begotten by the deity, a point left vague by later compilers.

Scholars declare that there is no trace of divine kingship in the Vedic hymns; it does not follow that divine kingship was then unknown. The Vedas are not a treatise on manners and customs, but allusive lyrics which assume in the hearer a considerable knowledge of the traditions of the wise men, to say nothing of those fundamental institutions which were familiar to the most ignorant. The island of Rotuma, north of Fiji, possesses hymns of a somewhat similar type. I doubt whether anyone would find in them traces of divine kingship, even with the aid of a prose commentary supplied by the most

[1] *The Odyssey*, xix, 111–3.

learned of the natives, yet from other sources I obtained undoubted evidence of divine chiefs. These other sources are lacking for Vedic times, and the silence of the Vedas is inconclusive. The later evidence is unambiguous; Indian kings are habitually addressed as *deva*—gods. Gray,[1] does indeed explain this away, contending that it does not imply "any divinity of the king, but merely that he is as much superior to the lower castes as the gods are superior to mankind". The explanation is forced, and Gray produces evidence against himself, for he quotes Manu as saying that "the king is a great deity in human form". In epic literature "a king or royal seer is called *nara-deva* (god of men); a priest is called *bhumi-deva* (earth god). It is only as a god that a king may accept a gift. He is Indra, Varuna, Kubera and Yama incorporate".[2]

The earliest records then show divine kingship in full flower, and indeed this religion must be very ancient to have spread over so great a part of the world, from Benin to the South Seas, and beyond them to Peru.

SUCCESSIVE INCARNATIONS

We have seen that kings were worshipped in their lifetime and after their death. In Egypt, "as a divine son of Ra, the dead king became a patron-deity, theologically distinct from the ancestor-god, though one of his manifestations". Here lies, I think, the germ from which has grown the idea of one universal god. I will first make a supposition.

Suppose the Kings of England are incarnations of Odin; then King Edward VII would be Odin incarnate, but temples would be dedicated to him under the name of Edward. King George VI would succeed him as Odin on earth, but would be worshipped under the name of

---

[1] *H.E.R.E.* s.v. "King (Indian)".
[2] Hopkins, *Epic Mythology*, p. 64.

George. Since King Edward and King George are both Odin, they must be one another, and also one with the many kings who have reigned since the Conquest.

Evidence that something of the kind has actually happened is scarce, and I have hitherto found none that is earlier than Indian mythology. Yet evidence from this shows that the process I have described actually takes place and is not merely fanciful. The Indian god Vishnu has ten incarnations. Each incarnation is worshipped in its own right, so to speak, but it is not forgotten that it is also Vishnu. One of the incarnations is Rama, whom legend represents as a king on earth. It makes little difference whether or not he is historical, for to the Indian he is a king, and to the Indian mind it is therefore conceivable that a king may be at the same time one of the great gods. Another of Vishnu's incarnations is Krishna, also represented as a man on earth. Rama is Vishnu and Krishna is Vishnu; therefore Rama and Krishna are one. This conclusion has been drawn, for there is a god called Rama-Krishna, just as there is a Krishna-Vishnu.[1]

Another incarnation of Vishnu is Narasinha, the Man-Lion. Now Narsing was a common name for kings in Southern India, and there also the Man-Lion is a favourite motive in architecture. There were Lion dynasties in Orissa and in Ceylon; the Ceylon kings were descended from a prince with a lion's hands and feet, the son of a lion and a princess.

A MODERN INSTANCE

The process can be observed in India at the present day. At Bodh-Gaya you may see a row of recent tombs erected over the remains of ascetics. When an ascetic dies "his body is buried in the sitting posture, cross-legged, with the hands in the lap, just as a man sits in meditation. . . . On the top of the grave a *lingam* of Siva

[1] Hopkins, *Epic Mythology*, p. 3.

is fixed. The idea is that the *sannyasi* (ascetic) has not died, but has become one with the universal deity Siva (or Parabraham). . . . The *lingams*, especially those on the graves of the *Mahants* (abbots) and influential men are daily worshipped in the same way as the god Siva is worshipped. . . . The offerings made and the *mantras* uttered are the same as those used in Siva worship".[1]

The Germ of Monotheism

This custom, I suggest, is the germ of monotheism. This is how it may first have dawned on man that many gods were the manifestations of one. Monotheism is usually taken for granted, and no explanation is ever offered for its first appearance; it is supposed to be a natural growth, sufficiently explained by the magic word evolution. Yet, when we come to consider it, there is no obvious reason why there should be one god rather than many; once man has come to believe in gods, why should he ever cut their number down to one? In some ways it is easier to believe in many than in one; it spares us endless theological problems, and makes religion more personal. Such an intelligent people as the Greeks seem to have been well content to have many gods.

The theory which I have outlined at all events explains how the oneness of God first occurred to men. It is based on a custom which can be traced as far back as early Egypt and Sumer, the custom of worshipping kings in their own names.

Monotheism by Conquest

The idea once vaguely conceived was doubtless confirmed and expanded by other causes, conquest being one of them.

[1] Information from Mr S. Bhattacharya.

Let us return to our supposition that the Kings of England are incarnations of Odin. They conquer India, and assume the title of Emperor of India, but in taking the title they are taking far more than the mere name; they are assuming the divine attributes which go with that name. They become, let us suppose, Indra. King George, then, is Odin, and also Indra; therefore Odin and Indra are one.

Professor Sethe and Dr Blackman both recognise that conquest may have helped to fuse gods together, though they conceive the process somewhat differently from that which I have outlined. "Owing to the political predominance gained by Buto over Heliopolis in the predynastic age, Horus, originally the god of Buto, came to be identified with the Sun-god, the local god of Heliopolis. Since the king was regarded as the embodiment of Horus, he was also regarded as the embodiment of the Sun-god." [1] The idea seems to be that the gods were first identified with one another, and that the king, being the incarnation of one, naturally became the incarnation of the other. It is by no means clear, however, why the political predominance of one city over another should cause their gods to become one. May I suggest another explanation? It may be contrary to the evidence at the disposal of scholars, but perhaps my suggestion will have brought forth this evidence, and thus definitely settled in what way conquest leads to fusion of gods. In the meantime this fusion may be accounted for mechanically thus: the Horus-king of Buto defeats the Sun-king of Heliopolis, and assumes his dignities. These dignities are the outward signs of his divinity as representative of the Sun-god, so that when the King of Buto assumes them he becomes the representative of the Sun-god. Henceforth he is Horus and he is also the Sun-god; therefore Horus and the Sun-god are one.

[1] A. M. Blackman, in *Proc. Soc. Biblical Archæology*, Mar. 1918, p. 60.

I am emboldened to make this suggestion, ignorant as I am of the facts, by my knowledge of Fijian usage. Divine chieftainship, somewhat obscured, has extended to Fiji, and Fijian history may therefore be consulted with advantage. We find there that titles are not made or assumed at will. In Europe any man who can unify Italy can proclaim himself King of Italy, but Fijian titles are in the gift of certain families, who alone can perform the rite of installation. Thus the people of Levuka bestow the title "Lord of Levuka" upon a chief who is not one of their own people, but one of the tribe of Mbau which, coming down from the hills, first subdued and finally expelled them; they still go one hundred and fifty miles by sea to install every new chief of Mbau. That chief also receives the title of "God of War" from his own tribe. He therefore combines two divine personalities in himself, not because the two gods have become identified with one another, but because his own people have raised him to one god-head, and the people of Levuka to another. We cannot, however, follow these implications in their consequences, because in Fiji the theory of divine kingship has unfortunately so far decayed that it has to be reconstituted largely by inference. Indeed, South Sea Islanders, and probably savages generally, are unsatisfactory witnesses in this respect, for, not having a class devoted to intellectual pursuits, they never develop systems of thought such as have been produced in Europe and Asia; they supply us with hints, but seldom give us the theory. In Europe and Asia, too, political unity has been achieved with a thoroughness unknown to savages; petty states have been absorbed into mighty kingdoms, and it is easy to see how, under these conditions, the idea of one supreme god, of whom all others are but aspects, must have been strongly promoted by the existence of one supreme king uniting in himself the divine attributes of all the petty kings whom he has displaced.

Conquest also acts indirectly in that it removes the king and rulers further from the people, and weakens the personal tie. It accustoms people to give allegiance to principles rather than to men, and turns their devotion to abstractions. The clansman fights for his chief, but the modern British fight for freedom or the Empire. In the formula "for King and Country" the king is a mere survival, the country the reality.

MONOTHEISTIC ENTHUSIASM

We have seen that the germ of monotheism lies in the doctrine of divine kingship, and that conquest helps it to develop. In the end it comes to pass that personalities and attributes are multiplied beyond reason, as king after king is added to the list. There is a limit to man's memory and to his powers of attention. A multitude of facts and interests is a burden to the mind. When these grow too numerous men seek to reduce them, and, if they delay too long, they do so violently and enthusiastically, sweeping away suddenly the prolonged tyranny of accumulated tradition. Such a movement was the French Revolution, which made a fetish of system and simplicity because both had been unduly neglected in the past. It is difficult to serve more than a limited number of gods, and especially difficult when the attributes of the gods are hopelessly mixed up, when every god is similar to every other. It is only necessary to read a treatise on the religion of the Vedas to realise how dull and annoying a religion may become when the personalities of the various gods cease to be clearly distinguished. Some minds are content with confusion, but others rebel against it and embrace with enthusiasm any movement which would sweep it away.

It is difficult, however, to understand the tremendous success of monotheism if we look upon it as merely an abstract doctrine. As such it might stir up strife among philosophers and those who quarrel about mere ideas, but the mass of mankind has too much sense for that. People would not take all the trouble that they have taken to assert that there is only one God, and no more, if behind that dogma there was not a tendency, a new spirit, which was worth fighting for. At first sight men seem hopelessly foolish to kill and be killed for the sake of pure abstractions, but closer scrutiny shows that it is not that they are foolish but that they are unable to express themselves and therefore to do justice to their cause. They feel a great deal which they cannot put into a few clear words, yet they require a few clear words as a war-cry with which to rally their forces; so we hear a great deal in history about the shibboleths of dogma and ritual which distinguish parties, and very little about the apirations which impel them. But we must judge the past by the present. If we look at the sects of our own time, we find that the distinction between them is deeper than points of dogma or ritual. You can almost tell what sect a man belongs to by his general outlook on life, his politics, his tastes, his speech, and even his morality. But a man can scarcely support one fellow-man and fight another in the name of social standing, or manners, or artistic tendencies, so he takes points of dogma as symbols of elusive traditions and feelings. If we judge past ages by our own we may feel sure that the quarrel over *homoiousion* and *homoousion* involved much more than an iota.

We could be quite sure, then, that the struggle between monotheism and polytheism was more than a philosophic disputation, even if our evidence did not furnish abundant hints to the contrary. It is significant that the monotheistic party in Israel was the party of union, while the polytheistic party was for secession. "Jeroboam said in his heart, Now shall the kingdom return to the house of David: if this people go up to offer sacrifices in the house of the Lord at Jerusalem, then shall the heart of the people turn again unto their lord, even unto Rehoboam, King of Judah." Those who had the same god would have the same king.

The attributes of Buddha are closely copied from those of a universal monarch; in fact, tradition declares that he had the option of becoming either a supreme Buddha or a universal emperor, and preferred to be a spiritual Lord of the World. The expansion of his creed was favoured by the greatest empire of Ancient India.

The Christian Church has a similar conception of its founder:—

"And kings sat still with awful eye,

"As if they surely knew their sovereign lord was nigh."
He was born at the time when the most powerful empire of the ancient world had been consolidated, and that empire spread the new creed. In the break-up of the Middle Ages the Church still kept alive the ideal of a Universal Empire. It is significant that the teaching of Mohammed resulted in the founding of a great empire. The idea of a Universal King and that of a Universal God go hand in hand. This is a survival of very early days. Kings at first were gods; the two terms were interchangeable. Now they are so no longer, but the ancient bond still persists.

Religion and politics are inseparable, and it is vain to try to divorce them. Originally one, they seem to have parted, but they have not really done so; their common origin still operates on men's minds. Monarchists must necessarily uphold the Church, and ardent believers in one God will help to build up large nations. The belief in a Supreme God or a Single God is no mere philosophical speculation; it is a great practical idea. But, like most other conceptions, it took some discovering. Men did not search for it at first, any more than they searched for the art of writing; they were led to it almost by accident, and it was a long time before they realised whither they were being led. Some have not realised it yet.

The doctrine of gods and their incarnations produced a group of gods who were but aspects of the same god; thence arose the belief that all gods were in reality but manifestations of one. Some peoples never got any further, but the bolder nations took the step of simplifying the Universe by sweeping away the multitude of gods which had become useless by their very numbers. Monotheism then became a definite article of faith to be fought for and to be established in all the world.

CHAPTER VIII

The Divinity of the Guest

THE observances of the Greeks towards strangers and guests are well known to those who have read their classics, but I may be excused if I recapitulate those of them which are important for a comparative study.

The Greeks did not distinguish between a host, a guest, and a stranger, but used the same term for all three, for the simple reason that they were not distinguishable. In Homeric times there were no hotels, so any stranger coming among a foreign people had to throw himself on their hospitality. They might drive him away, but to do so was considered wrong, the act of those who had no regard for the gods, for "from Zeus are all strangers and beggars"; "Zeus is the avenger of all suppliants and strangers, Zeus patron of strangers, who accompanies venerable strangers". So conscious were they that Zeus was present with the guest and suppliant that when one came they made a libation to Zeus. Not only is the god present with the stranger, but the stranger is often a god; it is dangerous to ill-treat even a wretched wanderer in case he might be some heavenly god. For gods in the guise of strangers from foreign lands, assuming every shape, visit cities, observing the insolence of men and their respect for the law. This possibility was a very real one, and it was not mere flattery when Odysseus, cast ashore on the Phæacian coast, asks the unknown Nausikaa, "Are you some god or a mortal"? To "the hospitable whose mind is god-fearing" every stranger is a guest and is "equivalent to a brother", "he welcomes him and provides a guest's fare", and on his departure selects from his stored wealth some gifts "as is meet and right with strangers". These gifts are not free gifts; the guest in time will make a suitable return, and if for some reason the host's hospitality is not returned his presents are deemed to have been given in vain. If the stranger has been shipwrecked, he owes to the person who takes him in "presents in return for life", a term also used of offerings to gods on recovery from sickness. It would seem that in such cases the person who received the castaway stood to him somewhat in the relation of a god, for Odysseus says to Nausikaa, "I will pray to thee as to a god". Had he merely said, "I shall remember you as a god", it might be taken to be merely a high-flown compliment, but why "I will pray"?

Anyhow the guest became the potential host of his host, and the bond thus formed between two men was perpetuated by their descendants; a hereditary guest-friendship is established by the hospitality of one man to another; their descendants will invoke it when they visit each other, and even on the field of battle they will trace the bond that unites them back to the ancestors who created it. Out of this hereditary guest-friendship developed in historical times the consular system. A state would in recognition of services rendered to its nationals by a citizen of a foreign state confer upon him the title of *proxenos* or state-host. This meant that he became the official protector of all their citizens who visited his state. He played the same part as a modern consul, the chief difference being that he was always a citizen of the state he lived in, whereas a modern consul is usually a citizen of the state the interests of which he represents.

The divine patronage of the stranger seems to have excited little surprise among readers of the classics. Brought up as we are from early childhood in the idea of a God who upholds justice and protects the weak and helpless, we regard it as quite natural, and therefore as requiring no explanation, even as the fall of a stone seemed to require no explanation until some perverse minds insisted that everything, however familiar, requires an explanation. Familiarity makes us overlook the vast implications that are contained in the idea of Zeus or Jupiter, patron of strangers. First of all, it implies a belief in one or more gods, a belief that is so far from being obvious that for centuries philosophers have been vainly labouring to justify it by basing it on pure reason. Secondly, given a belief in gods, we must have the idea that such gods are interested in protecting the weak, and this is so far from being a necessary attribute of gods that there are many of them about the world who do not concern themselves about the rights of the weak or indeed about any rights at all, while some even encourage taking the head of any stranger who may come along. Thirdly, if love of right is inherent in all gods, why should protection of the guest be the particular attribute of one? If kindness to strangers had been ingrained in the Homeric Greeks it might be natural that they should conceive the deity to be equally kind, but it is perfectly clear that this kindness was by no means a common virtue. The chief or king seems to have welcomed and protected suppliants, but on his way to the king's house the stranger was exposed to the gibes of the people he met. The Phæacians were a specially virtuous people, yet their princess was not sure that the stranger would meet with a favourable reception unless he threw himself upon the mercy of the queen, a lady of great understanding and influence. We should as a matter of course be well disposed to a stranger, and should not dream of insulting him merely because he is a stranger, but we do not invest him with any divine character, or believe the deity to be more interested in him than in any other human being. Evidently the idea of a god who accompanies strangers was not the outcome of a hospitable disposition, but rather a useful check in an inhospitable age.

We shall never understand origins as long as we confine our attention to one country. It is only when we compare the different forms which an idea takes among different peoples that we can hope to find a clue to the problem, or even to realise that there is a problem at all. When we pass over to India we enter a region the customs of which have become known to us only since we grew up and therefore do not appear to us as obvious and natural as those with which we became familiar at school. In India the stranger or guest is not merely, as in Greece, a man accompanied by a god, but is himself a god, or rather gods, for he is "compounded of all the gods". The *Taittiriya Upanishad* enjoins: " Be one to whom his mother is a god, be one to whom his father is a god, be one to whom his teacher is a god, be one to whom his guest is a god". Earlier still, the *Atharvaveda* works out the divine character of the guest in great detail, identifying every act of hospitality with some phase of the sacrifice to a god: "When in truth the host meets with his eyes the guests he looks at a sacrificing to the gods. When he greets them he enters upon consecration; when he offers water he brings forward the sacrificial waters . . . in that they prepare lodgings, they so prepare the sacrificial tent and the oblation-holders. In that they strew a couch, that is grass on the altar", and so on. Since waiting upon a guest is equivalent to worshipping the gods, it has the same virtue; the guest by receiving a sacrifice obtains possession of the universe, and through him the host also "conquers worlds rich in light". Manu counts the "honouring of guests" as one of the great sacrifices which form part of the householder's daily worship, the other four being the reading of the Vedas, the sacrifice to the Manes, the burnt offering to the gods, and the thrown offering to the creatures. The *Anguttara Nikaya* distinguishes five offerings: to kinsmen, guests, departed spirits, kings, deities. The offering to the Manes includes a reception of guests; it is specially laid down that such guests must not be friends. These guests are seated on the sacred kusa-grass which is strewn in sacrifices for the gods to sit on; they represent the Manes, and through them the Manes eat of the feast. Now these guests are selected according to one of two rules: the primary one is that the guests should be learned and virtuous Brahmans, but there is a subsidiary rule that "a man may feed his mother's father, his mother's brother, his sister's son, father-in-law, teacher, daughter's son, son-in-law, maternal relation, both the sacrificial priest and the institutor of the sacrifice". In other words, the guests may include all those related through females. This rule contradicts the rule that the guest must not be a friend, and one cannot help suspecting that the growing insistence on moral and intellectual qualifications has relegated an ancient practice to the second rank. Anyhow this rule is an important one to remember.

I have elsewhere made out a case for believing that the Pacific Islands preserve many remnants of a civilisation which they share with India, and that they often preserve them in a more archaic form. Let us see what these islands think about guests. Fijians call a stranger or guest *vulangi*, which means heavenly ancestor or heavenly god (these being the same to a Fijian). There is no need, however, to insist on an etymology which is not quite certain, for we have in the legend of the Lady Langi a close parallel to the meeting of Odysseus and Nausikaa. The Lady was dropped by a monstrous bird on an uninhabited island; a man and his son finding her there, and taking her for a spirit or goddess, addressed her "You stand there a spirit; we come as men". To which she replied: "You come as spirits; I stand here as man".

That episode, however, belongs to the mythical age. The Fijians are now all Methodists or Roman Catholics, and the divinity of the stranger or guest is to be inferred rather than seen. It can be inferred from the ceremonies which are observed at the reception of a guest. There is always an exchange of gifts between guest and host, but the gifts take the form of mutual offerings. They are offered with a form of entreaty, and received with a prayer for the success of the undertaking in hand. Even the stranger's formal account of his journey is treated as an offering, and received with a ritual formula and ceremonial clapping. A feast is made by the hosts for the guests, and is offered up and received with the usual ceremonial. Shipwrecked persons are presented with gifts called "a change of clothes", and owe "presents in return for life" (*ka ni mbula*), a term also used, like the Greek *zoagria*, of offerings made to gods on recovery from sickness. In some parts a stranger on arrival greets the natives and is greeted by them with a salutation elsewhere reserved for gods and chiefs (who are divine) and which contains certain syllables commonly used in worship.

We shall completely misunderstand Fijian hospitality unless we bear in mind that in Fiji there is, or rather until the British annexation there was, no intercourse except between kinsmen. Tribes not related by blood did not "go to one another"; did not "know one another"; so much so that the word used for acquaintance means kinsman, and indeed among certain tribes is the only word for kinsman. In their foreign intercourse tribes always followed "the path of kinship"—that is, if they wanted to visit another tribe, they would go to a clan with which they could trace some relationship, however distant, and through it get in touch with the rest of the tribe. Hence arose a system of guest-friends or consuls; in each tribe there was a clan or family which was hereditary envoy to some subject or friendly tribe, which it was said to "face". Members of this group were sent on missions to their particular *vis-à-vis*; entertained visitors from it, introduced them to the chief, and forwarded their interests. These guest-frienships or consulships can often be traced to a marriage, which is often repeated generation after generation. The ties of kinship between tribes vary, but there is one bond which interests us particularly here: it is usually traced to gods, and carries with it the same privileges as are allowed to descendants of a brother on the one hand, and of a sister on the other. They include the privilege of plundering one another, and the visitors are under the protection of the gods, who are angry if they are interfered with. This relationship is called *tauvu*, which means "people who are gods to one another".

Even in Fiji a guest-friendship may arise between two unrelated persons, especially since the annexation has widened intercourse. A man who has been hospitably entertained by strangers will ask them, if they visit his tribe, to put up at his house. But the parties will agree to be kinsmen, for a Fijian does not understand hospitality apart from kinship. If there is no true kinship it must be feigned, but if intercourse is kept up there will probably be intermarriage, and then the families will become cross-cousins.

Thus we see in Fiji how the Homeric system of hospitality could develop out of customs governing the intercourse between intermarrying tribes; in fact, we might almost say that the British peace is tending to bring about the transformation. On the other hand, it is hard to see how the narrow system of the Fijians could be derived from a wider intercourse such as we find in Greece. If the two systems are related, the Fijian is the more archaic.

But why should these two systems be related, coming as they do from regions so remote from one another? India is the link. On the one hand, Greece and India derive their languages from a common source, and if both countries accord divine honours to guests or strangers, the presumption is that this custom is derived from a common source, and the burden of proof is on those who would deny it. On the other hand, India recognises offerings to kinsmen and to guests, who in Fiji are one and the same. At an Indian funeral feast the guests are relatives through females, and these represent the Manes. It is very significant that Manu enumerates as guests those very relatives which a Fijian would reckon as such in a tribe which he is visiting, or which is visiting him. In Fiji to speak of a related tribe is to imply relationship through females, for even if two groups are descended from brothers they will sooner or later intermarry, and so become to each other as descendants of a male to descendants of a female; each side will find on the other its fathers-in-law and sons-in-law, maternal uncles, sisters' sons, and so on. Also the Indian conception of a guest is intermediate between the Greek and the Fijian; while no longer restricted to kinsmen, it does not extend to all humanity. Even a wretched vagabond may be a god in Homeric Greece, but a Brahman does not recognise a man of lower caste as a sacred guest; he will indeed receive him and give him food, but not as a guest to worship so as to obtain "wealth, glory, long life and heaven".

The hypothesis, then, is that the divinity of the guest is derived from the divinity of those kinsmen who stand in a cross-relationship to the host; with the breakdown of the kinship organisation and the extension of intercourse beyond its bounds, the rites observed towards kinsmen were extended by way of fictitious kinship to any stranger who found favour. This hypothesis certainly fits all the facts produced, the hereditary character of guest-friendship in Greece, the Greek consular system and Manu's rules. I admit that the basis of fact is a narrow one, but my excuse is that facts will always be hard to find as long as attention is chiefly directed to the writing of chronicles and none can be spared for the history of customs. But if all hypothesis is withheld until the materials have been collected, we shall wait in vain, for materials will never be collected until it is realised that there are problems to be solved. Slight as may be the present foundation for a hypothesis concerning the origin of the guest's divinity, it may serve as a pointer to those interested in the solution of such problems.

CHAPTER IX

Yakshas and Väddas

MODERN science cannot accept the existence of super-natural beings like the *Yakshas*, demons good and bad, which figure so largely in Buddhist writings. The historical critique which was in vogue at the end of the last century, and is still very powerful, would have argued thus: "Demons do not exist. Therefore traditions of demons are false." Certainly, but though demons may not exist, there exist men who are believed both by themselves and by others to be demons.

The ancient ritual books of India inform us over and over again that those who take part in the sacrifice "pass from the men to the gods", that he who is consecrated draws nigh to the gods and becomes one of the deities.[1] Contrariwise, the *Sūdra*, those who are excluded from the sacrifice, are *asura*, demons.[2] This idea can be traced back to the *Rigveda*. See viii. 48, 3. "We have drunk *soma*; we have become immortal; . . . we have found the gods." *Dasyu* means both demon and heretic. The idea is indeed much older than the *Rigveda*, since it is found among many peoples who cannot all either have given it to the Indians or derived it from them. Robertson Smith proved it for the Semites. It exists to the east of India.

It is a natural consequence of such a doctrine that the god or the demon and his worshipper are interchangeable in speech. In Fiji, for instance, the priests were often spoken of as "the gods", and the gods were sometimes referred to as "priests". When the Christian converts

[1] *Satapatha Brahmana*, ii, 2, 2, 9; iii, 2, 2, 12; and innumerable passages.
[2] *Pancavimsa*, v, 5, 17; *Taitt. Br.*, i, 2, 6, 7.

were taught by the missionaries that the native gods were
devils, they proceeded to call the heathens "devils", and
in some parts they now call the old gods "heathens".
The old-fashioned critique would reject all the stories of
wars against "the devils" as historically valueless; yet
we know them to be perfectly reliable accounts of wars
against the heathens.

Just so, when the chronicles of Ceylon speak of *Yakshas*
inhabiting the island of old, they are merely recording the
fact that the Sinhalese (by which I mean the invaders led
by Vijaya) were preceded in the island by demon-
worshippers, that is by heretics who did not follow the
cult of the Brahmanic gods. To the present day, as the
headman of a large jungle district pointed out to me, the
villagers of the remoter parts are, at bottom, *Yaksha*-
worshippers, often with no Buddhist priest to nurse
their orthodoxy. One may commonly hear a dull lout
impatiently addressed as "*Yako*"—demon.

This conclusion holds out the hope that by collecting
all the statements the *Mahāvamsa* makes about the
Yakshas of Ceylon we may reconstitute the prehistoric
civilisation of that island. But this task is not as easy
as it seems at first sight. Since *Yaksha* means indifferently
"demon" and "heretic", it is often difficult to know
which is intended. For instance, when we are told that
Yakshas eat men, are we to understand that the heretics
were cannibals, or merely that the demons enter a man and
eat up his inside so that he dies? Personally, I believe
that cannibalism and the belief in man-eating demons are
part and parcel of the same system of ideas, that wherever
we meet with one, the former presence of the other must
be postulated; but this remains to be proved, and, until
it is proved, we cannot build upon it securely. Till then
we may feel confident that cannibalism once prevailed
in Ceylon, but we cannot be positive.

A further difficulty is that we do not know how far the

old legends of Ceylon are really indigenous, how far
imported. Some we know are not indigenous. Thus,
the story of the one-pillared house, which the *Mahāvamsa*
embodies in Sinhalese history, is by the Jātakas located
in India. Just as the Javanese have placed in Java
the scene of the *Ramayana*, so the Sinhalese have attached
to their new home some of the legends which they
had heard in India. We cannot therefore accept
without more ado the *Mahāvamsa's* picture of the
witch Kuveni spinning at the foot of a tree as evidence
that spinning was known in Ceylon before the advent of
the Sinhalese.[1]

Legends related in India about Ceylon are not open to
the same objection, and can be more safely used than the
traditions of Ceylon itself. The belief, still firmly held
in the north of India, that the inhabitants of Ceylon
have tusks suggests that the early inhabitants used
tusked masks, as the Sinhalese still do in their demon
worship.

It is not my purpose, however, to discuss here in detail
the information that can be gleaned from the Buddhist
writings concerning those early inhabitants; but only to
define the outlines of their civilisation so as to clear away
the misconceptions that obscure the prehistory of Ceylon.
The *Yakshas* are invariably described as having kings,
and generally having a well-developed and sedentary
civilisation. The *Mahāvamsa* even names their city.
There is not the slightest hint that they were cave-
dwelling hunters. If the immediate predecessors of the
Sinhalese had been just a wandering jungle folk, it is hard
to explain why all traditions should agree in describing
them as anything but that. The *Mahāvamsa* does refer
to hunters, under the name *Vyādha*, the Pali original of
Vädda, but they live just outside Anuradhapura in a street
and are evidently a caste.

[1] Mhvs. vii, 11.

However divergent the views held about the Väddas, writers are unanimous in assuming that the *Yakshas* and the Väddas were identical. The implied reasoning is: "The Väddas are the remains of an aboriginal race. The *Yakshas* inhabited Ceylon before the Sinhalese. Therefore the *Yakshas* are the Väddas." There is no disputing the first proposition: physical anthropologists are agreed that the Väddas differ in physical conformation from the Sinhalese. The second proposition we have assented to. Yet the conclusion does not follow. There may have been several predecessors of the Sinhalese, not one. The *Mahāvamsa* does mention another race as having occupied the north of Ceylon, namely the Nāgas, whom we must take, on the principle that worshipper and worshipped are identified, to be cobra-worshippers.[1] Ceylon lies at the southern extremity of India and on the track of ships from the Arabian Sea to the Gulf of Bengal: it would be a wonder if no race but the Väddas had found their way there before the Sinhalese. Immigration has been constant in historic times; and there is no known reason why it should not have taken place in prehistoric times.

The appearance of the Kandyan Sinhalese confirms this inference: it does not seem possible to explain many types as Indian, or as Vädda, or as a cross between the two. There seems to be at least one more element.[2] That is, however, a matter which we must leave to physical anthropologists to unravel, when their attention is less exclusively devoted to the Väddas.

Archæologists have never even thought of doubting that everything pre-Sinhalese is Vädda. Implements of quartz and chert are common in Ceylon. They are very crude. They have been straightaway assigned to the Väddas. When the Sarasins discovered pottery mixed with these implements, they gave up, not the

---

[1] I, pp. 44 ff.
[2] *Ceylon Journal of Science*, sec. G, i, 83.

assumption, but the fact, and coolly declared, without proof, that the pottery had nothing to do with the implements. The same pottery, however, has been found in conjunction with the same type of implements in the Malay Peninsula, and it is no longer possible to deny a connection.[1] The obvious conclusion is that the makers of the implements were also users of pots, if not actually potters, and this is not in agreement with the usual conception of the Väddas as primitive hunters. It is in accordance with Foote's view that the implements are neolithic, if by neolithic we mean a civilisation that combines stone tools with pottery. It is important to note that the type of pottery found with these implements is one that persisted among the Sinhalese right down to the twelfth century or later. It is found as far as Japan, if the labelling in the Cambridge Museum of Archæology is correct.

It has also been assumed without demur that the cave-dwellers who were not Buddhist monks must have been Väddas, and that all pre-Buddhistic finds in caves are therefore the work of Väddas. But there is good evidence at Vessagiriya, just outside Anuradhapura, that, before they were handed over to the monks, caves were owned, not as part of the land on which they stood, but independently.[2] If they were owned apart from the land it must be that they were used for some purpose. Things found underneath a Buddhist floor may quite well be Sinhalese. Mr John Still found quartz fragments, such as have been ascribed to the Väddas, underneath the floor of a monastic cave-cell at Tantrimalai, which lies between Anuradhapura and Mannar, in the regions first settled by the Vijayan invaders.[3] Similar quartz

---

[1] I. H. N. Evans, *Papers on the Ethnology and Archæology of the Malay Peninsula*, p. 155; *Ceylon Journ. Sci.*, sec. G, ii, 94.

[2] *Ceylon Journ. Sci.*, sec. G, i, 58.

[3] *Ibid.*, i, 57; *Journ. Roy. As. Soc.*, Ceylon Branch, xxii, 74.

fragments were found at Mantai, near Mannar, in strata probably of the eleventh century. As Mantai was a bead-manufacturing centre, they may be spoils from workshops.

A dolmen and cists have recently been discovered in Ceylon.[1] Their date cannot yet be fixed; but they prove the existence of a culture different from that of primitive hunters. Another neolithic type, the trilithon, is still erected at the present day. Indeed, we must be prepared to find that other neolithic types, including quartz and chert implements, persisted among the Sinhalese country-folk much later than was ever suspected, perhaps down to the Gneiss Age.[2] They cannot have derived these from a pure hunting population.

The Väddas could only be identical with the Yakshas on one condition, namely that the Väddas were not always hunters, but were once upon a time cultivators whom the disorders that laid waste the north and east of Ceylon in the thirteenth and following centuries drove to a jungle life. This theory has actually been put forward by Parker in his *Ancient Ceylon*. I would not say that it is impossible; but Tennant and the Sarasins have produced literary evidence of a jungle people in the fourth, seventh, and eleventh centuries.[3] The name *Besades* or *Bithsades* which is there given them, coupled with the descriptions, does seem to indicate the Väddas. Parker is so far right, however, in that the Väddas must, at one time, have been in much closer contact with the Sinhalese than they were when they attracted the attention of the Europeans. Their country, now so deserted, was once dotted with Buddhist monasteries and with artificial lakes. It was here and there commanded by rock fortresses such as Nuvaragala. They cannot have gone far without

---

[1] *Ceylon Journ. Sci.*, sec. G, ii, 94 and 96.
[2] *Ibid.*, ii, 78.
[3] Collected in Dr and Mrs Seligman's *The Veddas*.

meeting with a village or monastic settlement. In the twelfth century the capital of Ceylon was right on the borders of what is now Vädda-land. These hunters occasionally come there now (the arrival of one was once reported to me); but whereas ten years ago there was but a miserable village, seven hundred years ago there was a splendid capital. They now haunt occasionally on Gunner's Coin, a cave with interesting frescoes that was once a monastery.

There is the evidence of the language. The Väddas speak an archaic dialect of Sinhalese.[1] A careful comparison of this dialect with Sinhalese literature should enable us to determine the exact time at which they began to be cut off.

The Seligmans have sought to minimise the importance of language. They point out that a people may adopt a language without the corresponding culture. But in addition to the language the Väddas have taken over the kinship system of the Sinhalese, a system that extends over South India and right into mid-Pacific. It is not a mere set of terms for various relations, a mere vocabulary: it is the expression of a social system, to adopt which is to carry out a revolution in the structure of society.

The Väddas in their ritual make use of coconuts and rice, agricultural products which should not appear in a primitive hunting ritual. The Seligmans have felt the difficulty, and have tried to explain it away thus: "We have shown that many of the *yaku* (=*yaksha*) ceremonies are essentially acts of communion uniting the living with the spirits of the dead, and we have hinted our belief that the reason for rice and coconut being almost essential parts of the offering is that they are the foods of which the Väddas are especially fond." [2] But in explaining away, the authors have affiliated the Vädda religion to

[1] *Op. cit.*, pp. 424 ff; *Ceylon Journ Sci.*, sec. G, i, 186.
[2] The Veddas, 419, Cp. 130.

that of the Aryans, or rather to a very widespread religion of which the Aryan is a derivative. I have touched upon this doctrine at the outset, and so need not dwell upon it further here. There can be no question here of an autochthonous religion.

Ecstatic dances are an important part of Vädda ritual. They do not differ essentially from those that may be witnessed close to Colombo. How far they differ in detail can only be determined after a close comparison of the two. Unfortunately we possess no published accounts of ecstatic Sinhalese dances other than masked demon dances. In one important point of religion the Väddas differ from the Sinhalese. The *Yakshas* worshipped by the Sinhalese are demons. The Vädda *Yakshas*, according to the Seligmans, are spirits of the dead.[1] Before we knew this we could not help suspecting that the *Yakshas* of Brahmanic and Buddhist literature were originally spirits of the dead: they haunt cemeteries, and generally play the same part as spirits of the dead play in countries farther east whose culture is certainly akin to the archaic culture of India. The doctrine of transmigration, which has taken such a hold on India, has no place for spirits of the dead: every man who dies is immediately reborn, it may be as a man, or as an animal, or as a god. Thus in Indian literature the *Yaksha* has become just one of the innumerable forms in which a man may be reborn. We know that this has been the fate of the *preta*. The word originally means "departed", "deceased", "ghost", but under transmigration it describes a bad form of incarnation, one inflicted as the wages of sin. As the word *Yaksha* is not found in the *Rigveda* in the sense of spirit or demon, we must conclude that the *Yakshas* are the departed spirits worshipped by non-Aryan races in India, that as the invaders became better acquainted with the religion of these peoples they

[1] *Op. cit.*, p. 30.

either adopted their indigenous term, or used a Sanskrit word in a new sense to designate the spirits worshipped by their heretic forerunners.[1]

The Väddas, then, have done the historian of religion a service in preserving the *Yakshas* in an earlier form than does the literature. Yet their religion, though more archaic in this respect than the Sinhalese, cannot claim even in this particular to be aboriginal. It just represents the religion of the *Yakshas*, possibly of the Sinhalese themselves, before transmigration came to transform it.

The various strata of Vädda religion cannot be determined on general grounds: nothing but a careful analysis and comparison with the rest of Ceylon and with South India, to say nothing of Indo-China, can settle points of detail. Pending this comparison we have enough evidence to satisfy us that it is vain to seek among the Väddas a primitive hunter's culture. They have been too much in contact with their neighbours. They are not even regarded by these as a separate people. The term Vädda is not racial: it merely means hunter. The *Nitinghanduva* enumerates them among the Sinhalese castes, second in the order of precedence, consisting of "kings or prime ministers who betake themselves to the forests". The Seligmans reject such traditions; but tradition cannot thus lightly be set aside, however impossible it may seem— what seemed impossible often proves to be merely our misunderstanding. In this case there is nothing impossible in the tradition. The *Mahāvamsa* mentions numerous cases of kings and rebels of high rank seeking refuge in the hill country, which is described as very wild in the twelfth century. It is quite in accordance with what we know of the Indian temperament: the blood of the jungle tribes is still strong in Indian veins, and the jungle always calls to men of a certain temperament. It is

[1] Etymologies of *yaksha* seem vain. It may not be a Sanscrit word at all.

only by accepting Sinhalese tradition that we can understand the high status which is accorded, so contrary to our expectation, to a destitute and broken jungle population that lives by taking life.

The conclusion we have come to is that the Väddas are descendants of an earlier population than the Sinhalese, possibly the earliest population that now survives.[1] They have been diluted with Sinhalese blood of the very bluest, but not to the extent of obliterating their racial characteristics. They have, however, been incorporated in Sinhalese society as a hunting caste, and, by reason of their noble blood, have been assigned a higher rank than should fall to destroyers of life. Of their original culture it is doubtful if anything remains, so deeply have they been influenced, first by the *Yakshas* (a term which may cover more than one race), then by the Sinhalese.

As regards the *Yakshas*, the *Mahāvamsa* gives the impression that the whole country was Sinhalese in the third century B.C., and became completely converted to Buddhism in the twinkling of an eye. The *Mahāvamsa* often conveys a wrong impression simply by its omissions (it almost completely ignores the Portuguese and the Dutch). It may be that, when the excavation of stratified sites has proceeded further, we shall find that the *Yakshas* persisted much later than was usually supposed.

---

[1] The late Mr Lewis told me he had been told in the south-east of small cave-dwellers who were exterminated in the last century by the Väddas because they were wont to kill people in their sleep. Were there pigmies in Ceylon as in the Malay Peninsula?

CHAPTER X

Money

WHY does the King's effigy appear on our coins? We are so used to seeing it there that it never occurs to us that it might be otherwise, and that it requires an explanation. If anyone asked us we should probably say that the coin is issued and guaranteed by the state, and that as the King is head of the state, he appears on the coins as its symbol. But a reason put forward to justify a custom need not be the reason that originally prompted it. The House of Lords is justified by its supporters as a useful check on the Commons, and it is on this ground that other countries have introduced a second chamber into their constitution. If we had no history of the constitution we should no doubt be told that the second chamber was devised for that very purpose. History shows us, however, that the Lords are older than the Commons, and at least till Tudor times were far more powerful.

There are many ways in which a state could indicate its guarantee of a coin: a map of the country, as appears on some stamps; a scutcheon, as often appears on the reverse; or merely the name of the state. The device of putting the king's head on was not obvious to the ancients, nor is it to the Chinese. The Greeks commonly stamped the national god on one side and his symbol on the other; thus the Athenians had Athene on the obverse and her owl on the reverse. The Athenians might indeed be excused from putting their chief magistrate on coins, since he was changed every year, but the Lydians were said to have invented coinage, yet coins of Crœsus bear a lion and a bull but no effigy of the king. The Indians began by stamping religious symbols, such as the tope, sun, wheel and svastika. They sometimes stamped the king's head after they had been introduced to the Macedonian coinage which was so stamped, but mostly continued to use religious symbols.

What, then, the Greeks and Indians have in common is the religious character of the symbols which express the guarantee. Is this the clue to the problem?

Ancient coinage is so restricted that if we confine ourselves to coins we shall make little progress. We must examine all the currencies of the world. The old school will protest; the new may have qualms. They will say that I have no right to argue from Samoan mats to Greek and Roman coins. Why not? The materials are indeed very different, but are they more different than a sovereign and a pound note? We know the note to be merely a substitute for the gold. It is not the material that is important, but the purpose, the idea that underlies its use. Weaving is weaving, whether you use the hair of an animal or the fibre of a plant. We build ships of steel, but do not claim for them an origin independent of the old wooden ships. So money is money whatever it is made of.

In the Solomon Islands they use shell rings as currency. These are of various sizes; some are thin and may be worn on the arm; others are thick and are simply stored. These rings are constantly used for religious purposes. After a burnt offering to the dead a man will take an arm-ring and hold it up in the air; suddenly his arm will whirl round and round; the spirit has alighted on the ring and is impelling his arm. When a man dies his soul is caught on a small ring; this ring is known as the "soul", and is placed in the skull-house with the skull of the deceased. Rings are hung on skull-houses and shrines, and are regularly given as a fee to priests or to anyone who performs or teaches a charm.

In Samoa and Tonga they had no regular trade, but

families preserved fine mats to use as gifts on great occasions. These mats had each a name, and their value did not depend in the least on their state of preservation; an ancient mat all falling to pieces might be preserved as a priceless heirloom. One story which I was told explained their value and their names; it mentioned a mat in which there abode a god.

In Fiji also there was no trade, but there was interchange of gifts. The place of fine mats was taken by whale's teeth, which were called *tambua*, from *tambu*, holy. There is a story of a very large *tambua* which was made of stone. In Eddystone they also had stone ones, but it is interesting to note that they were not used for exchange, but only kept in skull-houses and shrines.

Do the South Sea Islands yield the clue we are seeking? Did the coins of the Greeks bear the head of a god to show that the god was present in them?

There was a sacred quality about gold. The Vedic Indians believed it to be the seed of Agni, the fire god. It evidently partook of the nature of the sun since it could be substituted for it in ritual. For example, water for a certain rite had to be drawn before sunset, but if this had not been done a firebrand or a piece of gold could be held above the water; the officiant "makes it the image of him who shines yonder". At another point in the ritual a gold plate is made, "For this gold plate is the same as truth. Yonder sun is the same as truth. It is made of gold: for gold is light, and he (the sun) is light; gold is immortality, and he is immortality; it is round, for he is round. . . . Indeed this gold plate is the sun". This passage suggests a common origin for the gold coin, the crown and the halo, all three being merely representations of the sun's disc; it also explains the circular form of our coinage. This shape was not always in such favour as now; in India they originally preferred a square, a form which in religion has always been a rival to the circle; in

Ceylon as late as the thirteenth century they used wedges and possibly gold rings, and as late as the sixteenth silver hooks; in Fiji we have found conical objects in favour; the earliest Egyptian currency consisted of gold rings. Is it possible that rings were originally worn as sun shrines to protect against evil, and degenerated into mere ornaments?

We can now understand why in Greece "mints were set up in the temples of the gods, and forgery was sacrilege": why in Rome in 269 B.C. a silver currency was introduced and a mint for it set up on the Capitoline Hill in the temple of Juno Moneta, Juno the admonisher, whence our word money.

But why did the heads of sovereigns appear on coins? Because they are the representatives of the god.

The theory I have outlined runs counter to generally accepted views as expounded in manuals of political economy and elsewhere. Those views are not founded on any evidence, but on an inveterate habit of tracing all customs and institutions to utility as we conceive it. In the main it is doubtless true that men are guided in their activities by reasons of utility, but their conceptions of utility differ widely. The circular shape of our coins is supposed to have been preferred on account of its convenience, but such a kind of utility may carry no weight with people who believe that the magical efficacy of an object depends on its shape; they will consider that shape most useful which imitates most closely the object they wish to control, no matter now awkward it may be to carry. When the economist and the anthropologist say that the circular shape of coins is due to convenience, they are looking at the matter from the point of view of the modern European, who has secularised coinage. When they say that currency was devised to overcome the limitations and inconveniences of barter, they are imputing to ancient man the motives which would sway a modern financier. They are victims of the dangerous fallacy that because a custom serves a certain purpose it was invented for that purpose. If we divest ourselves of our modern preconceptions and study the evidence, we are driven to the conclusion that currency had a religious origin, that it began with amulets which were worn or stored because they contained a protecting spirit. Economists tell us that gold is used for coinage because it can always be melted down and used otherwise, but contrary to their teaching the essence of currency was originally that it had no material utility, but was of the highest supernatural value. If gold is of any material use to-day, it is because its supernatural value has led to its being used for ornamental objects and has endowed it with a prestige which it cannot lose even after the reason for it has been removed. The manifold advantages of gold for purposes of coinage have enabled it to triumph over rival materials such as shell, stone, and mats, but they were not the reasons for its original selection. It began its career as one of many materials used to contain the god; a little of it was given away in exchange for quantities of stuff because a few ounces of divinity were worth pounds of gross matter.

If currency is of religious origin, it follows almost inevitably that trade must be. Fiji, Samoa, and Tonga may perhaps give us an idea how men managed before trade was invented, for these islands have no trade, not even barter. It may be that they lost the art of trading, or it may be that they never learnt it; I know of no evidence either way, but the map favours the supposition that they never learnt it; trade extends over the greater part of Melanesia and stops short of these three groups of islands. In the following sketch of the origin of trade I shall assume that Fijian economy represents a state of affairs antecedent to the invention of trade.

This is how the Fijians proceed. I belong, let us

suppose, to Lakemba, an island well provided with good soil but deficient of the best timber, such as is used for canoes and bowls. I am much in need of such timber, therefore I and my clan set to work to plant on a large scale, so that next year we may have a large surplus to give away. I warn my cousins of the island of Kambara, where food is short but good timber abundant, that I am coming to hold a festival in their honour. These cousins may be very remote. The connection may go back to prehistoric times, that is seven or eight generations, or more, but it is so useful that the memory is preserved. Being warned, our cousins set to work to fell trees and make canoes and bowls. As one side represents the male and the other the female line, there is great rivalry, and it is not a question who will get most but who will give most. Each side hopes that the stuff which it gives will exceed that which it receives; not enough in excess to make a bad bargain, but just enough to give them the right to crow over their opponents. The time comes; I sail for Kambara with my family; we are received with much ceremonial, ceremonial clearly religious in origin; they present us with whales' teeth and a coconut; they present it as an offering; our master of the ceremonies receives these offerings and prays over them for the success of the visit. We are hospitably entertained and then proceed to offer up the food we have brought with us. If we were hillmen we should mention at the end of the offering prayer the name of our hosts' temple, but being coast-men we merely end with "Let it be offered up". This offering of food is accompanied by an offering of whales' teeth; there are always whales' teeth; the master of ceremonies on the other side acknowledges them with a prayer. Then we dance to our hosts. Next day it is their turn to make offerings of what they have; canoes, bowls, timber, mats, followed by some whales' teeth. Then they dance to us. After that we go home, feeling victorious or defeated according as our offerings exceeded or fell short.

I suggest that here we have the origin of trade. Of course there may always have been private exchanges, though even these are scarcely known among Fijians; if they want anything they beg for it and it is not refused. But organised trade, trade surrounded by forms and usages, trade which stands under the protection of a god, must have begun in something which would account for its formalities and its obligations. I think we have found that beginning in the exchange of offerings. One group makes offerings to the gods of their kinsmen—that is to say, the gods of their mothers; these offerings are always accompanied by special ones which are not for use, but which contain the god, and are stored by the recipients on account of their divine efficacy until they are required to be given away on the occasion of another ceremonial. Sometimes no stuff is presented, but only shrines or amulets which, being sacred, are equivalent to large quantities of profane material. Convenience would encourage this practice. I met with a case of the giving of a god's shrine in return for ordinary gifts; a Fijian who was taught an elaborate cure by a spiritualistic medium, and was presented with a club in which resided the spirit which effected the cure, gave his teacher a present.

The theory which I have outlined identifies the original form of money with the fee paid to the priest who performs a sacrifice. This fee in India was not an ordinary gift; it had to be an object which partook of the nature of the god to whom the offering was made. For instance, "if a cake is offered to Agni, Fire", the priest's fee for that is gold; for that offering is for "Agni, and gold is Agni's seed. He gives it to the Fire-kindler, for he, the Fire-kindler, is the same as Agni". In other words, the officiating priest represents the god, and is presented with some object in which the nature of that god abides. The sacrificial fee is assigned to a deity; it follows the sacrifice to the world of the gods, and thus creates a bond between the gods and the sacrificer.

Note.—The quotations are all from the *Satapatha Brahmana*.

CHAPTER XI

Modern Critique

IN a very sound article on "Patricians and Plebeians at Rome"[1] Professor H. J. Rose makes a statement which sums up Modern Critique so well as to form a very convenient text on which to base a critique of that critique. He says: "In the matter of the origin of the plebs we have to handle Livy or Dionysius as we do Niebuhr or Binder; as theorists, that is, who must bring forward facts to prove their theories."

The premise, that Livy and Dionysius are theorists, is unimpeachable; but I demur to the conclusion that they are to be treated just like Niebuhr and Binder, for, beyond being theorists, the two pairs have nothing in common. Livy was heir to a continuous Roman tradition; Niebuhr belongs to an entirely different lineage, to a small degree Roman, but largely Oriental, Celtic, Germanic, the whole very much transformed by centuries of development culminating in the destructive rationalism of the eighteenth century.

A theorist is the child of his own times, or rather a brother of his own and the child of former ones. His theories may differ from those of his forefathers, but they have gradually developed out of them. Niebuhr and modern critique developed out of the eighteenth century and therefore their theories conform to the canons of Pure Reason, approve what seems rational to a nineteenth-century European, and reject what does not. Their theories are, therefore, very good evidence for the state of mind of the nineteenth century, but not for the manners and customs of Ancient Rome. Livy, on the other hand,

[1] *Journal of Roman Studies*, 1926, p. 106.

was saturated with the traditions of earlier generations, which themselves derived their traditions from earlier generations, and so on to the source.   When he theorised, therefore, he was bound to theorise along traditional lines, to imagine such motives as impelled his own contemporaries, or as he was accustomed to hear of as impelling his ancestors.

Let me illustrate my meaning by an example taken from actual experience.   There is in the island of Lakemba, in Fiji, a large cave.   There are no traditions of any kind about it, but just out of curiosity to see what he would make of it I asked Master Tarongi how the cave had been formed.   He thought a moment and then answered: "Perhaps the ancestor-god shaped it".   That was just his theory and was put forward as such, but shall we say that his theory is of no more value to the historian than one I might conceive?   Obviously no, because my theory would be framed on the analogy of theories current in the Europe of my own time: it would talk of erosion, disintegration and so forth; in default of other evidence a historian two thousand years hence could use it to reconstruct the geological theories of the twentieth century, but it would tell him nothing about Fijian history.   Master Tarongi, on the contrary, drew upon ideas of causation which he had imbibed from his elders: over and over again he had heard natural features ascribed to the actions of some ancestor-god; when asked to produce a theory where none existed he applied the teachings of his forbears as automatically as I should apply the lessons of geological manuals.   His theory, then, illustrates the beliefs of his people not only in the twentieth century but for many generations earlier.   The only question is: How many generations?   The same type of legend prevails in the Solomon Islands, Ceylon, Northern India and many other parts, so that it must go back such a distance in time as to make the interval between Livy and Romulus dwindle into insignificance.

It so happens that we have a considerable collection of legends such as served as model for Master Tarongi; so that we can dispense with the copy. This is only of interest as an example of formation by analogy, a process familiar to comparative philologists, and destined to become equally familiar to anthropologists when they cease to study processes in an imaginary being called primitive man, and turn their attention to the real men around them.

There is, near Kandy, in Ceylon, a square temple of stone with a pyramidal roof and surrounded by a wall pierced with trefoil windows. An enthusiastic amateur, widely read in European archæology, writes that a priest has begun to roof over the space between the shrine and the outer wall. Vandalism! The plan is examined and turns out to be that of numerous Kandyan temples of wattle and daub: a square sanctuary surrounded by an outer wall supporting a roof so as to form a covered deambulatory. The top of the wall is examined and traces of the insertion of a roof are found. The priest was right. He was only a theorist like the amateur, for he had never seen that temple in its original shape, and no one had, since it was built some centuries ago; but whereas the amateur approached the architecture from the outside, and thus failed to grasp the essentials in the midst of unessential peculiarities, the priest approached it from inside tradition; he had his ideas moulded by little modern village shrines and, even more, by habits of worship which demanded certain features. He did not reason things out, but just had a feeling for the right thing, and an ounce of such feeling is worth tons of critique.

When, therefore, Sinhalese villagers tell us that it was King Mahasammata who ordained that the men of the drummer caste should carry out the propitiation of planets, we shall realise that they are theorising, but at the same time we shall not treat their theory exactly as we should those of Senart and Risley, because the Sinhalese have inherited their theories in an unbroken line from the facts, whereas Messrs Senart and Risley are not the heirs of tradition. The first thing we have to settle is how old this theory is. Mahasammata is well known in Buddhist literature; he is the original ancestor of the solar line. Yet, so far, neither inquiries among the learned nor a search among indexes have produced any confirmation. Even so, I still put my faith in the villager. Literature is only a fragment of what has been, and it is largely accident whether it preserves a fact or not. However, let us suppose that this is purely a local theory; it must have been framed on the analogy of earlier ones, and those on the analogy of still earlier ones. We can be sure that those earlier ones have not left just one derivative in an obscure corner of the Ceylon jungle: we must seek elsewhere. The result of a search through Brahmanical literature, inscriptions, caste legends, modern customs, is to reveal the king as the head of the caste system with the power to promote and degrade, award titles and privileges. Thus the theory of the villagers is not far removed from the truth; it is merely a distortion of it. There is no reason to doubt the existence of Mahasammata, and if he existed he must have been the fountain of honour, assigned new privileges, extended or restricted duties. The distortion consists in making him appear as the inventor, instead of a regulator or administrator. It is as if, having lost all records previous to 1900, we mistook the birthday honours list of that year for the first institution of the peerage.

Having gained our experience among the living, we can now apply it to the dead. Dionysius says (II, 8): "Romulus, when he had marked off the better people from the inferior, next decreed and defined what each should engage in, the well-born to sacrifice, and rule, and judge, and with him administer the state, confining themselves to the affairs of the city; the plebeians to be released from these duties, neither having any experience of them nor, on account of their poverty, any leisure, and to cultivate and breed cattle and to practise money-making crafts." Plutarch concurs, and also ascribes to Romulus the institution of patrons and clients. Fustel de Coulanges, who generally defends tradition, deserts it here. He argues that the institution of clients must be much older than Rome, since it existed in other Italian cities, and his argument is unanswerable. Yet, even so, I would back the opinion of Dionysius and Plutarch against Pauly-Wissowa and the most up-to-date critical historians. After all, de Coulanges' argument applies no less to Dionysius's theory than to the clientship: whenever the Greeks or Romans (to say nothing of the Indians) speculated on the origin of grades of society they invariably concluded that it was the work of some king or sage. Therefore the theory is vastly older than Dionysius; in fact, than Rome itself. It had evidently become a habit of thought over a large area of the world, and there could not be so much smoke without a fire. I think we have already discovered that fire in India: early kings are law-givers rather than administrators; they merely expound the law, which is in society the counterpart of order in nature. The king upholds the constitution, but for Greeks, Romans and Indians the constitution is the division into classes, and the apportionment to each of proper rights and duties. When we establish a new colony the first thing we do is to frame a constitution of which the Governor is considered the author, though he may merely be approving of what his coadjutors have copied from other constitutions. I see no reason to doubt and every reason to believe that when Rome was founded the king promulgated the laws he proposed to rule by, laws which from ancient times had been considered necessary for the prosperity of every state. It is not suggested that he arbitrarily classified the people according to his own will: the greatest potentate cannot ignore existing class distinctions; but men are perpetually organising and reorganising, and for the ancients any organisation involved castes or classes. The kings of Rome certainly had the power to adjust the classes, and to promote or reduce within the system, since we find that that prerogative was exercised by the elder Tarquin, on a very large scale by Servius Tullius, and finally descended to the Censors. The story of Marcus Livius and Caius Claudius shows that in theory the discretion was absolute, though in practice it was expected to be tempered by custom, good sense, and public opinion, like the king's power of creating peers, or any theoretically unbounded prerogative.

Thus Dionysius is right after all, except in one particular: he may have mistaken the first exercise of the prerogative for its first institution.[1] Is it quite certain however, that he did? When a modern historian says that Tsar Nicholas II gave Russia a constitution he does not mean that Nicholas invented constitutional government, parliament, or the peerage; nor does the statement that Wolsey framed statutes for Christ Church, Oxford, and established studentships, necessarily imply that he invented the collegiate system. The ancients were perfectly well aware that the clientship existed in other cities besides Rome. Plutarch recognised that it was older than Rome, since he mentions a theory that it was derived from one Patronus, who came with Evander. The ancients were, besides, undoubting diffusionists, and

[1] Modern historians are not free from this fallacy; many opinions are based on the first appearance of an institution in our records, as if first appearance were the same as first occurrence. A custom may exist for a thousand years before it happens to get into our records.

if they found the same institutions in two places did not talk of its being natural or invoke the uniformity of the human mind, but concluded that one had borrowed from the other. Lykurgus was credited, rightly or wrongly, with the whole constitution of Sparta, yet at the same time he was supposed to have borrowed its main features from Crete.

Whatever may have been in Dionysius's mind, he has preserved for us a valuable piece of information concerning the constitutional powers of kings, powers which go back to a very remote antiquity and which play a great part in the history of human society, but for which we shall search in vain through the pages of the critical school.

Dionysius does more: he definitely disproves the racial theory which Professor Rose has laboriously demolished. For him the division into patricians and plebeians was the result of social organisation (we may add, for our part, along traditional lines), not of conquest. Diversity of origin is, in my experience, one of the most tenacious memories a people can have. If foreigners come and settle, whether peacefully or by conquest, among another people, they will remember that, if nothing else. Even decayed rustics living a precarious existence on the edge of the jungle remember that, long ago, the people of the next village came from overseas under seven princes; yet all difference of custom and language has vanished! We may be quite certain that if the Romans did not believe the patricians and plebeians to be distinct peoples it was because they were not, and it should take a good deal more than facile theories of race fusion to shake us in that faith.

The fundamental vice of the critical school is that it assumes traditions to be wrong until they can prove themselves right. To Mommsen they are mere "romances dressed up as history", so he dismisses them without even giving them a chance of establishing their innocence. That is not the attitude of the wise judge.

There are countries where false evidence is the order of the day; where even a man with a good case will lie to make it better. Yet even in such countries the judge does not set aside the evidence and evolve the facts out of his own brain. No, he listens patiently to the whole farrago, knowing it to contain lies, but knowing also that even lies are based upon facts. He hopes by the application of common sense to eliminate inventions, leaving only the truth. Thus a man brings a charge against his mistress of having absconded with property belonging to him. This charge may be true, but experience warns that it is probably a false one, brought in revenge for her running away. Let us, however, not prejudge the case, and since the man is our only witness, we cannot get at the truth without his aid. His statement is noted, and an inventory taken of the articles alleged to have been stolen. It includes a woman's bodice, clearly a gift made by him to her, which he is spited at having bestowed in vain. Thus the evidence contains its own correction, for the whole story is true except for one small but vital fact—the articles had been given.

If a man cannot get away from the facts when he is trying his best to do so, how much harder must it be when he is cleaving to them with all his might? Are we not at least as safe as the judge in accepting the evidence and using it to correct itself? The plain man trusts his senses, and when he finds them at fault uses them to correct their own errors: it is only the philosopher who rejects their evidence altogether on account of some manifest failures, and proceeds to construct a universe out of his imagination. So also the critical historian, having caught out tradition once or twice, sweeps the whole away and proceeds to fill the vacant space with what he himself thinks self-evident, but what succeeding generations will recognise as the prejudices of his time. Grote thought he was reducing Greek history to reason:

we now see that he was reading Victorian liberalism into Athenian politics. Yet Grote was moderation itself compared with the destructive activities of later generations, whose excesses in reversing anything the ancients had declared are already bringing about a reaction. Already I hear Sir Flinders Petrie rejoicing that "the passion for denial which reigned from Niebuhr to Cheyne has had a salutary check in many countries".[1]

It is when a people's habits of thought are remotest from ours that we should treat them most tenderly, yet it is precisely then that Modern Critique becomes most high-handed: whole aspects of thought are liable to be ignored or denied simply because they do not square with European rationalism. In vain pundit after pundit comes forth and states in no equivocal language that the Indian king is a god, or even several gods; the European scholar will not accept their assurance; these statements, he explains, do "not imply any divinity of the king, but merely that he is as much superior to the lowest caste as the gods are to mankind".[2] Why cannot the Indian mean what he says? One suspects that the true reason is that such a doctrine sounds like blasphemy to unaccustomed ears.

Even the sounder and more moderate among those bred in the critical school allow prejudice to creep in under the guise of reason. Thus when Sophocles's "Antigone" argues that a brother is more precious than a husband or children, because she can produce more children but not another brother, our taste is naturally shocked. Admirers of Sophocles cannot bring themselves to believe that so perfect a dramatist could have suffered such a lapse, and the blame is laid on some argumentative and tasteless copyist. It has, however, been discovered that

[1] *Antiquity*, 1928, p. 234.
[2] *Hastings's Encyclopædia of Religion and Ethics*, s.v. King (Indian).

the argument was a tragic dilemma which has appealed
to more than one age and people. It is a theme of song
in the modern Balkans; it is related with admiration in
a Buddhist story which is doubtless pre-Buddhistic. It
is obvious that it made a very wide appeal to the ancient
world, and a dramatist working it into his tragedy would
be renewing old feelings. Perhaps Sophocles did not
work it into his tragedy, but found it already worked in.
Anyhow, does it really matter whether he wrote it or not?
He who reads him as literature can bracket the passage
and skip it when he gets there, but the historian of civilisation will be thankful that someone put it there. Modern
Critique has wasted on questions of authenticity which
are quite immaterial much time which it could more wisely
have spent in extending its knowledge, for one of its great
weaknesses was that it thought it knew a great deal more
than it did; it had no conception how scrappy its information was. There is a story of a German professor who
emended milch-cow to milk cow, because, he argued,
there was no such word as milch in English. We may
smile at him, but might not the Romans of the monarchy
laugh at Professor Beloch when he argues that the names
of four kings are plebeian, and therefore the lists of kings
are not trustworthy? Would it not be wiser to recognise
that we do not know everything, and that if we knew
more we might see an excellent reason for these plebeian
names? Even in our present state of knowledge it is not
difficult to imagine one. May not some of the kings
have been plebeians? There were low-caste kings in
India from early times; why not in Rome? As a matter
of fact, Ceylon presents us with an excellent parallel: it
has recently come out that the names of some of the early
kings belong to the third or agricultural caste, not to the
first or royal, and we have besides a legend that the first
king of Ceylon was of the third caste. Though our use of
the word "tyrant" may disguise the fact, democratic

kings in Corinth were succeeded by an oligarchy of the royal caste.

There was some excuse for the presumption of Modern Critique when it began its career: its adherents had no knowledge of human ways and thought outside their own circle, the cultivated middle class of Europe. Since then anthropology has extended our knowledge so fast that historical thought has not been able to keep pace with it, but we are beginning to realise that there are more ways in which men can think and act than were ever dreamt of in the philosophy of Niebuhr or even of Mommsen, and that things which seemed fabulous to them do actually happen. Thus a little knowledge leads away from tradition, but much knowledge brings us back to it, and we have to thank Professor Rose for placing our widened experience at the disposal of Greek and Latin scholars.

It is not, however, only knowledge that Modern Critique lacks, but also the faculty of entering into the point of view of other ages and other races, of adopting their premises and reasoning from them, for to do so requires a constructive mind, and critique is destructive. Hence the failure to do what, in retrospect, seems merely putting two and two together. Thus Muir put the student of civilisation under a great obligation by assiduously collecting ancient Indian traditions as to the origin of caste, but, though his subconsciousness evidently felt such texts to be worth collecting, his reason found them so contradictory that he rejected them as untrustworthy. One set of traditions derived the castes from the various members of a god, while others traced the castes to the sons of one man, not always the same man. It was impossible that both could be true. This verdict does not seem to have been called in question, and no one seems to have attempted to take these traditions seriously. Muir, like every Sanskrit scholar, was well aware that, according to Indian thought, the members of the higher castes are born twice—first, after the flesh, from their father and mother; a second time, by initiation, from the Veda—but he never entered sufficiently into the spirit of such a creed to argue from it and to conclude that castes have a double origin, temporal and spiritual, that there is no more contradiction in saying that the Sunaka Brahmans are descended from Sunaka and that Brahmans in general are born from Purusha's head, than there is in saying that John Smith is the son of George Smith, and yet, as a baptised Christian, is a child of God and a member of Christ.

Sometimes the contradiction lies not in the facts recorded but in the use made of them. Thus Plutarch gives three alternative theories for the word "patrician": he says that patricians were so called (1) because they were the fathers of legitimate sons, (2) because they knew their own fathers, and (3) on account of the patronate. If any one of these etymologies is true, the other two cannot be, but the actual facts may all three perfectly well be true. Comparative evidence suggests (it is as yet no more than a suggestion) that the "fathers" were the heads of noble families, men who had gone through the sacred marriage rite, which is at the same time an installation in a higher rank, and thus begot children qualified to carry on the sacred rites who carefully kept their pedigrees in support of the claim; moreover, they stood in a relation analogous to that of father towards the family serfs. Thus the three rival theories preserve three facts which are mutually complementary, and become conflicting only when used for the same etymology. It will generally be found that when men want a theory they draw from facts.

Thus I believe that, as our knowledge extends beyond the limits of one people to as much of the world as our minds can embrace, many problems will solve themselves which critique can never solve.

CHAPTER XII

In the Grip of Tradition

TRADITION is unpopular at present; in fact there is a revolt against it because it has become too rigid and also because it means discipline. Such revolts may play a useful part in society, sweeping away the obstacles to adaptation. It is unfortunate, however, that science should lend its support to doctrines which are taken up merely because they promise emancipation from the past. Men, dissatisfied with their condition, are anxious to make a fresh start, and therefore readily believe that they can do so. They eagerly accept the assertions of the psychologists, who attach no importance to heredity and ignore tradition. Every difficulty in the way of understanding racial characteristics is welcomed, and their very existence is hotly denied because it would imply predestination. The linguists have caught the infection, and there are some who believe that there is a complete linguistic break between each generation and the next. Similarly, there are anthropologists who want every individual to create his culture *de novo*, and fanatically oppose any inquiries into origins, any suggestion that the present is conditioned by the past.

It is time that an effort was made to repel this invasion of desires, resentments, and egotisms from the realm of science. Science is based on observation, and observation involves sinking one's own preferences and surrendering to the facts. Let us then observe; let us open our eyes and ears to what is going on about us, and we shall find that, in spite of its protestations, Europe is held as fast by tradition to-day as in any other age. Man is a traditional animal, and must always fall back on tradition for his means of expression. Even his longings cannot take on concrete form unless tradition gives them shape. In fact, this revolt may be a last struggle to escape a gradual ossification of culture, a last effort of age to persuade itself that it is still young.

Whether we like it or not, the great passions of these times still pour themselves out into channels which existed thousands of years ago. The banks may shift, but the general course remains the same. I shall select for demonstration two examples from the politics of the present day.

The Good Queen

Now that the constitutional crisis of December 1936 has passed into history we may be able to examine it as coldly as we should the deposition of a Pharaoh or a Grand Mogul.

If we are to understand the premises that were accepted or attacked, and the passions that were released, we must grasp two facts. The first is that the monarchy remains essentially a ritual institution. The king signs administrative documents, but that does not make him primarily an administrator. Bishops and clergymen also sign administrative documents. It is true that the king is popularly regarded as part of the civil administration, as opposed to the ecclesiastical, as temporal rather than spiritual, but this classification does not correspond to the facts. The real line of demarcation runs rather between the civil administration on the one hand and the royal ceremonial and the church ritual on the other, the two last being intimately connected and often overlapping, as in the coronation ceremony.

The second fact to remember is that our ritual belongs to a type which may best be described as ethical, a type to which those of Buddhism and Islam also belong. The objective of such a ritual is a morally good life rather than a prosperous one. All the principal features of the prosperity ritual are to be found in those of the ethical type, but their material aspect has been changed into a moral one. To take an example which bears specially on our theme, the victim and the worshipper (the two are interchangeable) must be free from blemish. The blemish was physical; it is now moral. The king is the supreme worshipper, and there are still people who will not have a halt or a blind king. We *prefer* one that is handsome, but *insist* that he be good. Our king is less a purveyor of prosperity than a pattern of character, and must be as far as possible an ideally moral figure. Here a conflict arises between earlier tradition and later morality. Morality has become identified to a great extent with chastity or monogamy, but on the other hand the idea that the king is abounding in fertility has not quite died out. A compromise has been arrived at: a king's amours are secretly admired, ecclesiastically deplored, and officially ignored. This compromise must not on any account be violated, or it may be the worse for the king.

There is no compromise possible in the case of the queen. She must be, like Cæsar's wife, above even suspicion. Public opinion does not like her even to have been lawfully wedded and lawfully parted by death. So few widows have become queens that it is difficult to test public opinion in practice, but I think we should all feel disappointed if the heir to the throne were to marry one. For a king to place on the throne a woman whose first husband is still living is unthinkable; it would be a breach of the close connection between queenship and chastity.

During the constitutional crisis one heard the view expressed that the king had the right to marry whom he liked. The king has never possessed such a right; he is on the throne not to please himself, but for the good of the people. If the good of the people is prosperity, he must

not, in marrying, commit such a breach of the rules as
would end prosperity. If the good of the people is their
moral elevation, he must not marry anyone who could
not be idealised as a good queen. If what was meant was
that the king ought to have the right, that is quite another
matter, one that lies outside the scope of science and
belongs rather to philosophy. We are not here concerned with what ought to be, but what is. We are not
here to alter tradition, but to describe it. We can only
note that tradition requires of the queen certain qualifications, and still requires them as firmly as ever. The
qualifications may vary, but qualifications there have
always been.

It would seem that at one time the queen had to be of
earthly descent to balance the king's celestial nature.
We know that more generally she must be of royal descent.
We have but recently done away with this rule, or rather
reverted to an older practice, according to which the king
could marry the daughter of a nobleman. But whatever
changes are made, there is one fact that remains unchanged,
and that is that the queen is the king's partner in a sacred
marriage, and that to be an effective partner she must have
no commerce with anyone else. India supplies an
apparent exception. The Ancient Indians seem to have
thought it too much to expect of a queen that she should
always be virtuous, so before she could play her part in
the rite of Varunapraghasa she had to confess her lapses,
because "when confessed the sin becomes less, since it
becomes the truth". By confession, that is, she became
ritually pure.

Marriage has now spread to all classes, but it remains
sacred and the wife has to confine herself to her ritual
partner. Among some West African tribes a bride, if she
has been unchaste, has, like the Indian queen, to confess.

Attacks are now being made, not for the first time in
history, on the institution of marriage. An institution

which has spread to all and sundry naturally loses some of its pristine rigour. In the royal circles from which it originally spread, however, it retains its strictness and elaboration, if only because these are almost the last distinguishing marks left in this sphere between royalty and its humblest subjects. When, therefore, an attempt was made to relax the royal marriage to the same degree as the common, that attempt was decisively repelled.

The reasons given were not those which would have been given long ago, or by the still existing tribes who think that any relaxation of the queen's virtue would bring disaster on the crops; the British repelled it because their ritual is ethical, and the queen must be a paragon of virtue.

Yet the British ritual is not as purely ethical as the British themselves imagine. Three days before the coronation these words were heard at the Central Methodist Hall: "England has always been blessed when it had a ruler of noble character, and the people should realise that fact. Such a king was a benediction of God." What is to be blessed? The word is conveniently vague, but we can discern behind it a suggestion of material prosperity. The Bishop of London hailed the new reign "with Christian hope because the Throne is occupied by a true Christian man and a true Christian woman". That is left even vaguer than at the Central Methodist Hall, but this very vagueness is a sure sign of strong emotional reserves in the background. Experienced observers of men would have taken care not to provoke these reserves into action.

No one who was acquainted with the history of marriage and of the way in which theory has been replaced by emotion would ever have put forward the compromise of a morganatic marriage. The whole point of a wife, as opposed to a mistress, is that she takes part in the ritual even when it degenerates into ceremonial. We have lost the belief that a man cannot perform certain rituals without a mate, but we have got instead a vague feeling that a bachelor is unsuitable as a leader of pageantry. There is something unsatisfactory about a queenless king, even about a wifeless governor. Even the modest pageantry of the household seems incomplete without a mistress of the house. Once a mistress of the house has been duly consecrated she must take part in all "functions", and her absence has to be explained and excused. We can give no reason; we just feel like that; but if anyone imagines that a traditional feeling is less powerful than a reasoned theory he has learned very little about human nature.

A mistake which many people make is to suppose that a practice for which we can give no satisfactory reason is for that very reason stupid, and being stupid can easily be done away with by a little reasoning, or failing that by decree. They forget that communities, like individuals, form habits, and that habits are more deeply ingrained than reasons. Reasons come in at the beginning when they are necessary in order to establish a habit, but, once the habit is thoroughly established, the reasons drop out. The habit may then surround itself with a body of emotions which reasoning lacks, and so when reason interferes it often gets the worst of it. One of the best examples of this is the incest taboo. The reason for it is completely forgotten, but the custom has dug itself in so securely that even the most advanced thinkers have not dared to disturb it.

Queenship and marriage are less secure, and some therefore have attempted to disturb the ancient rule that partnership in the royal ritual is exclusive and indissoluble. In so doing they have provided the student of social phenomena with valuable material.

The constitutional crisis showed precisely how the people can be moved by attacks on traditional ways—

ways which appear to the highbrow to be quite out of touch with realities and therefore of no importance. It was curious to watch how the highbrows themselves were carried away by the wave of feeling, while all the time they imagined themselves to be above such things. Men who in normal times looked down upon the monarchy with lofty tolerance descended from their pedestals and joined in the fray. Blood-shed in Spain and international perils were displaced from the headlines, and men hurried to seize the daily paper as they probably had not hurried since 1918. It was no use arguing that kings come and go, and really make no difference, for human nature rose up against reason, insisted on being impassioned, and thus made the monarchy important. Importance resides not in things but in ourselves; a thing is important because we make it important. The British public made the crisis so important that the fate of the Empire was involved. Not the least surprising fact was that the "new" countries such as Australia and New Zealand, those most republican in their reasoning, showed themselves most monarchical in their feeling, and became the most ardent supporters of a point of view of which they had forgotten the meaning. They were so ardent because they had forgotten; when you do a thing because you have thought it out as the best means to an end you do not get fanatical about it, but when you do it because it is the tradition of ages gradually adjusted to fit desires, then it is that emotion is most intense. No one quarrels over the best design for a carburettor—men just argue about it; but they will quarrel bitterly over marriage with a deceased wife's sister precisely because there is no basis for argument. Persuade a man, in accordance with a system of thought which he shares with you, that the land will prosper if the king unite with a queen, and the queen with no one else; he will adopt the suggestion as he might a new and better plough; he will be angry if the new rule is broken as he might be angry if anyone misused his plough. But it will be a very different sort of anger that his descendants will feel when they have forgotten the basis of the rule and have transformed it into a spiritual comfort, an ideal that cheers the soul. They will rise against anyone who attacks that ideal as against one who sets out to damage their souls.

THE DICTATOR

Sun-worship was once all the rage among mythologists; everything was solar. Then a critic reduced the fashion to absurdity by proving that Napoleon was a sun-god, and his twelve marshals the signs of the zodiac.

This parodist was much nearer the truth than he suspected. Napoleon was not a sun-god, but in some respects his behaviour was inherited from representatives of the Invincible Sun, and that is what made the parody possible.

Like all great men of action, Napoleon was a dreamer, and like all dreams his harked back to the past and were largely traditional. His ambition was to revive the Holy Roman Empire even as Charlemagne had done. Charlemagne had twelve peers, so his imitator must have twelve, but being a soldier he gave them the military title of marshal.

Charlemagne was not the originator of the imperial idea; he too drew his inspiration from the past. He merely revived the lapsed title of those Roman emperors who had been the earthly representatives of *Sol Invictus*, the Invincible Sun.

Nor did Charlemagne invent the twelve peers. Our fear of being thirteen at table has been plausibly traced to a company of twelve headed by a thirteenth, the king or prophet, doomed to die within the year. The Normans who conquered South Italy fixed at twelve the number of counts who ruled the country. Our jurymen still number twelve. It is not uncommon for Hindu religious teachers to have twelve disciples. The religious fraternity of Bayumi in Cairo has twelve coadjutors, neither more nor less. One important point to note is that of our twelve disciples eleven were good, the twelfth a traitor. It is important because it suggests a parallel with the earliest company of twelve that I have yet traced. In the course of his consecration the Vedic king calls on twelve successive days at the house of each of twelve court personages. The first eleven of these are called his jewels, but the twelfth is an obscure personage, a discarded queen who represents Nirriti, the earth as the abode of decay. There is no hint that these personages are associated with the zodiac, but each of them represents a god whom we know, from other evidence, to have been in charge of some star or constellation lying near the ecliptic, the only exception being the "Way".

Figures of speech and fancies are admissible as evidence, for they do not arise out of nothing. It is a safe presumption that metaphors were once facts, so we can cite the president of the Royal College of Constantinople in the tenth century. He "was named the Sun of Science: his twelve associates, the professors in the different arts and faculties, were the twelve signs of the zodiac".

In short, Napoleon's behaviour was to some extent conditioned by an ancient theory which assimilated the state to the universe. The state had to copy the normal universe in order that life might be normal. The exact form of such a state necessarily varied with the knowledge of the universe and with the direction of men's interests, whether they were engrossed by the weather, or the stars, or some new discovery about the sun. The facts which we have here put together point to a variety of the state in which emphasis was laid on the sun and the zodiac. The theory faded out so long ago that we are reduced to inferring it, but the habits acquired under its influence persisted in some measure right down to the beginning of the nineteenth century. The figure of an emperor with his twelve peers still made an appeal to the romantic imagination, and when that imagination was reinforced by genius the romance could still be translated into fact.

This, it may be, was the last time that the cosmic theory of the state made its appearance in European politics, but it was certainly not the last time that the Roman Empire supplied the stuff of which dictators' dreams are made. The evidence is in our daily paper, except that Mussolini goes back beyond Charlemagne to the Cæsars.

Here we must guard against the error of mistaking the symptom for the cause, as we should if we ascribed these dreams entirely to tradition. Dictators would have sprung up even if we had lost all memory of the Roman Empire, but they would have been cast in a different mould.

The Jews can claim a great antiquity for their dreams. The demand for a Jewish national home would probably have arisen if historical memory had been completely wiped out, but tradition suggested the exact home, and made a very bad suggestion. The Jews would not have picked out a tiny country already well populated if they had not remembered that their forefathers had once lived there, and if they had not continued to look upon Zion as a holy city; nor would the people of Great Britain have been so ardent in their support if the Old Testament had not created a habit of looking upon the Jews as the rightful owners of the land, and if the spirit of the Crusades did not still govern their attitude towards the Moslem world.

It is a peculiarity of man that his impulses cannot take a definite shape without a model on which to mould them. He may feel restless and rebellious, but he cannot give his rebelliousness a definite direction except by imitating previous rebels, who have themselves imitated earlier ones. He wants to hit out, but if he merely kills he becomes a vulgar criminal. He must cover his killing with the cloak of tradition; he takes Brutus and Cassius as the sponsors of his actions, and so becomes a traditional hero. History may do no more than supply an excuse for an impulse which is a child of the present, but an excuse must be lived up to and so it becomes a factor in his behaviour: he has to continue posing as a modern edition of a Roman patriot. Or suppose him to be touched with megalomania: his hormones, or whatever it may be, drive him on to cut a figure among men and to exceed them in their achievements, but he does not know how to set about it until he has studied the ways in which others have worked out their megalomania. The motive power is within him, but the machinery he has to borrow from his predecessors. He has learnt of empires in the past, and so he dreams of an empire like the one most nearly related to the circumstances of his time and country.

Or, again, take a community which has been humiliated so long that it wants to restore its self-respect by becoming a sovereign nation with a territory like other sovereign nations. It does not evolve an entirely new conception, but goes searching among its archives for a time when it was a sovereign nation. That age, always believed to be golden, supplies the concrete plan for its desires to work upon.

Man is in truth a most unimaginative creature, and his wildest flights are but copyings in which he does not depart very far from his model. It is his weakness, and at the same time his strength, that his impulses are so vague that they need example to give them definition. Hence his immense powers of adaptation. His impulses do not at once take concrete shape as does the behaviour which we call instinctive. They have no definite direction, so that he flounders about, instead of going straight to the point like a chicken just out of the egg. Yet in the long run he is the gainer, because he is free to go off in any direction which circumstances may dictate, and these circumstances are the product of traditions which are continually being adapted to meet present needs.

To give an example, he is equipped to make noises with his mouth, and noises he must make, but the kind of noises is not determined by the shape of his vocal organs or the nature of his brain. The young child does not know what noises to make, and if he is born deaf will never know, but will struggle angrily against his inability to express himself. Whether he calls a dog *dog* or *chien* or *hund* will be determined by the people among whom he lives. Thus he is not tied down to one region of the earth, and wherever fate places him he will be able to adapt himself. His impulses to emulate, to surpass, to resist, or to lead, are all as undetermined as his impulse to speak, and are as much in need of precedents to determine them. Nature is the mother of his aspirations, but tradition is the midwife.

CHAPTER XIII

Snobbery

THE desire to emulate one's betters has been a most potent, perhaps the most potent, force in the diffusion of customs. Yet it has received scarcely any notice from sociologists. Why?

In the first place we are not honest with ourselves. Few like to admit that they adopt new ways because they want to rise to a higher status or fear to drop to a lower one—in short, that they are snobs. It is especially difficult to admit as much in these days of equalitarianism, when only low people admit that they have betters, and it is part of the social rise to recognise no superiors.

Secondly, the study of culture has not yet emancipated itself from philosophy with its way of deducing, not from observation, but from first principles supposed to be absolutely and eternally valid. Now the philosophy which dominates the study of culture is still out-and-out utilitarian, so all theories of culture are based on utilitarianism and not on facts.

Take cars, for instance. If you ask anyone why cars have diffused so rapidly throughout society, he will not observe, but at once go back to his first principles; these include the axiom that men adopt new inventions because they are useful, whereby he means at bottom mechanically efficient. A car is useful; this utility is obvious, and so everyone wants a car. In all Europe the car has spread most rapidly among the English because the English are a practical people; it has spread still more widely in America because the Americans are still more practical.

Observation tells us a very different tale. In their book *Middletown* (New York, 1929) Mr and Mrs Lynd have collected a great deal of evidence direct from car-owners of the Middle West. Utility, in the narrow sense of the word, hardly figures at all among the motives for buying a car; it is the fear of losing caste that is the chief factor. The impulse comes mainly from the younger people; a young man simply cannot take a girl out on foot or in a bus. The family is compelled to get a car, so that their boy can take girls out and eventually find a mate. It may begin with a cheap car; then the young man will apply steady pressure to convert it into a more expensive, and so more impressive, car. Sex, then, is the prime mover, but sex only drives in the direction of a car because the car is a sign of wealth, and wealth is a proof of success, and the female will not look at a male who is not successful. Success in America is wealth. The pressure to buy a car is exercised even when sex does not come into play at all. I can speak from experience, because I have suffered that steady pressure. I have been urged, sometimes with the fervour of missionary zeal, to get a machine I did not want. I was made to feel that I was not living up to my class in dispensing with it.

Snobbery is even more in evidence in the matter of clothing. Why do girls in Middletown wear silk stockings? Is it because they last longer, are warmer, or are in any way more "useful" than those made of other materials? No, the only way in which they can be called useful is that they spare a girl the humiliation of appearing less well-to-do than her schoolfellows. She will sooner forgo education altogether than endure the disgrace. Food is really useful; it is the *sine qua non* of life, yet there are Middletown families that will pare down the food, that will be content with inferior substitutes for a good healthy diet, in order to provide a car and silk stockings. The reason is that indoor evidence of wealth, such as an ample board and prime food, does not help an American's status as does outdoor evidence.

In America status depends on wealth or the appearance of it, because in such a huge fluid population people "know money; they don't know you". In communities where the people you meet are mostly people you know personally, status depends much more on private qualifications such as birth. It often depends on the power to make rain, or to heal, or to make prosperity in a general way. The prosperity-maker, the king, as he is usually called, wears something on his head, so it is the ambition of every man to be like him and wear something on his head. There are communities where he alone, or only those who rank immediately below him, are allowed to wear some headgear. In our community everyone, even the poorest, has been able to fulfil that ambition; but in the presence of the king we are still reminded that originally only one man had the right to wear a hat. Where everybody enjoys a privilege it ceases to be one. If everyone wears a hat it ceases to be evidence of social status. Our young people look upon it as a nuisance, and so discard it. Yet there is a touch of snobbery even in this defiance of good form: it began, remember, in Oxford.

It seems highly probable that all clothing has been vulgarised in this way. Dr E. E. Evans-Pritchard reports that among the Burun of Dar-Fung "only the chief and two notables wore short pieces of cloth coloured with red ochre round the loins, the rest were completely naked" ("Ethnological Observations in Dar-Fung", *Sudan Notes and Records*, xv, 7). In most countries everyone wears something, but then the people at the top usually wear more. The spread of clothing from the loins to the whole body can to some extent be traced in art: the higher ranks always lead the way. In Ceylon the whole gamut can still be observed from the chief with hat, jacket, skirt, and shoes, all complete, down to the peasant with a loin-cloth and possibly a cloth above the waist, and still lower

to the outcaste Rodiya who is allowed to wear nothing
above the waist.[1]

In the Near East, European clothing is now associated
with government service, and government service is on a
higher plane than private enterprise. I have seen a daily
paid clerk change from a *dhoti* into trousers, coat, and
boots on the day when he first came to the office as a
permanent salaried official, thus sacrificing comfort on
the altar of snobbery. In Egypt it might be said "people
know clothes; they don't know you". If you wear a
skull-cap you are a peasant, if a turban a *sheikh*, if a fez
an *effendi*. Those of our tailors who cater for the
ambitious clerk are constantly reminding him that clothes
determine the status.

There is snobbery even in death. It is well known that
pyramids were originally royal tombs. Then great nobles
indulged in small ones. They disappeared long ago from
the upper classes, but have taken refuge among the
peasantry. Stepped pyramids, the oldest known type in
Egypt, are still to be seen in village cemeteries.

Snobbery diffuses not only etiquette and material
possessions; it can diffuse the law. It has, for instance,
driven "borough English", ultimogeniture, out of England.
Primogeniture cannot be said to be more "useful" than
ultimogeniture. There is much to be said for the
succession of the youngest son to the paternal house:
he is the last to reach maturity and so to be ready to go
forth in quest of fortune. Sentiment, too, is on the side
of the Benjamin, as witness numberless fairy-tales.
Borough English had, however, the misfortune of being
the custom of the conquered, primogeniture of the con-
quering aristocracy. "Consequently, if the tenement
descends to the younger son . . . the inference is sometimes drawn that it is not free" (Pollock and Maitland,
History of English Law, I, 374, 647). Borough English

[1] See also my *Progress of Man*, chap. viii.

became associated with serfdom, and then it was doomed: everyone who wanted to rise in the social scale copied the aristocracy.

Our marriage ceremony, that of the Indians and the Malays, and other related types are certainly of royal origin. In other words, we should not go through the marriage ceremony we know if it had not been an aristocratic privilege. Even now it has not quite ceased to be so, for it is still the upper classes that feel most acutely its omission, and proletarian revolts usually include an attack upon marriage.

Polygamy is certainly aristocratic in origin, and there are still places where it is confined to the chiefs. In Egypt, on the contrary, it is commonest among the peasantry, because it has proved profitable, as well as conducive to prestige: children begin to work early and so are an asset. On the other hand, the European is making it *bon ton* to have only one wife, so that, by a not uncommon reversal, it is monogamy that is becoming aristocratic, and polygamy, like the pyramids, is likely to find its last refuge among the lowest.

It may seem extravagant to claim for snobbery an important part in the building up of nations, but let us consider the facts. Language must be one of the chief binding materials of nationality, since nations correspond pretty well to linguistic areas. But how are those linguistic areas formed? By the diffusion of the speech of the best people. In that way English has displaced Cornish, Erse, and Welsh. We can still watch the dialect of the best people gradually driving out the local dialects, because the dialects are regarded as "bad" English. As a matter of fact they are perfectly good English, but they are plebeian, and so they, especially the cockney variety, are a bar to advancement. With the standardising of the language there goes a standardising of manners and customs, and increasing centralisation.

The success of missions depends largely on whether snobbery works for or against them. In the Pacific they made little progress until the chiefs or their influential relatives took up Christianity; then an order would go forth that everyone was to turn Christian, and the majority obeyed. Snobbery was not the only factor; loyalty and a sense of discipline certainly predominated; but there is also a strong desire to be with the people of quality. Many Fijians have an uncomfortable feeling that by being Methodists they do not belong to the King's church, and if free competition were allowed between sects the Church of England would certainly win many adherents by its royal character alone.

In India, on the contrary, the missions attack institutions which are the very hall-mark of good caste: suttee, child-marriage, the hierarchy of caste itself. The Indian, conservative as he is, is quite capable of conversion, as is proved by frequent conversions to Hinduism and the constant formation of new sects. But then, Hinduism works with snobbery, not against it: a despised tribe can raise its status by adopting child-marriage, vegetarianism, and other essentials of Hinduism, just as in England people often leave the chapel for the church in order to consolidate their social rise. Christianity is now becoming the religion of the low castes, so that its chances are getting smaller than ever.

It is because they ignore the force of snobbery that reformers so often fail. In India we have tried to abolish suttee by force, not by the slower but surer process of altering the ideas at the back of it, by making it appear vulgar, for instance. The result is it still goes on in secret, and aristocratic Hindus are still quite unrepentant on this score. Were we to withdraw force there is little doubt that the "best people" would revert to suttee, because we have repressed the manifestation instead of treating the cause. We have not realised that to forbid suttee is like

forbidding an officer to follow his code of honour, death
rather than surrender, going down with the ship, and all
that we associate with the character of an officer and a
gentleman. We should never succeed with him that way,
but we might if we could persuade him that his country
had need of him and that it was dishonourable to leave
it in the lurch.

Recently legislation has been passed in India to suppress
child-marriage. What was wanted was not repression,
but the patience to create a set of better people than the
best, one which did not marry its children young. That
is what is happening in Syria: the best people in the big
towns have largely given up marrying their children
before puberty, and as big towns set the tone for
little towns, and little towns for the country, child-
marriages may eventually die a natural death.[1]

Utilitarian philosophy has had an equally unfortunate
effect on our treatment of national problems. It has
completely ignored the snobbery of nations, as it has
ignored that of individuals. It has, for instance, accepted
it as an obvious axiom that nations go to war for the sake
of some gain real or supposed. Publicists have therefore
wasted a great deal of time trying to prove that war
always results in loss and not in gain, hoping thereby to
cure men of a desire for war. But if we do as in the case
of cars, if we go about asking Dick and Harry why they
are in favour of a particular war, we shall never find that
it is because they hope for some gain. On the contrary
if you urged them to support a war on that account they
would be most indignant. If any man seeks to drag a
nation into war because he hopes to derive some material
advantage from it he must carefully disguise his intent.
His best way is to persuade it that peace can only be
preserved at the expense of caste. What has rallied the

[1] In Egypt child-marriages are "repressed", with the result that
ages are faked.

French people year after year to support costly armaments since 1871? It has been the fear of dropping from the position of a first-class nation into the second class, or even lower.

The utilitarianism of the last century put commercial wars in fashion among historians. There is no doubt the rapacity of traders and financiers constantly leads to friction, but has any nation ever stood firm behind its financiers and traders because it expected to be in pocket at the end? Commercial quarrels only interest the mass when its vanity is at stake. Nations, like individuals, like to think of themselves as great merchants, and will make any sacrifice rather than be relegated to the rank of a shopkeeper. When statistics are published to show that British tonnage is losing ground compared with rival nations, are we downcast because we foresee ourselves less able to acquire "useful" things, or is it that we can no longer swell with pride at seeing the British flag everywhere and the rest nowhere?

Great Britain, a society-leader among nations, had once the fastest, the largest, the best liners furrowing every ocean on the globe. Lesser lights made up their minds to emulate it. All kinds of nations are now building better, faster and more luxurious ships. It is not that it pays, for they are generally run at a loss, which has to be made good by the taxpayer; but the taxpayer seems apparently to think it is well worth the satisfaction of outshining the best.

Great Britain, a society-leader among nations, has colonies. Her nearest rivals follow suit. It thus becomes the mark of a great power to have colonies, just as it raises a man's status to have a country residence as well as a town house. Therefore, any nation that has any pretensions has looked round for colonies. The first in the field have acquired rich and profitable territories. Later comers have taken anything that was going, regardless of cost; for colonies have become as necessary to a nation that would hobnob with the best, as evening dress is to a man who would move in good society.[1]

We may think it all very ridiculous, but it is not the sociologist's part to decide whether the behaviour of states is sensible or absurd, only to find out what it is and why. He deals in facts, not in moral judgments. National snobbery is a fact, and it has never been one so much as at the present day.

It is a fact which the colonial policy of Europe has consistently ignored. All our great proconsuls have been permeated with utilitarian philosophy, with the conviction that all a people wants is prosperity. Give it prosperity and it will be content. In actual practice prosperity has always bred discontent. There are many reasons, but one is that with prosperity come national pretensions. A very poor community, precariously wringing its subsistence from a niggard soil, has no leisure for thoughts of national greatness. Give it a margin above mere subsistence, and it will begin to give itself airs, despise those that still struggle on in its former condition, and think itself deserving of yet higher rank. Eventually it will want an army, a navy, an air force, shipping lines and industries of its own, not that it is really interested in such things, but simply because all the best nations have them. But above all things it will want independence, because you cannot be a gentleman among nations unless you are independent. It is as useless to argue that independence can only be purchased at the expense of prosperity, as it would be to argue with a slave who wants to sink all his savings in buying his freedom. Status is dearer to most peoples than prosperity, so the argument misses fire. Of course, they want prosperity very much, but they want the status of a sovereign state so intensely that nothing

[1] "It is a matter of honour for Germany to regain her colonies." —*Deutsche Allgemeine Zeitung.*

will ever convince them that independence is inconsistent with prosperity. On the contrary they will readily persuade themselves that they are not prosperous now, but would be if they were free. Attempts to disabuse merely irritate, because they imply a permanent inferiority, a constitutional inability to rise, and that is what no climber can admit. Collective status is called "civilisation". A nation is civilised if it dresses, builds motors and flies like the best. All but a few nations are determined to be "civilised", whatever the cost.

Since argument is of no avail there seems no alternative but repression. That, however, is the method of ignorance. Growing knowledge has discredited it among psychologists. It is time it fell into disrepute among students of society. It should be possible to achieve better results by harnessing snobbery to policy than by violent attempts to suppress it. After all, snobbery is only bad when it is overdone. We laugh at it under the name of snobbery; we admire it under the name of emulation. It has been the purpose of this essay to show that it has played a very important part in the growth of civilisation. In individuals we constantly turn it to good purposes; it should be possible to do the same with nations.

CHAPTER XIV

Chastity

A SACRED marriage forms part of many rituals. Chastity
is strictly enjoined by others. These two rules seem completely opposed to one another; yet, paradoxical as it
may seem, there is now good evidence that ritual chastity
is merely a form of sacred marriage.

Some of the evidence has long been familiar, but its
bearings have not been perceived.[1] I owe it to Mohammed
Gamal-ed-Din Hamdi Eff, that he has enabled me to put
two and two together.

Describing that well-known ecstatic ritual known as the
zār, [2] he says: "If a woman is married, she must abandon
sexual relations with her husband, for she is supposed to
be married during this time to the *sayyed* (spirit) for whom
she performs the *zār*". This is confirmed by others who
thus explain why women are possessed by male spirits and
men by female. In short, the woman must be chaste
because she is reserved for a sacred marriage with the
spirit or god.

This statement at once awakens other facts that had
lain dormant. In Peru there were "Virgins of the Sun"
who had to remain virgins because they were the brides
of the sun. The wife of the god or king is available to no
other man. Among the Tshi-speaking peoples of Africa
"a priestess belongs to the god she serves, and therefore
she cannot become the property of a man, as she would
be if she married one ".[3]

[1] For references see *Enc. Rel. Eth.*, index s.v. "Marriage 'sacred'";
my *Progress of Man*, pp. 143, 242, 260; my *Kings and Councillors*,
index, s.v. "Sacred marriage".

[2] Miss W. S. Blackman, *The Fellahin of Upper Egypt* (London,
1927), p. 198.

[3] A. B. Ellis, *Tshi-speaking Peoples*, p. 121, as quoted by *Encyclopædia of Religion and Ethics*, s.v. "Chastity", iii, 485.

Our nuns are mystic brides. Of such brides St Catherine of Siena and St Catherine of Alexandria are outstanding examples; more recently St Theresa of Lisieux.

In monotheistic religions the god is male, and so in Europe there can be no mystic marriage for male priests and ascetics; but in South India this is no obstacle, and in their hymns to Siva some of the South Indian saints borrow the phraseology of love and evidently feel some of its ecstasy.

Thus the same theory can arrive quite logically at opposite results.

The priest as well as the king is identified with the god. He may therefore carry out his duties. Next door to the Tshi-speaking peoples dwell the Ewe folk. Their priestesses "are the wives of the god, but prostituted to the priests".[1] This prostitution may go further, for the worshippers themselves are commonly identified with the god so that the priestesses are at their disposal. A young girl of the Mysore Nattuvans, for instance, goes through a marriage ceremony at the temple; "she is wedded to the deity for temple service, and to no other man in particular". She can never be a man's wife, but receives lovers.[2]

Since logic leads to opposite goals it is clear that logic alone cannot explain either vows of chastity or sacred prostitution.

Clearly there is some other factor which impels logic in one direction or another.

When we come to think of it why should a custom develop in any direction at all? Why should it not stay as it is? Why should not the sacred marriage continue

---

[1] A. B. Ellis, *Ewe-speaking Peoples*, 1890, pp. 140 ff., in *Enc. Rel. Eth.*

[2] L. K. Ananthakrishna Iyer, *The Mysore Tribes and Castes*, iv, 425. *Cp.* E. Thurston, *Tribes and Castes of Southern India*, iii, 37 ff.

indefinitely in its original form? Clearly all that comparative history has done has been to describe the successive manifestations of some underlying tendency. It does not fully explain why a carnal act which is the desire of every normal man should turn into an aversion for the ways of the flesh; it only shows how it was justified and so encouraged.

It must not be imagined that these justifications play no part in the development of an institution, that they are mere appearance without any influence on the underlying stream. They raise a lust or an aversion to the dignity of an institution. Where there is no mystic marriage, as in Fiji, there is no organised asceticism. In such countries those who are averse to sexual intercourse must either submit to it or live single and despised. The theory of the mystic marriage has turned the tables on the normal individual by raising the celibate to a plane above him, that is, provided the abnormality is accompanied by a considerable activity and force of will. Mere coldness, mere negation is never esteemed, but only the substitution of mental intensity for sexual vigour.

It is here that the psychologist can make himself useful. The comparative historian gives him the sequence of development; it is for the psychologist to delve below the surface and discover the mechanism. That he can do by the study of living specimens. He has, however, further to learn from the comparative historian the fact that this preference of the mystic love to the fleshly is not found always or everywhere with the same frequency. It is unknown among the Fijians, for instance. Among other peoples it is always present, but in varying degrees; it seems to increase with centralisation, urbanism, emotionalism in art, relaxation of morals and various other phenomena which seems to go together. This escape from the flesh then appears to be not an isolated fact, but one symptom of a psychological change which has many other symptoms.[1] That psychological change seems to be the prelude to a gradual decline in reproduction and so in population. It is a problem, then, which even a combination of the historian and the psychologist cannot solve; they must call in the biologist.

[1] Chap. xxx.

CHAPTER XV

Saviours

IN many countries, especially in Africa, there is a rule that only the sons born to a king after his consecration are allowed to succeed. More commonly, sons born before the consecration are allowed to succeed, but even then a special sanctity or prestige attaches to sons born after the coronation; hence such titles as the Byzantine *Porphyrogenitus*, "Born-in-Purple". If a Sinhalese king was born from the womb of an anointed queen, the inscriptions are careful to lay stress on the fact.

The king is merely one species of the genus Head-of-the-Ritual. He is head of the national ritual, and minor rituals have minor heads. Is the above rule, that only sons after installation can succeed, peculiar to the species, or is it common to the genus?

The father is head of the family cult. No son can succeed to the headship of the family who was born before his parents had gone through the sacrament of marriage. In Western Europe this rule has recently been relaxed; bastards are now generally allowed to succeed to the family name and estate if the parents afterwards marry. The marriage has been made retrospective, but still there must be a marriage or there is no succession.

The point of this insistence is not very obvious in this country, where the household cult either has disappeared completely or survives only in the attenuated form of family prayers. It is very obvious where the household cult is in full vigour. In India a man and a woman by marriage come into possession of a family hearth. At their wedding they are king and queen, and thereafter they preside over the family cult, as the king does over the state cult. So much so that the Sanskrit *pati* means both king and husband. The Siamese king is father of the country, as the householder is father of the hearth.

Our rule thus covers both cases: "A man may not succeed to a dignity unless he was born while his father held it"; or better: "A man cannot procreate offspring fit to carry out a ritual until he has himself been consecrated to carry out that ritual". We should perhaps get still nearer to the fundamentals if we said: "A son cannot attain to a life to which his father had not attained before the son was born". For the ritual confers life, and each step in the ritual confers a higher life than the step before.

Since it is the aim of science to reduce as many facts to as few principles as possible, it would be a distinct achievement if we could show that this rule applies to all ritual.

Let us begin with the first step, the birth ceremony. Infants cannot procreate, and so we cannot test the rule unless the ceremony is omitted or delayed. But such ceremonies are seldom omitted, because they are simple and cheap, and because they are women's rites and women cling to them. There are people who are not baptised, but they are the children of unbelievers, who care nothing for the ritual and its rules. The Church cares very much, however, and yet it does not prohibit the child of an unbaptised man from being baptised. On the contrary, it is delighted to baptise him in order to save him. The rule does not, then, apply in this country, but neither does the rule about the king's son, and that about the ordinary man's son is being relaxed. This is not, then, a very good country in which to test the rule. It would be interesting to know what happens in countries where birth ceremonies are taken very seriously.

Initiation at puberty is the next step. An uninitiated boy is often old enough to procreate. He is generally forbidden to do so, but if he breaks the rule what will be the consequence for his child? According to the rule we laid down that child should be incapable of initiation; he should remain an outcast. He was born before his father was made into a man, so he can never become a full man. That is exactly what happens in India. There is a time limit there for the initiation of a Twice-born. If he is not initiated before a certain age he becomes a a Vratya "deprived of the morning prayer and despised by the aristocracy". The sons of Vratyas cannot by initiation recover their fathers' lost status of Twice-born, but remain outside the pale.

In India, then, our rule holds good for initiation. It is to be hoped that observers will look out for cases elsewhere; they are necessarily scarce.

Our first impulse is to pass over death rites, since a dead man cannot procreate. This is a mistake, for there are cases in which dead men begot offspring. There is, for example, the sacred marriage of Isis and the dead Osiris from which Horus was born to avenge his father on the adversary Set and reign in his stead. For those who still believe myths to be pure fantasy and not records of fact there is the sacred marriage of the queen and the dead horse in the Vedic horse-sacrifice, which is a fact. The horse is identified both with her living lord, the king, and with the god Varuna, who reigns both in heaven and in the underworld. Unfortunately, there is only one case (to my knowledge) where the results of such a union are known: the Queen Kausalya becomes pregnant with the god Vishnu in consequence, and he is born as Rama. Rama is not an ordinary king, he is an *avatar*—that is to say, one of the forms which Vishnu takes when he comes down into the world in order to smite the demons and save the world.

It is worth while making a search for more instances. Among the kings of Ceylon two stand out above the others as the saviours of the Sinhalese nation. Popular tradition has remodelled their lives to some extent on the pattern of mythical heroes. The first, Dutthagamani, in the first century B.C. is born after a visit of his mother to a dying monk—he is the monk reborn. He is to be the future Buddha. The second one, Parakrama Bahu I (tenth to twelfth century A.D.) is born of the sacred marriage of the queen and a live elephant, but a dream one.

Both cases come near to our requirements, but not quite. We have to go to Mexico for a perfect example. Brasseur de Bourbourg's *Popul Vuh* tells us at great length how the virgin daughter of a king, apparently of the underworld, conceived from the spittle dropped into her hand by the head of a man destroyed by her father.[1] She gives birth to twins who grow up *to avenge their father and rid the world of demons*. They are of the nature of saviours or avengers.

When we go into the details of the career of these twins we find that they fit in remarkably with Lord Raglan's pattern of the hero,[2] as will be seen in the following analysis, in which I have kept his numbers for comparison.

1. Their mother is a royal virgin. Her father is obviously king of the underworld.

2. The story opens with the pedigree of the father. It traces him back to the Creator and Creatrix.

4. The father is killed by the future mother's people. His head drops saliva into her hand, whereupon she conceives.

5. See 2.

6A. An attempt is made to destroy the mother, but a substitute is produced for her heart.

---

[1] A similar story comes from Iraq; a Yezidi girl conceives after drinking from a river into which her brother's head has been thrown (R. H. W. Empson, *The Cult of the Peacock Angel*, p. 78 (ed.)).

[2] *Folk-Lore*, 1934, p. 212; also *The Hero*, p. 179.

7. She goes to the home of the father of her children and gives birth to twins.

6B. Their elder brothers seek to destroy them.

10. When they grow up they perform miracles and acquire their father's regalia.

11. They are challenged to a game of ball by their mother's people. They go to the underworld where they are put through various ordeals, but triumph. In the end they are put to death by burning, but are reborn with greater miraculous powers, and destroy their mother's people by the same means as Medea used against Pelias.

15A. Then they rid the world of demons.

These facts suggest the following hypothesis: Lord Raglan's hero is a super-king, a saviour, born of a dead king. That is inconsistent with one item in his pattern: he believes it to be part of the original pattern that the hero slays his own father on coming of age.

I think that on this point Lord Raglan has been misled by the myth which he took as his starting-point, that of Oedipus. There the hero (and saviour of Thebes) does kill his own father, but in the majority of myths he is his father's avenger. From Egypt eastwards it is not his father that the hero slays or defeats, but his mother's brother. The struggle is between the hero and his mother's people, or with his future wife's people, who in a cross-cousin system are the same. It is a part of the dual organisation.

But why, it may be asked, should the Oriental version be the original one? Why not the Greek? Because it is easy to explain the facts on the first hypothesis, but, so far as I can see, impossible on the second. Can anyone suggest a plausible way in which the father could have been altered to the mother's brother? On the other hand, we do know that the elders on the mother's side do get confused with the elders on the father's side; the "uncles" with the "fathers". I have seen this happen even in that region of highly developed cross-cousinship, Fiji, especially among the children. Thus it becomes impossible to tell whether the "father" of the myth is on the mother's side or the father's side unless the genealogy is preserved. Let the term "father" be narrowed down to progenitor, and the mother's brother is mistaken for the father. I have tried to show elsewhere that such has been the history of Greek kinship; that it has developed, like all Aryan kinship systems, out of a classificatory system, ultimately out of one which distinguished the mother's side from the father's.

The point is important, because the psycho-analysts have made great capital out of the Oedipus myth. It would serve them right if it turned out that originally it was not the father but the mother's brother who was killed, for they will rush into history without ever consulting the comparative historian.

We can now sum up our results and Lord Raglan's in the following hypothesis, subject to further verification:—

I. Each sacrament confers higher life and power. A man cannot normally attain to a degree of life not reached by his predecessor (I say normally, because there are always accommodations). The highest degree can be reached only by the son of one who has reached the highest, namely the death rites.

II. A king can be put to death by the other side of a dual society. His posthumous son will have power above all living men. He is the man of destiny, the avenger and saviour. He conforms to the pattern sketched by Lord Raglan except that it is his mother's people, the other side of the dual society, and not his father, whom he smites.

CHAPTER XVI

The Age-Limit

In the preceding chapter I quoted the Indian rule that the son of a man of sacrificial rank must be initiated by a certain age or drop into the rank of those not admitted to the sacrifice. We cannot, however, be content with isolated cases, but must compare in the hope that from the comparison the purpose of the rule may emerge.

As usual, the rule is to be found without going outside Western Europe. The investing of a knight was once, according to M. Marc Bloch, subject to an age-limit. There was a time when "the son of a knight participated in his father's rank up to a certain age, after which he had either to arm himself or sink into the crowd".[1] Arming oneself consisted in going through the ceremony of *adoubement*, which preserves very fully the initiation pattern, or rather the ritual pattern generally, since initiation ceremonies have the same pattern as others. This age-limit is thus the exact counterpart of the Indian, for that applies to the royal or knightly caste as well as to the priestly. Evidently the rule is not purely local.

We have still to find a rule or rite that is peculiar to any one sacrament. There could not be, for there is no sacrament which can always be distinguished from others. Marriage and coronation often coincide: in Fiji a funeral is at the same time a circumcision ceremony; in Siam a royal funeral is obviously a coronation. We can be confident, therefore, that our age-limit will apply to other sacraments.

Among the Slut Bedouin a man who remains a bachelor after twenty is considered to be without dignity. In

[1] *Annales de l'Histoire Economique et Sociale*, 1936, p. 372.

Lane's *Egypt* not to be married at a sufficient age was improper and disreputable. Hence child-marriages; they ensure against family disgrace.

We have no time-limit for marriages now, but it is not long ago since it was a reproach for women not to be married in the early twenties. The French are more definite: a woman who is not married at twenty-five is said to "coiffer Sainte Catherine". This evidently has something to do with St Catherine's mystic marriage and suggests withdrawal from the world, but the exact meaning and origin of the phrase I leave to specialists in the lore of saints. Such an inquiry might well repay the trouble by throwing some light on the meaning and consequences of the age-limit.

Those who have set ideas as to what is possible or impossible in the matter of customs would never stop for an instant to consider whether there is an age-limit for funerals. Yet such an age-limit has been familiar to us all for some time but under a different name, the killing of the king or the dying god. The age-limit is here not fixed in years, but according to bodily signs. Counting in years is unknown to most cultures, and is quite unessential; it is the physical development that matters. The Indian king was expected to die fighting; the time of life is not specified, but he must forestall disease.

At first sight it may seem perverse to talk here of an age-limit for funerals; evidently it is an age-limit for efficient ruling, like our retirement at sixty-five. If that were so, why should the king not just retire, like our civil servants? Evidently it is not sufficient that he should cease to reign; he must die. But mere dying never did anyone any good; in fact, it is generally harmful, and therefore much feared. Some rite has to be performed. Sir James Frazer has collected many illustrations of this, but the classic example is that of Antigone, who braved death rather than let her brother go unburied. There were also the Athenian admirals who were condemned to death for not collecting the bodies of the slain for burial. Rites are performed even for enemies; in fact, the whole point of a man-hunt is to have a ritual that will bless the people. To die for the good of the community, your own or the enemy's, you must die as part of a ritual. Like the sacrificial ox, the king is killed not to get him out of the way but as a necessary part of a ritual, which to be effective must be performed while the king is still vigorous.

Royal customs spread downwards, and what was the age-limit for the king may become the age-limit for everyone. According to Strabo, for example, the age-limit among the Caspi was seventy, those reaching that age being shut up and starved to death.

In India death seems to have been commuted into retirement from the world. Buddhist tradition tells of a king who retired to an ascetic life on the appearance of the first grey hair. Every householder owning a sacrificial hearth is a miniature king, and therefore retires to the forest when wrinkles and grey hair appear, or when he becomes a grandfather. But note that he does not just retire, like our officials, but spends his time in the performance of rites. This fictitious death is, like real death, a ritual.

There is no fundamental difference between human and animal sacrifices, so it is not surprising that we hear of age-limits for animal victims—in *Leviticus*, for example. A common rule is that the victim should be without blemish, which is another aspect to the age-limit, for the point of the age-limit is that the central figure of the ritual should be in a suitable physical condition.

If the killing of a sacrificial victim were the only case of an age-limit, the explanation would seem to be within our reach. One explanation has already been suggested, and is certainly right as far as it goes, but it has to be extended to cover initiation, marriage and possibly other sacraments, and I confess that I do not yet see how this can be done.   There must be physical fitness in each case, but physical fitness does not necessarily consist in being in the prime of manhood; there are other physical states which are propitious for other sacraments.

There is one direction in which we may profitably look. Ritual is closely bound up with the seasons of the year and the crops.   It involves an initiation of the world with its seasons, and the critical periods in man's life may well be equated with the critical periods of the year, the clearing, the sowing, and the reaping.

CHAPTER XVII

Childhood Ceremonies

CHILDHOOD ceremonies have been much neglected. They deserve more attention.

Miss Fletcher and Francis La Flesche have told us what the eighth day ceremony was supposed to achieve among the Omahas; it introduced "the child into the teeming life of the universe". The authors of *The Omaha Tribe* [1] give an invocation in which the priest announces successively to heaven, air, and earth that "Into your midst has come a new life". The regions of the world are to make its path smooth so that it may attain to the four ages of man (four is the ritual number of the Omahas; seven is ours, so Shakespeare has seven ages). This ceremony, Miss Fletcher comments, "voices in no uncertain manner the Omaha belief in man's relation to the visible powers of heaven and in the interdependence of all forms of life". [2] One cannot help wishing she had let the Omahas voice that belief to us direct instead of transmuting it for us into her own semi-mysticism. No doubt she preserves the general ideas, but so dressed up that they certainly appear to us somewhat differently to what they would appear if we had verbatim reports.

We get nearer to the naked truth in Dr H. G. Quaritch Wales's article on "Siamese Theory and Ritual connected with Pregnancy, Birth, and Infancy". [3] He tells us that, when born, the infant "is still believed to be closely connected with the world of *phī* (spirits). . . . To prevent the

[1] Twenty-seventh Ann. Rep., Bur. Amer. Ethn.
[2] *Ibid.*, pp. 115 f.
[3] *Journ. Roy. Anthr. Inst.*, 1933, p. 441.

phī from claiming it" an old woman picks up the cot "with the child and begins whirling it round with a circular movement, at the same time reciting the traditional formula, 'Three days child of *phi*, four days child of man, whoever claims it let him take it.' At the same time she drops the basket hard enough to startle the baby and make it cry loudly. The object to giving the child this shock is to make it forget its previous lives and claim it definitely from the world of *phī*".[1] The child is thus separated from the dead.

This, then, is a reversal of the separation from the living which takes place at a funeral. This is probably a very common episode in funerals, but it has not been noticed because generally it is not very explicit. In India it is very explicit. It takes place after the burning to the accompaniment of the words: "These living ones have separated from the dead."[2] The Koryaks, whose cremation shows a close resemblance to the Indian, draw a line which represents a stream between them and the cremation ground. The Kiwai Papuans dismiss the dead with words such as these: "You devil (spirit) now; you no come back this place; what road belong you—you go; woman (and) pickaninny belong you he stop house, that road you shut him; me fellow look moon he light, sun he go up; you go Adiri [the land of the dead] now—all same sun he go down."[1]

Thus the dead man is cut off from the living that they may have long life. When he is reborn he is cut off from the dead so that he may have long life.

Perhaps if we had the Omahas' own words we should find what Miss Fletcher calls cosmos and universe is really the world of the living as opposed to the world of the dead. It is no use speculating however; it is more profitable to

---

[1] *Journ. Roy. Anthr. Inst.*, 1933, p. 446.
[2] Asvalayana, *Grihyasutra*, iv. 4, 10; *Rigveda*, x. 18, 3.
[3] G. Landtmann in *Essays Presented to C. G. Seligman*, 107.

look for further evidence in the form of actual spells with a native commentary noted verbatim.

We can now distinguish the following stages in the life of a man:

WORLD OF THE DEAD	Separation from the dead: making the spirit into a human being.
WORLD OF THE LIVING	Puberty initiation: makes a child into a man.
	Marriage: makes a man into a householder.
	Birth of firstborn: makes a householder into a father.
	Separation from the living: the father becomes a spirit.
WORLD OF THE DEAD	Deification: makes an ordinary spirit into a god.
	Separation from the Dead.

And so we begin again what the Indians call the wheel of existence.

Between the separation from the dead and puberty initiation come various childhood ceremonies of which little is known. Between marriage and birth there are the pregnancy rites. And finally a man may rise from householder to be village headman, priest, king, emperor, or whatever his office may be. These promotions, however, are not given to all. In the above table are included only those rites which everyone must go through, except deification, which is optional, but which I have added to show that promotion does not cease with death.

CHAPTER XVIII

Baptism by Fire

THE curse of human studies has been endless classifications, definitions and distinctions till almost every single fact has become a category in itself. That is not science, for science consists in reducing the welter of facts to as few principles as possible. Every time we succeed in bringing two sets of facts under one heading we have made a step forward.

The section on baptism by fire in Vacant's *Dictionary of Catholic Theology* helps us to do this with baptism by water and the ritual use of fire. The gist is that both have been long recognised as variants of one process, baptism, which imparts life, or a better life, by the application of an element (in the old sense of the word).

The details are as follows:

1. The disciples of Simon Magus and others maintained that baptism by water is incomplete without baptism by fire, basing themselves on Acts ii, 3. This fire was merely an apparition at the time of immersion.

2. Some Gnostics used a real fire; they applied a red-hot iron to the ears of the baptised. This local application which we call branding or scarification, is found all over the world and is a feature of initiation.

3. The Bezpopovtchina sect in Russia practised total immersion in fire in order to purify themselves. This meant burning themselves to death, which they did in large numbers.

4. The Albigenses solved the problem of total immersion in fire without hurt to the neophyte by baptising them surrounded by torches in a dark place. Their sectarian opponents suggested that they might do it more thoroughly

by burning them, and unkindly reminded them of those who had undergone such a thorough baptism by being burnt at the stake.

5. Origen, like other Fathers, believed in total immersion in fire, but after death. According to him, Christ will plunge the dead into a river of fire, even as John the Baptist plunged the living into the waters of Jordan. Those baptised with water will not require baptism by fire. The two rites are evidently conceived as alternatives. We may note that in the Greek Hades there were rivers of fire as well as rivers of water.

The application of water and the application of fire are thus regarded as interchangeable or complementary. They have the same purpose, and differ only in the element used. The nature of the element, of course, conditions the application: fire destroys, so that total immersion is impossible for those of the living who do not value consistency above their earthly lives. Fire-walkers come as near as possible to solving the problem of total immersion in fire without hurt, so near that fire-walking is considered miraculous and therefore sensational. This is unfortunate, because it has fallen into the hands of the journalists, and so has been lifted out of its context. It is not therefore generally realised that it is merely one episode in a ritual of the usual pattern. Inanimate objects and the dead bodies of men and animals can, of course, be freely immersed in fire, and so are.

The following categories, which are always treated separately in books, are now seen to come under the single heading of life-giving by means of fire—toasting, scarification, throwing brands, burning heretics, cremation, burnt offerings, fire-walking. This life-giving by means of fire is merely one variant of the process of life-giving. It differs from life-giving by means of water only on account of the different physical properties which make a complete identity of technique impossible. How nearly identical the techniques are in spite of this difference in the elements appears in the following parallel:—

LIFE-GIVING

BY WATER	BY FIRE
Immersion	Cremation
	Burnt offering
	Burning at the stake
	Fire-walking
	Toasting
Sprinkling	Throwing brands
Touching with water	Scarification
Drinking (Siam)	Fire-eating

The last is well known to us as a circus trick, but in Lane's *Modern Egyptians* there are instances of fire-eating as part of a serious ritual.

We thus have a complete picture of the development of the ritual use of fire from a well-worked-out theory of vivifiers, of which fire is one of the most popular, down to mystic conceptions and mere metaphor. When soldiers talk of the baptism of fire they are not repeating the product of a brilliant poetic inspiration, but merely preserving the last degenerate vestige of a once living system of ideas of far-reaching consequences.

The reader can deal with other substances in the same way—blood, sand, oil, wood, etc.—and can use Professor M. A. Canney's *Givers of Life* for the purpose. Let him particularly note the alleged effects, whenever there is any information on this point. I am confident that he will fail to find any fundamental difference between them. Such an inquiry inevitably leads to the conclusion that all ritual application of substances boils down to one process varied by three factors:

1. The properties of the substance, whether liquid or solid, edibile or inedible, etc.

2. The extent of the application, whether total or local internal or external, etc.

3. The character of the people, whether given to hysteria or not, whether sensitive or insensitive to pain, whether squeamish or not (as in the case of cow-dung), etc.

The properties of the substances, however, make less difference than might be expected. Gold is neither edible nor soluble, yet it is drunk in India and Siam. We have seen that even the painfully destructive nature of fire can be disregarded in mass hysteria. But common sense generally prevails over the passion for consistency, often by way of compromise, as in toasting as a substitute for total immersion. The chief desire of men is to live long and live well, and they will seldom take a life-giver in a manner that defeats its purpose.

CHAPTER XIX

Initiation and Manhood

THEORIES of puberty rites abound, but why not first ask the people who practise them? The Fijians call a boy "man" after circumcision. Howitt saw Kuringals drive away grown-up men before an initiation ceremony began, because they had not been initiated; they had not been "made men".

Such examples might be multiplied indefinitely, but we all know already that boys come out of the ceremony as men, so we should be no wiser if we went on on this tack. My purpose here is to draw attention to cases which show clearly that it is no mere manner of speaking, nor a mere moral transformation.

The Loritja, a Central Australian tribe, allow an initiated youth to keep an uninitiated boy, because that boy is not reckoned a man.

Omaha boys fast and cry in the wilderness. If they dream that they receive a woman's burden-strap, they feel compelled to dress and live henceforth in every way as women. Such men are known as *mixuga*.

Clearly a boy cannot become a man just by growing up: a ceremony is needed. But surely these people do not believe that initiation fixes the anatomy. They know quite well how a boy is made. Nor will plain facts allow them to think that the changes which take place at puberty await the performance of a rite. In Fiji, circumcision used to be so long delayed that boys were physically men before they underwent it, and some had already had intrigues with girls. Howitt's outcasts had wives and children. Miss Fletcher tells of one Omaha whom an omen had forced to live as a woman, but who none the less reared a family.

If the ritual makes no difference physically, what does it do? Ask the people. The Omaha tells us that a boy who prays and fasts is seeking "happy life, good health, success in hunting; in war he desires to secure spoils and to escape the enemy". The general purpose is not peculiar to initiation: all rituals have as their end Life (with a capital L) and all that conduces to it. Thus the Omaha consecrate their little children "to walk long upon the earth", to obtain "light of many days". The general purpose of the childhood rite and the puberty fasting is the same. One sacrament differs from another merely in the scope and degree of life and power which it confers. As usual, we need not have gone outside our own country to learn that; any theological treatise will give us the sacramental ladder and the exact kind of grace each step confers. "Grace" is a supernatural gift by means of which eternal "life" is conferred.

Putting two and two together, we conclude that the Omaha initiation gives a boy the common gift of all ritual—life, but in its own specific form a *male* life. By the Turning Ceremony the child acquires just length of days; later by fasting the boy acquires a manly life, one dependent on male occupations, such as hunting and war. He is henceforth qualified to play a male part in the ritual and to wear male insignia. That is, of course, if he has passed the ritual successfully. This cannot be known without a test, which in this case is a dream. If the dream indicates that the boy is now a man, well and good; if it points to his not having acquired a male life, or "grace" as we should call it, he cannot live as a man and wear male insignia.

Thus the sensational custom, like all sensational customs, resolves itself into a straightforward application of a general rule. The rule is that a ritual blesses only those who are qualified to undergo it; it blasts those who are not holy enough.

To take a concrete case, no one who is not qualified may take the royal consecration. Many a man has been blasted, or involved his kingdom in a drought, by his presumption. In the same way, no boy who has failed to achieve a male grace can wear male garments, or follow male pursuits like hunting and war, in which success depends largely on successful rites. If he ignores the dream, he is blasted. "Instances have been recorded", says Miss Fletcher, "in which the unfortunate dreamer, even with the help of his parents, could not ward off the evil influence of the dream, and resorted to suicide as the only means of escape."

It is no use calling in mental pathology to explain the *mixuga*. They are not inverts in whom the wish was father to the dream. It is quite plain that the rôle of *mixuga* was repugnant to most of the men, but there was no alternative except the ill-luck which besets the man who assumes a rank into which he has not been successfully consecrated. Miss Fletcher records the case of one *mixuga* who was so manly that he broke out now and again, dressed as a man, and went to the wars and then, after distinguishing himself there, resumed a woman's life, except that he had a wife and children.

No, it is not a case of pathology. It merely shows with what rigour ritual theory can be carried out; quite naturally, because you cannot trifle with life and death.

Initiation, then, confers not manhood but manliness, if by manliness we understand success in all the pursuits of men, in achieving women, in rearing a family, in war, hunting or whatever may be considered man's work.

Fishing is man's work in Eddystone of the Solomons. That is why the Eddystonians believe that if a man is woman-shy he cannot catch fish. A woman-shy man is not manly, and therefore he cannot be successful in the manly work of catching fish.

Spinning for bonito is especially manly, and women are not allowed in canoes dedicated to it. Before a youth can take up the art he must be inducted . In Eddystone there are no generalised puberty ceremonies, ceremonies that confer a general patent of manly efficiency. There are only specialised initiations, that is initiations into special systems, the bonito ritual, the war ritual, and so on. The Eddystonians have apparently ceased to think a ceremony needful in order to confer manliness in general; boys grow into marriageable men without it, but not into successful fishermen, or warriors; specialised initiations are required for success in these specialised pursuits of men. It sometimes happens, however, that a boy fails to develop manliness; he is woman-shy, and has a smell which the bonito does not like. This condition is removed by special charms, and I have met a man who was thus cured; he married and was able to catch fish.

I possess a full, but unpublished, Rovianese charm for the condition of woman-shyness. The prayer runs: "I stroke this man; I stroke away the woman-shyness, the smell. . . . Let this man abide—catch fish; let him overturn turtle; let him catch bonito; let him marry. Thus be it with the man whom I stroke. Be effective for him, you spirits."

The purpose is more generalised than that of other medical charms, those for head-hunting and bonito fishing. It makes an unmanly man into a manly one. We may then regard it as a puberty initiation which has fallen into disuse, but is revived whenever a man fails to develop manliness without its aid.

CHAPTER XX

Initiation and Healing

I KNOW a young lady who was not baptised as a baby. She kept ailing and so she was baptised; she has thriven ever since.

Here is a case in which an initiation ceremony is used for healing. This comes about as follows: all rituals confer weal, and therefore the ritual of initiation does so. It may be omitted for some reason, such as slackness or growing scepticism, and if no illness or other calamity ensues, more people become bold enough to omit it. If, however, there is illness or other calamity, conscience pricks; people look round for an omitted ritual, and proceed to repair the omission. As omission becomes more and more frequent, the ritual becomes more and more restricted to pure healing; it becomes medicine.

This explains how it is that a ceremony similar to the old Maya baptism "is still in use among the modern Mayas of British Honduras to cure sickness".[1] It is a pity that we have not the details to compare point by point, but it is clear that though the missionaries have succeeded in weakening faith in the old initiation till it is no longer a matter of course, the Mayas still have enough faith in it to fly to it in case of illness.

I have sought to explain in the same way the Eddy-stonian cure for woman-shyness.

The same explanation may hold good for the Fijian custom of carrying out as a cure the same operation as that which the Australian Blacks use for initiation. As is generally known, many of the aborigines of Australia

[1] T. Gann and J. E. Thompson, *History of the Maya*, London, 1931, p. 139.

have an initiation in two parts, the first including circumcision and the second subincision. The Fijians have the first part only, but it has been said that the hillmen of Viti Levu, who are strongly Australoid, make use of subincision as a cure. This is not quite accurate, so far as my information from Kandavu goes. The operation is less drastic than subincision, but there can be little doubt that it is a variation of the same operation. It would seem, then, that the Fijians have dropped the second part of the initiation, but revive it in special cases.

Blood-letting is probably another illustration of the same process. We know that it was widely practised in ritual, particularly in initiation ceremonies, long before it became limited in our country to the healing of specific complaints. We have done the same as the Fijians, except that we did not draw blood from the penis.

Revival in a scare is then, as we have seen, one way in which initiation may be narrowed down to medical treatment. There is another way; a man tries all the rites that he has been brought up to believe in and finds no relief, so in despair turns to the possessor of some foreign ritual, as we turn to foreign specialists. That is how the Fijian nobleman Vuetasau was converted to Christianity, and through him the whole island of Lakemba. He and his people were baptised because, after his own gods had failed to cure his daughter, the Christian god succeeded. Many conversions come about in this way.

Professor M. A. Canney mentions a case in which a Hebrew on receiving Christian baptism was cured of his disease.[1] Naaman was cured by a Hebrew baptism when the rites of his own country had failed.

The history of circumcision in our country illustrates a third process. Circumcision, as we all know, was originally part of a system of initiation. It still is, as a

[1] *Journal of the Manchester Egyptian and Oriental Society*, xix, p. 41.

general rule. It is only one episode out of many that go to make up the initiation ceremony, but is the most sensational episode for those who practise nothing like it; they are so fascinated by that one rite that they overlook the rest. They want to explain what seems so strange, and proceed to do so in the manner in which theorists always begin; that is they look for some reason that appears "rational" to them; in other words, one which agrees with the philosophy of their own time and class. The only purpose which to the philosophers of the eighteenth century was sensible in their own eyes was that of cleanliness, so circumcision was ascribed to some wise legislator who devised it as a method of improving the health of his people. Any connected rites and myths, if noticed at all, were explained as cunning devices to get the reform adopted by a people unable to appreciate health but eager for hocus-pocus. This interpretation grew in favour as the craze for hygiene grew. As a result of that craze, many Christians have adopted circumcision without the accompaniments which were originally as indispensable as the operation itself. As the purpose is for them purely hygienic, all the other rites have become irrelevant.

Here, then, we have a clear case of ritual becoming a surgical operation—that is, of a complete initiation rite, vaguely aiming at manliness, being whittled down to one episode applied definitely and exclusively to the pursuit of cleanliness.

The process by which this has come about is not the same as in the first case. There a disused ritual was revived under the influence of fear. Here a people who did not practise the operation have lifted it out of its context because the context did not interest them or fit in with their system of thought. The operation alone interested them, because it seemed to fall in with a fad of their own time.

When a ritual episode is thus taken out of its setting

and provided with a new interpretation and a new use, it becomes in the eyes of the adapters a "rational" act, as opposed to magic. That is natural, since they give it a new use because they believe in that use and not in the old one, and what they believe in they think rational. If the new use consists in narrowing down from general weal to the cure of a particular disease, it is regarded as rational medicine.

These terms are unfortunate because they proceed from a false psychology which divides the mind into two compartments, one rational and the other magical. This school of thought imagines a time when the rational compartment almost filled man's mind. Then the magical compartment grew and grew, extending to all man's life: "religion got mixed with all his doings", to speak the language of that school. Then of course we moderns have come along and pushed back the limits of the magical till it has completely disappeared, and our minds harbour nothing but the rational.

If, instead of philosophising, we trace out actual cases from the beginning to the end, what we find at one end is a vague general quest of life, a quest ill-adapted to secure any particular component of weal, but generally helpful in life; at the other end appear highly specialised techniques concentrating on one specific objective, the slaying of enemies, the catching of fish or even of one kind of fish, the cure of belly-ache, or whatever accessory of welfare it may be. As a result of this specialisation these techniques *may* become highly efficient for their own limited purpose, but they are useless for any other. The generalised state ritual of Fiji is a great social tonic; it is useless for blood congestion. Blood-letting has no social value, but it may conceivably relieve congestion.

Our theories of culture, however, are still so near to philosophy, so little based on observation, that the hard-and-fast division into rational and magical still pervades them all. It is the accepted doctrine that a "rational" custom must have a rational origin. Recently Dr Hugo Horwitz, in one of the best articles on technology of recent times,[1] asserts that a technical invention cannot come into being through mythologico-ritual concepts. It is strange that such statements can continue to be made with the example of circumcision under our very noses.

The idea of "magical" and "rational" is purely subjective, and therefore unknown to the biologist. What he does know is generalisation and specialisation, which are purely objective concepts. Specialisation leads to greater efficiency at the expense of breadth and adaptability. In an age which worships efficiency specialised forms therefore appear rational, but they may appear irrational in the next age. The student of culture has not to approve or condemn, but to trace development, which can provisionally be sketched somewhat as follows:—

GENERALISED RITES FOR WEAL

Communion, etc.	Mutilation	Chants	Moral effect
Medicine	Surgery	Literature	Specialised moral ritual
			Pageants

Since the above was written I have come across the following illustration of the manner in which a sacrament can be revived to heal. A Shawnee says: "We hadn't gone by the rules in naming Arthur the first time; we just sent for two old women who stayed overnight and gave Arthur his name. . . . But when Arthur got sick we made up our minds that we'd do it better, and so we had him given a new name at a peyote meeting." [2]

[1] *Anthropos*, 1933, p. 729.
[2] *American Anthropologist*, 1935, p. 626.

CHAPTER XXI

Tattooing and Healing

Soot is not uncommon in ritual. Cuts figure widely, especially in puberty ceremonies and at funerals. Tattooing is a combination of the two, and makes its first appearance in the life of a man at maturity—that is, as a general rule. Its purpose, like those of other rites, was originally a full life.

In Egypt, tattooing has come to be far more specific in its use; it is often used to cure ailments the cause of which can be narrowly defined; for instance, those due to the fumes from fishcooking. Miss Blackman has found tattooing also used for such specific ailments as headache, toothache, weak eyes, and possession.

What evidence, it may be asked, have we that these specific uses are derived from the initiatory use? The evidence is that other uses of tattooing in Egypt and neighbouring countries retain an initiatory colouring. Miss Blackman [1] has the impression that in Egypt tattooing is still a sign of manhood. It is also used for sex appeal.[2] Comparative evidence tells us that initiation confers manly or womanly welfare, which includes sexual potency and the power to procreate. Tattooing thus acquires a sexual connotation which may be emphasised at the expense of other elements of life-giving. This preparation for a sexual life comes out very plainly in a custom recorded from parts of Upper Egypt, where, we are told, they paint tattoo patterns on the face and hands of a maiden who has died ripe for marriage. "She is adorned in this way because, if she was good, she will

---

[1] W. Blackman, *The Fellahin of Upper Egypt*, p. 23.
[2] J. S. Wilmore, *The Spoken Arabic of Egypt*, p. 365.

become a houri in paradise." [1] In other words, she is prepared to be a bride.

In Iraq tattooing is used to induce pregnancy.[2] This use also derives naturally from the initiation rites which confer manly or womanly fruitfulness. Without them a man or woman is not successful in the things pertaining to his or her sex.

An Iraqi woman who has lost several children in succession thinks that she can save the next by having it tattooed. Naturally, since initiation, like other general-ised rituals, confers a long and vigorous life. Another theory, however, has crept in here, the theory of the evil eye. The patterns on boys in one village are tattooed like those of girls to avert the evil eye by making the boys look as if they belonged to the less favoured and so less envied sex. This procedure is in flat contradiction to the original purpose of the rite, which was to make boys into men by endowing them with all that belongs to men.

There are critics who will not be satisfied because they cannot *see* the initiatory use of tattooing being gradually narrowed down to specific ends. Such critics will never be satisfied, because if they could sit waiting till doomsday they would never see development. They think that they can see evolution because they have been brought up to believe in it, but all that they really see is a great variety of forms the existence of which can be satisfactorily explained only on the supposition that they have all developed out of the same originals. That is all that we have the right to expect in the development of human institutions; a theory that will explain all the variations in the simplest possible way without invoking any processes that have not been observed.

We know that initiation confers a successful maturity, and we know from records of circumcision and the evidence

---

[1] H. A. Winckler, *Bauern zwischen Wasser und Wuste*, p. 133.
[2] *American Anthropologist*, 1937, p. 54.

of our contemporaries that a single ceremony may be lifted out of the ritual of initiation and used for a specific purpose. It is quite possible, then, that tattooing has been isolated and narrowed down in this way, and if we assume that this has happened we can fit all the pieces of the meaningless jumble of facts into a simple and intelligible picture. We cease merely to collect and begin to connect.

All the uses of tattooing which we have reviewed are labelled by the anthropologists as "magical", with the implication that they do not really work. If they did work, they would be labelled "rational medicine". But supposing it turned out, as may happen any day, that tattooing does work in some cases? Suppose, for argument's sake, that our medical men struck a new trail which led them to the discovery that tattooing did remove some causes of headache. Then we should have to transfer that use of tattooing to "rational medicine" while leaving all the others in the department of "magic". Obviously we cannot base our classifications on mere opinion, which may change at any time, and the classification into rational and magical is purely a matter of opinion. The Egyptians are of the opinion that tattooing works, and they can give you plenty of concrete cases in support of that opinion. The European physician has never even tried to justify his opinion, and no doubt he is quite justified in refusing to do so. In refusing to examine the claims for tattooing he is saving himself from what would probably be a wild goose chase after a new remedy for headache. Still, his opinion is only an opinion, and it may be reversed at any time; there are more things in heaven and earth than are dreamt of in our medical schools. We must have something more stable and more objective than opinion on which to base our classifications.

There is one objective difference between our hygienic

12

use of circumcision and tattooing in Egyptian medicine; after detaching circumcision from the system which we describe as initiation we have worked it into another system which we call hygiene. In Egypt, tattooing has broken loose from initiation without attaching itself to any other system, at least it seems so as the evidence now stands. But it must be remembered that, at least so far as I know, no attempt has been made to get at the underlying principles. Perhaps these have dropped out, and the different uses of tattooing not only seem but are *disjecta membra*.

However that may be in Egypt, in Iraq we found a case in which tattooing was caught up into a different system of ideas which we may sum up as the evil eye. The new interpretation may seem to us as "magical" as the old one, but the process is the same as that which has led from the old initiatory to the new hygienic use of circumcision, namely the reinterpretation of old practices in the light of new theories. Processes are objective things, and it is on processes that the science of culture, like other sciences, must be built.

CHAPTER XXII

Kinship Systems

WHEN we explore a new language, we infer the meaning of words from the objects to which they are applied. The first object gives us a preliminary definition. That may chance to be right, but further experience may compel us to revise it. Thus I may first hear the word "table" used of a list of facts in a book, and so translate it "page". By degrees I shall learn better.

This caution is generally borne in mind by students of literary languages, but it is too often lost sight of in the study of non-literary languages. A great many investigators never get beyond the first use of the word that happens to come their way. Miss Lucy Mair has produced a striking example in the *Bulletin of the School of Oriental Studies*, vii, 918. An investigator heard the Uganda word *obuko* applied to palsy. He entered it in his dictionary as "palsy". It really refers to marriage rules, to a breach of which palsy is the consequence.

One of the most flagrant cases is the translation of the so-called classificatory kinship terms. The person most commonly called *tama* in Melanesia, the one most in evidence, is a man's father. He is the man who will be named if you asked, "Who is your *tama*?" So *tama* has been duly set down as "father". The same has been done with other kinship terms in Melanesia and elsewhere. It was soon noticed, however, that other men besides the father are called *tama*. By all rules the first translation should have been dropped, and a new one found to cover all the different *tamas*, and thus express the essence of *tama*-ship. Unfortunately, no single word can do so, and it has remained in the literature of the South Seas as "father", with the proviso that it is "extended" to cover father's brother, father's father's brothers' sons, and so on. Ever since we have been racking our brains to explain how Melanesians can call their uncles, and even remote cousins, "fathers".

The effect on theory has been disastrous. The order in which we have learned the uses of *tama* and similar words has been confused with the order of development in actual history. Because we first took it to mean father we slip unwittingly into the assumption that it meant father originally.

This fallacy has now received official expression in the term "kinship extensions". That expression implies that the meaning father is primary and that all other uses result from extending the term to an ever-widening circle of kinsmen.

It is curious that this doctrine, which is historical since it describes a process of development in the past, is championed most stoutly by those who are forever gibing at origins, evolution, historical reconstruction. This is a historical reconstruction, or what is?

The only way of proving that a process has taken place in the past is by recognised historical methods: either produce documents or resort to the comparative method. It is perhaps fortunate in this case that we have little documentary evidence and so must rely on the much more reliable comparative method.

Before we can apply it we must get our facts right. To that end let us forget all we have ever been told about the meaning of classificatory terms and rediscover the language, taking Fijian as an example. Evidently *tama* cannot mean father since it includes cousins to the nth degree, even cousins too young to have children; in fact, a man is born a *tama*. We notice, however, that all those cousins have one thing in common: they are once removed; in other words, they are of the generation next to Ego, and, to be more precise, to the one immediately before. Not all the members of this generation, however, are *tama*. There are two sides to that generation, the father's and the mother's; only those on the father's side are *tama*. That is evidently the meaning of *tama*, so our final definition will run:

tama = all males of the previous generation on the father's side.

Repeating the process we go on.
vungo = all males of the generation immediately above and below Ego on the mother's side;
tavale = all males of the same generation on the mother's side.

And so on. When our list is complete we find that all the terms fall into two sets, one set belonging to the father's side, the other to the mother's. Each term refers to a particular generation within one side. In short, these terms do not express consanguinity, as we have unfortunately been accustomed by Morgan to believe, but they fix the place of any relative according to generation and side. If I call a man *tuaka* it is clear that he is of my generation on my father's side, and senior to me; a *wati* is a woman of my generation on the side from which my mother comes.

This last term affords an excellent illustration how a particular use is mistaken for the true one, and the true one comes to be looked upon as an improper one. A Fijian introduces his wife as *wati*, so the word is noted as "wife". When it is found there are hundreds of *watis* who are not his wives, the first translation is not abandoned, but all other uses are explained as extensions: these women, it is explained, are called wives because he might marry any of them if the family so decided; they are wives by anticipation, "potential wives".

Upon this muddled lexicography has been built up a whole edifice of primitive promiscuity.

Exactly the same usage exists in Arabic. Arabic-speaking husbands can often be heard addressing their wives as *bint 'amm*; but they also call their paternal uncles' daughters *bint 'amm*. We do not translate "wife", "potential wife", because we know that *bint* is daughter, and *'amm* is paternal uncle; therefore *bint 'amm* means "cousin on the father's side". When a man marries his cousin, as it is best to do, he goes on calling her "cousin" as he has been accustomed to since childhood. The Fijian and the Ashanti do exactly the same.

We can remember the time when an English youth would refer jocosely to his father as "The Governor". No one has ever suggested that this was primary and that the word has been extended to colonial administrators.

All our difficulties spring from a preconceived idea that kinship terms everywhere try to express the same thing as they do in Aryan and Semitic languages, and that in those languages they show the place on the family tree. The result is that in a certain African language the term *nana* is rendered father's father, father's father's brother, and so on through thirty-four European relationships, and then it does not exhaust all the possibilities. And what is the outcome of all this painstaking? We have a list of cases, but we have not got the meaning. It is as if a dictionary under "hot" told us "the sun is hot, pepper is hot, *A*'s temper is hot, the discussion is hot", and left it at that. If we go to the trouble of extracting the meaning of *nana* from the cases we find it simply means "any relative two generations above or below".

At this point we may be asked what evidence have we that the people themselves understand kinship terms in this sense. The same evidence as we have for the meaning of any word, what is common to the cases in which it is used.

As regards the Chinese system we have more, we have

the definite statement of a Chinaman. Mr H. Y. Feng produces documentary evidence that the Chinese system was once a cross-cousin system, and so it is akin to the Fijian. As in cross-cousin systems the kinsfolk are still divided into two: those of the same patronymic, and those of another. These sides he chooses to call "sibs". Besides this vertical division, there is a horizontal one into generations. "These two factors, sib and generation", he sums up, "not only pervade the whole system but regulate marriage". A man marries a woman of another patronym of the first generation.[1]

The hill tribes of Viti Levu, Fiji, indicate very clearly what their kinship terms mean to them. Every hillsman assumes all other hillsmen to be his kinsmen. He is not concerned how near or how far related a stranger may be; he does not search the pedigrees to find out how they are related. All he wants to know is their respective generations. That is easy, because the whole population is divided into two alternate generations called *tako* and *lavo*. If both are *tako* or both *lavo* they are of the same generation, and then the senior is *tuka*, the junior *tadhi*, terms which have unfortunately been translated (by myself among others), as elder and younger brother. Evidently they mean nothing of the kind, since a man's grandfather is his *tuka* as well as his elder brother. The words simply mean "of the same one of the two generations, on the same side, senior", or "junior", as the case may be. If one man is *tako*, the other *lavo*, then they are related as *tama* and *luve*—that is as one generation to the other. In the case of relatives who are known, and whose side is therefore known, two sets of terms exist, just as in all cross-cousin systems. The line and the generation is what the Fijian looks for in his kinship system, not propinquity.

[1] "Teknonymy and the Chinese Kinship System", *Amer. Anthr.*, 1936, p. 60.

Why should he be so interested in the generation and so little in the nearness of kin? Because nearness is of little importance in public affairs; generation and line are all important. If a chief, chieftain, or priest dies it is not the next of kin that succeeds, as with us, but the next senior of his generation, no matter how distant; if the deceased was the last of his generation, then it goes to the most senior of the next. A Lauan expresses the rule thus: "X was not made chief, because his *tama* was living". We are not rendering the meaning at all by translating *tama* "father", because X's father was dead. What is meant is that X could not succeed because there was still a member of the previous generation on his father's side to come before him.[1]

We now understand why members of the same generation and side are so carefully distinguished as senior and junior (commonly rendered "elder brother and younger brother, classificatory"). The order of seniority is all important. With us only one of a group of brothers has to have his status made clear in royal and titled families; so among such families he bears a special title "heir" which singles him out; the rest are lumped together as brothers, for their seniority is normally of little importance, since they drop out of the succession. It is only when the holder has no issue that the seniority of his younger brothers need be remembered.

It is not the whole of a generation that succeeds, but only those in the male line. Therefore the female line has to be distinguished from the male by special terms. Since the female line is completely excluded, seniority does not come into consideration at all in their case, so no distinction is made between senior and junior.

---

[1] These remarks apply equally to the Aranda who have the same system of succession, according to Strehlow. It is also found in Ceylon where the classificatory system prevails (*Ceylon Journal of Science*, sec. G, i, 75; Geigler, *Culavansa*, i, 20 ff.

Generation, line, and seniority decide not only succession, but everyday behaviour. The duties in the ritual are fixed in the same way.[1]

In short, what we seek most is the next of kin, and so we run up and down the family tree. The Fijians (and the Australian aborigines, and the rest) do not, because there is no point in doing so. All they want is such information as will enable them to place each man on the correct side in the right generation. An inquiry proceeds thus: "How are you related?" "Of the same side and generation." "Why?" "Because our fathers were of the same side and generation." Or else: "We belong to successive generations on opposite sides, because he is of my mother's side and generation."

If the users of classificatory systems can get on without pedigrees, surely the field-worker can. He would be all the better for it in working out the system. He would cease to see the system thus:

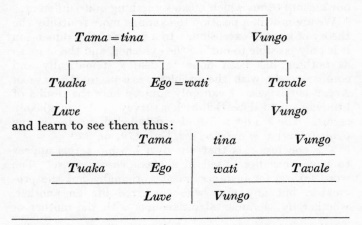

and learn to see them thus:

	Tama	*tina*	*Vungo*
Tuaka	*Ego*	*wati*	*Tavale*
	Luve	*Vungo*	

---

[1] See my *Lau Islands*, pp. 35 ff., and *The Progress of Man*, pp. 259 ff.

I do not mean that pedigrees are useless. There are many investigations that are impossible without them, but they have exercised a pernicious influence on the theory of classificatory systems.

Some systems are more complicated, some less, than the typical cross-cousin system from which our illustrations have been drawn, but the principle remains the same. It is all a matter of how many lines and how many generations are distinguished.

Since classificatory terms have no real equivalents in our language we must either use cumbrous circumlocutions or condensed symbols. We must chose between saying: "A boy is circumcised by a man one generation up on the opposite side"; or else represent that man by something like this: $\frac{1 \ Op}{Ego}$ I leave it to others to work out something on these other lines. It would be easy enough but for the Australian systems. Anyhow we cannot go on identifying these classificatory terms with our kinship terms which mean something quite different.

We are now in a position to examine more fruitfully the theory of kinship extension. In a paper of this dimension it is only possible to outline the evidence, and the more so as nothing has been done to deal systematically and comparatively with the problem, except in the case of Aryan languages. I can only sum up here the results of bringing up to date Delbruck's survey of Aryan kinship terms. The reader will find a detailed discussion in the *Ceylon Journal of Science*, sec. G, i, 179; ii, 33.[1]

The conclusion is that our own kinship terms appear to have once been used in a classificatory sense. The word father, for instance, meant originally not the procreator, but any man who conferred life on another, whether by sacramental intercourse with the mother or

[1] R. S. Rattray made a move in the right direction by dividing up his kinship terms into generations; but he stopped half-way. *Ashanti*, pp. 24 ff.

by some other ritual act, but not by the mere unconsecrated infusion of semen. It also applied to all the kinsmen of the father's side and generation, because they are ritually interchangeable with the father. At a very early date, before the splitting up of the parent Aryan tongue, this and other terms were narrowed down to their present use; but the original use still persists in connection with ritual, *e.g.* godfather, lay brother, etc. The present usage is thus a result of contraction, not of extension, and is based on modern physiology, not on a theory of sacraments.[1]

The Semitic evidence wants working out in detail, but a superficial examination provisionally points the same way.

Are we to believe that speakers of Aryan and Semitic started with a classificatory system and ended with a genealogical one, while the rest of the world reversed the process, extended terms which meant properly begetter, bearer, begetter's begetter, and so on, to cousins so distant that kinship is only presumed? It is hardly probable, but if anyone believes it happened so, let him produce some evidence.

He might point out that classificatory terms are constantly used like ours, that in Melanesia *tama* is often understood to mean the father and no one else. Is this the original use, as is constantly assumed by the "extensionists", or is it the beginning of contraction? Only definite cases can decide this question.

If a Fijian asks, "Have you a *wati*?" it is obvious he cannot mean, "Have you kinswomen of your generation on your mother's side?" because, where kinship is unbounded, no man is without such kinswomen. What is meant is "Do you own such woman?"—in short, "Are you married?" There is not a boy who has not got kinswomen two generations before him, so the statement

[1] Supplemented by my *Progress of Man*, pp. 261 ff.

"he has a kinswoman two generations up" can only refer to one of them, the nearest. The meaning is: "He is a boy who has been much under the care of his grandmother, and so known a good deal of old women's lore". This is an excellent example how the meaning of words is filled in by the rest of the sentence and by custom. Here custom narrows down the dictionary meaning not only to one person, but to one characteristic of that person. If a Frenchman talks of "ma femme" he refers to one woman only, not any woman connected with him, not his servant, or even his mistress, but the one with whom he has contracted a permanent alliance recognised by the state, and possibly by the Church. No one has ever suggested this is the original meaning of the word, and that it has been extended to all women. It is not always necessary to have a possessive. If an Englishman says "The King", everyone understands he means the King of England. It does not follow that originally the title meant that king only, and has been extended to other kings.

In all these cases words designating whole classes of men are restricted by the singular, the definite article, or some other sign of definiteness to one person, the context and custom further define who that one person is. "My *tama*" is the *tama* of the family circle; "the Captain" is the commander of the speaker's company; "herself" is the speaker's wife. It is easy to see how, as the household emancipates itself from the clan or kindred, kinsmen outside the household drop more and more into the background, the direct line father-grandfather monopolises the attention, and so the kinship terms. The father always stands out among the men of his generation; but he stands out more than ever when the household forms a closed body with its own household cult. That cult now no longer descends from brother to brother, but from father to son, so that the other members of the father's generation can no longer be regarded as being on the same footing as the father.

In the use of *tama* to mean "father", *wati* to mean "wife", we have the germ, not the survival of a genealogical system.

A short review of the facts thus raises a presumption that the classificatory terms are not due to extension, but that our habit of denoting nearness of kin is the result of contraction.[1] Finally, to establish this presumption it would be necessary to show that it fits all the facts, not only of kinship, but of social organisation generally. Among the most important facts are the ritual functions of kinsmen. The first task is to collect them all and to try and find the underlying principle why it is, for instance, that the men of the father's side and generation provide the regalia for initiation, while the men of the mother's generation and side carry out the operation. Until that has been done all discussions as to the ultimate meaning of classificatory systems, or indeed of kinship systems in general, must remain idle guesswork.

Note.—Miss Margaret Mead has made a very intensive study of these functions in the Admiralty Islands.[2] Only a comparative study, however, can explain.

I only know of one serious attempt to prove the extension theory, that is, if I have understood Prof. E. E. Evans-Pritchard aright. In his paper on "The Nature of Kinship Extensions"[3] he shows with admirable objectivity how the Azande child learns to extend the terms and the behaviour from the immediate family

[1] From a manifesto by Infante Don Alfonso Carlos and King Alfonso's reply it appears that the Royal House of Spain can use "Uncle" and "Nephew" of second cousins once removed, as in classificatory systems.

[2] "Kinship in the Admiralty Islands", *Anthr. Papers of the American Museum of Natural History*, vol. xxxiv, Pt. ii, 240 ff.

[3] Man, 1932, p. 7.

circle to wider circles. Presumably these children are repeating the phylogenetic evolution. But our children begin by calling all adult men *dada*, and are taught to limit it to one man. There is obviously a flaw in an argument that leads to contradictory results. The flaw is that the conditions under which a child learns a language, or behaviour, generally do not reproduce those under which evolution has taken place. As Vendryes says: "Children only teach us how an organised language is acquired; they do not give us an idea what language can have been at the beginning of its evolution." Substitute "behaviour" for "language", and the statement remains equally true. Biologists have for some time recognised the fact that the growth of the human body does not exactly reproduce the evolution of the race. The chief merit of Prof. Evans-Pritchard's paper is that it gives us the Azande point of view in their own words and actions, and does not romance about what is going on inside their minds.

CHAPTER XXIII

Blood-Brotherhood

PROFESSOR EVANS-PRITCHARD has revolutionised the conception of blood-brotherhood. His evidence makes the term a misnomer, because the relationship is definitely not brotherly; it is, as he points out, a joking relationship. Now this joking is very characteristic of moieties and cross-cousins, but it is quite inconsistent with the etiquette of brotherhood among the Azande, with whom Professor Evans-Pritchard's paper [1] deals, no less than elsewhere. With them, just as with the Fijians and others, "intercourse between brothers is always coloured by notions of seniority. . . . On the other hand, blood-brothers have an egalitarian status and treat each other with open familiarity across the usual barriers which Zande custom erects between members of society. Hence the behaviour pattern between a man and his brother is incompatible with the behaviour pattern between a man and his blood-brother, and a man cannot therefore be a kinsman and a blood-brother." Professor Evans-Pritchard gives examples of practical jokes quite characteristic of cross-cousinship.

Ideas and the customs that reflect them do not exist as discrete particles, but as organic parts of systems of thought and action. Whoever, therefore, finds a joking relationship will not stop there, but will look for the remaining members of a system of which joking is but a part. He may not find them, because the institution may have so degenerated that joking alone survives. He will, however, find them among the Azande. An Azande buries his blood-brother, marries his daughter, cadges from him, helps him, gives him hospitality,

[1] *Africa*, vi, 370.

"occasionally a man is largely dependent upon his blood-brother for the necessities of life. It is quite common, in fact, for Azande to contrast blood-brotherhood with kinship, extolling the first in comparison with the second. They say that a blood-brother is a much better friend than a real brother".

We have here, practically complete, the pattern of behaviour between two moieties: mutual aid combined with playful hostility, intermarriage, interburial. I have elsewhere [1] attempted to derive the whole etiquette of moieties from one fundamental principle—that, for some reason or other, there must be two parties to the ritual. We may call these "god and worshipper", "victim and sacrificer", "principal and ministrant, "king and priest", or by whatever terms we choose to fit the particular case; they are all mere variant applications of the principle. A further rule is that the two parties must belong to different lines. If one line is principal, the other must be ministrant.

The Fijians call such a reciprocal relation "mutual ministry" (more literally "facing one another", or "worshipping one another"), and I propose to adopt this term. It means that if the deceased belongs to one line, the other buries him (Winnabagoes), or mourns for him (Trobriands), or otherwise plays the *vis-à-vis*. If the bridegroom comes from one side, the bride comes from the other. If one line provides the principal, the other waits on him, brings him offerings, and so on. If the ritual is a cosmic one, one line is "sky", the other "earth".

Let us apply this to the covenant which the Azande seal with their blood. In the first place the two parties cannot be brothers; they must belong to different lines. The ritual in which both take part seems at first glance to stand apart from all others, but on close consideration we find that it is not so. A drinks B's blood. That is

[1] *Progress of Man*, pp. 242 ff.

nothing new; the drinking of blood is a very wide-spread variety of communion. Sometimes the victim is slaughtered, and sometimes blood is drawn from a live victim, especially if it be a man. In the latter case we do not call him a victim, but the difference is one of detail, and does not affect the main principle. This drawing of blood from a man is very common in Australia. The primary purpose is to impart strength, but it is also used for binding men together so as to prevent treachery; a ritual of wider import becomes a blood-covenant when used solely for the sake of the binding effect. The Azande blood-covenant does not differ in essence from the Australian or any other blood-communion. It is true that the drinking is reciprocal, but in this there is nothing unusual; on the contrary, it is fundamental to this mutual ministration that the sides alternate as principal-god-victim. The rôles are reversible. The only peculiarity here is that both parties are simultaneously principals and ministrants. This is difficult to understand as long as we think of a god as omnipotent, or, at least, immeasurably removed above man. It becomes quite simple if we realise that this point of view is by no means universal. If we think of gods as persons or things with life to give, we can understand that, if persons, they can give life to one another and so worship one another.

Blood is not the only substance used in the Azande ceremony; there are, besides, salt and groundnuts. Animal, vegetable and mineral are all represented, but whether this is accident or design we cannot tell. It is clear, at any rate that blood is merely the most sensational of a number of communion substances. This is true of other blood covenants. Joinville, for example, says that the Comans made covenants by drinking the blood of both parties mixed with wine and water. But blood is not necessary to a covenant; it may be replaced by other substances.

After the Azande blood-drinking, there is an investiture with a peculiar form of head-dress. And, of course, there is the indispensible word in the form of a conditional curse.

This ritual thus consists of the usual elements of ritual, and there are two parties. These are not drawn from two moieties; they may, in fact, belong to different races, but the ceremony *makes* them to be related in exactly the same way as moieties are elsewhere.

If you want to assign a ritual function to a man, you simply perform the ritual with him in that function. Thus, if you want to make him king, you make him go through the royal ritual. So, if you want two men to be related as ritual opposites, you just make them play their part as opposites, and they will be opposites. For instance, a band of kinsmen may find it advisable to split up into two groups which shall take opposite parts, instead of the same parts, in the ritual. They just carry out a rite in which they act as opposites. Professor and Mrs Seligman have described such a rite under the name of "splitting ceremony".[1]

On the other hand, total strangers may think it to their mutual advantage to become opposites from being nothing. They proceed to function as opposites. A common way is to celebrate nuptials between the two parties, who thenceforth intermarry. The Azande method is to carry out the communion part only, and intermarriage follows. This communion is apparently not repeated. Covenants, then, are merely rituals carried out to inaugurate the relationship which is involved in every ritual. It is an interesting example of how a custom which has a certain effect comes to be observed solely for that effect, and thus has its original purpose narrowed down.

Some societies may not care to use the ritual for the purpose, because existing bonds are quite sufficient for their needs. They are self-sufficient, because the dual

[1] *Pagan Tribes of the Nilotic Sudan*, pp. 207, 246, 264.

organisation is well established. Others welcome extensive connections, and so inaugurate cousinships very readily. Such are the Azande, and in consequence their covenant has declined to little more than a contract which is losing its potency because it has become cheap. The Fijians stand half-way; with them the dual organisation is not yet completely obliterated. In short, the blood brotherhood is no brotherhood. It is just a covenant in which blood is used, and covenants are nothing but two-party rituals used not for their proper purpose of giving fertility, life, strength, victory, but for the sake of the alliance which is one result of the ritual.

Fortunately, we have covenants which have not become atrophied like the Azande covenant, but which alongside the more restricted aim of alliance retain the original wider purpose—peace, prosperity, offspring, in short, Life. Such is the Hako ceremony of the Pawnees which, far from being atrophied, fills 278 pages in Miss Fletcher's fine monograph.[1]

The Hako is performed whenever one tribe seeks to ensure friendly relations with another, but it is also "a prayer for children, in order that the tribe may increase and be strong; and also that the people may have long life, enjoy plenty, and be happy and at peace." That is the characteristic objective of a generalised ritual, and a generalised ritual is a recreation of the world. Accordingly it begins with a reference to the creation myth, as every good creation ceremony does. It has all the usual episodes—sacred marriage, life-giving, rebirth and so on. It is not primarily a covenant, but a creation ceremony used with special reference to its binding effects. Different then, as the Hako and the Azande ceremonies may seem, they are related as a well-preserved ritual is to a decayed one.

[1] *Twenty-Second Annual Report of the Bureau of American Ethnology*, Part II.

CHAPTER XXIV

Covenants

In the last chapter two forms of covenant were discussed, one used by the Azande and the other by the Pawnees and called by Miss Fletcher "the Hako".

The Hako is very valuable for theoretic purposes since it represents a stage of development from the creation ritual to the covenant pure and simple. It has not ceased to be a creation ritual, but it is commonly resorted to in order to bind two tribes together. The blood covenant of the Azande, on the other hand, has become specialised as a means of binding; it has dropped all other purposes. As a consequence its technique has been pared down to fit its specialised purpose, whereas the Hako preserves the full pattern because it remains generalised.

There is another striking difference between them; the Azande rite causes the two parties to behave as we find cross-cousins behaving wherever cross-cousinship is recognised. The Hako, on the other hand, relates the two parties in the peace-making as father and son; those who take the initiative—the visitors—appoint one of their number as father; the hosts select one of their number to be the son.

At first sight this difference seems to forbid that we should connect the two rituals as derivatives of a common original, but a closer analysis of the ritual pattern leaves a common origin as the hypothesis that best fits the facts.

A complete ritual requires two parties, male and female. These need not be a man and a woman, for the two parties come together as god and goddess, and a god and a goddess may be represented otherwise than by a man and a woman. In modern India a male and a female idol may be bedded together, in Vedic India a dead stallion and the queen. There is a Vedic rite of mating the king with the earth symbolically. In the Hako [1] the Pawnees used two feathered pipes to represent the male and female, but the sacred marriage which gives birth to the Son takes place between the party of the Father and a corn-cob, which is called Mother Corn. Mother Corn is Mother Earth. "Our spirits," says the priest, "and the spirit of the corn come together and unite for the purpose of finding the Son." It is a sacred marriage of minds.

The male and female principals may even be represented by two men. In Vedic mythology two gods pair, and this is reflected in the ritual, or at least in the explanation of the ritual. In the royal consecration of the Igalas (of Southern Nigeria) Mr G. M. Clifford writes to me, one man lies on top of another and they "go through the motions"; the new king is then born from under the skirt of the man who takes the woman's part. In this case the Son is born from two men.

If all traces of sex are removed, and the Son is left out, the result is a covenant between two men who are related as members of intermarrying parties—that is, of two parties which perform the sacred marriage together. The male members of two intermarrying parties, if they are of the same generation, are cross-cousins, and there is evidence which suggests that the sacred marriage can take place not only between a male and a female cross-cousin, but between two male cross-cousins; a man's male cross-cousin is his male wife. Certainly the Loritja of Central Australia allow a bachelor of one moiety to keep a boy of the other. Among some hill tribes of Fiji a man calls his male cross-cousin "my cohabitor", though it is

[1] *Op. cit.*, pp. 52, 124.

only a manner of speech. The Jukun of Northern Nigeria have not only male wives but female husbands.[1]

We are thus led to postulate a parent creation ceremony in which two groups take part as male and female. If the male party is represented by a man from one group and the female by an inanimate object, and if the resulting son belongs to the female side, we have the Pawnee type, in which group A is father and group B son. If the father is inanimate and the mother human, as in the Vedic horse sacrifice, then group A should be son and group B mother. Unfortunately we do not know what actually happened, or whether a ritual of this type has ever become specialised as a covenant. The case remains for the present purely hypothetical.

In the Christian covenant there is only one *human* party, the congregation regarded as female.

If the parties are two men, cross-cousins, and the son is cut out as irrelevant to a ritual which is no longer creative but merely binding, we get the Azande type.

A creation ritual readily narrows down to a covenant, and as readily to a commercial transaction. In fact, covenant and commercial transaction are often indistinguishable, since it is chiefly with a view to the exchange of goods that communities like to get together.

In the Hako ceremony the fathers provided the garment and the regalia for the ceremony. These and other gifts remained with the children, who in return made gifts of ponies to the fathers. The things brought by the fathers were taken by the children "to some other tribe, when they in turn become the fathers. Thus manufactures peculiar to one tribe are often spread over a wide territory".

The Fijian ritual also provides opportunities for exchange. What is a consequence of the ritual often becomes the purpose; ceremonial visits of condolence,

[1] C. K. Meek, *A Sudanese Kingdom*, pp. 71, 116.

"the casting off of mourning", were made the pretext
for an exchange of commodities. While I was in Lakemba
the death of the chief's little daughter was seized upon
by the people of Ale in Kandavu as an opportunity for
opening up commercial relations with the richest state
in Fiji. There had never been any relations between
Kandavu and Lakemba; "they did not know one
another". But the wife of the chief of Ale was related
to the chief of Lakemba, and arranged with him that she
should come to hold a potlatch. She thus opened a
"path"—a ritual one—along which henceforth the
people of Ale and Lakemba could travel to and fro on
ceremonial and profitable visits. Such was the hope
which the leaders of Ale expressed in their speeches, but
the Lakembans did not like the idea, because the balance
of trade would have been against them. By this I mean
that their exports would have exceeded their imports.

The Azande also use their covenants for commercial
purposes.

This change of function, this specialisation, has been
completely ignored in works on "primitive" trade, in
which a wedge is usually driven right through the life of
the people, splitting it up into "economics" and "ritual".
This artificial severance has recently been made the basis
of an otherwise excellent survey of typical cultures. The
defence pleaded is that "religion and ritual may frequently
have little genetic relation to the broad elements of
economic and social life".

It is the fact that in our community there are men who
have narrowed down their pursuit of welfare to the
buying and selling of shares, while others have narrowed
down their interest to church ceremonial. It is therefore
possible for some theorists to specialise in economics and
others in ritual. Though it is possible one may doubt
if it is wise, and our economists might have been less
bewildered by events since 1914 if they had not separated

economics so completely from life at large. However that may be, there are other communities where such specialisation of studies is quite impossible, because it does not exist in the objects of study. There every individual engages, more or less, in a common, vague pursuit of welfare in a way which cannot be described as ritual, or commercial, or political, because it is all of them at once. Such are our Fijians and Pawnees, whose activities have not branched out into economics, religion, diplomacy or other specialisations, but remain undifferentiated. Like all generalised activities, they may seem to us highly inefficient. A Fijian potlatch distributes wealth, binds tribe to tribe, entertains, circulates news, stimulates travel, all at the same time, but it does none of these as efficiently as our highly specialised shops, embassies, theatres, newspapers and tourist agencies. Yet it somehow "gets there" without the violent crises, the mal-distribution, the top-heaviness, the worry, the boredom, and all the other ills attendant on intensive specialisation.

CHAPTER XXV

The Uterine Nephew

ANTHROPOLOGISTS are familiar with the curious custom which allows a Fijian sister's son to help himself freely to his uncle's property. The case is famous because it is supposed to be a manifest survival of a time when a man inherited through his mother, and succeeded to his uncle's property and not to his father's. So satisfactory has this theory appeared that little trouble has been taken to collect further facts that might confirm or disprove it.

In a paper on "Chieftainship in the Pacific" I pointed out that the custom had been imperfectly described, and that the evidence, when recorded in detail, contains many facts which cannot be explained by this theory, if they are not actually inconsistent with it. These facts are:

(1) The deliberate excesses by which the custom is marked.

(2) The beating which the nephew receives from his cousins whenever he exercises his rights.

(3) The offering which must be made before the right can be exercised.

(4) The definite statement made by natives of the North and West that the right is not exercised at random, but only at "offerings" (*solevu*). Even in those parts of Fiji where the limitation is not expressed, the natives, in describing the custom, always appear to have in mind the visit of a nephew from abroad, when ceremonial exchanges and offerings are the rule.

(5) Lastly, there is the strongly religious character of the custom.

Now it should be the ambition of all of us who are

interested in the comparative study of customs to aspire to such a perfection in our science that its theories will explain the facts as rigorously as is the way in the older branches. We are far from having reached that condition, because our study is a new one, but we can gradually go towards that ideal by refusing to entertain theories which do not explain the facts as satisfactorily as students of language explain the forms of words.

I tried to set an example by propounding a theory of the uterine nephew's right which I believe to be better than the orthodox one because it explains more. I fear that that theory was still-born; but far from losing faith in it, I feel more confident than before that it is a step in the right direction; that there is a very good chance of its being right, whereas the other cannot possibly be. I have, indeed, no new evidence, but my attention has been attracted by a detail which I had overlooked in the old evidence, and which carries the theory still further back towards origins.

First let me recapitulate the theory—Fijian witnesses from the North and West definitely state that the sister's son steals only what has been offered up on the village green at a ceremony, and that he gets a beating for it. In the neighbouring island of Tonga the sister's son comes forward at a kava ceremony and carries away, quietly, the offering laid before his maternal uncle or grandfather. Among the Thonga of South-East Africa the uterine nephews steal the offerings made to the gods, and are pursued and pelted. All these peoples have classificatory systems of kinship similar in type. I have no hesitation in believing that all these peoples derive their kinship systems and the customs associated with them from a common source. Why not? The language of Madagascar is akin to that of Fiji; why not the customs just over the straits from Madagascar? Comparing, then, these customs, I concluded that the original custom

consisted in the uterine nephews stealing the offering, and
that the practice in South-Eastern Fiji was an extension
due to divine kingship. There I left it, overlooking one
very important sentence in Mr Junod's book on the
Thonga: "Uterine nephews are representatives of the
gods, as we shall see later on, and they assert their right
by stealing the offering and eating it up." Elsewhere he
tells us: "Any man who has departed this earthly life
becomes a *shikwembe*, a god." These gods, then, are
spirits of the dead, who receive offerings through their
representatives, the uterine nephews. It seems to
follow that it is also as representatives of the dead that
the uterine nephews are pelted. But why should the
spirits of the dead be pelted? Why, to drive them away
so that they shall not haunt the place of offering.

This custom of the nephews' stealing the offering is
part and parcel of the same system as the customs connected with cross-cousinship. I have described how
cross-cousins abuse one another, beat one another, and
all with the greatest good humour. I insisted on the
fact that the custom stood under the sanction of gods or
ghosts, but exactly how or why was not clear. Another
puzzling fact was that the word *tauvu*, cross-cousin,
means properly "god to one another"—that is to say,
related as ancestor and descendant, or god and worshipper;
for *vu* means god, ancestor, and *tau* is a reciprocal prefix.
Now if a man is a representative of his mother's gods or
ghosts, he is a god to his cross-cousins, and since the
relationship is reciprocal, his cross-cousins are gods
to him.

The statement which I have quoted from Mr Junod
explains why the uterine nephew eats the offering. It
may well be the clue to the whole problem, for it also
explains—

(1) The excesses; for the nephews or cousins are
imitating the ghosts which they represent.

(2) The beatings and at the same time the good humour with which the cousins insult and rough handle one another; there is no hostility on either side.

(3) The statement made to me in North-East Fiji that if a man reproaches his cross-cousin for helping himself to anything, that man will die. Why should he under the old theory?

(4) The great prestige which a chief's sister's son enjoys in Fiji: he represents the gods. In Tonga he is definitely of higher rank than his uncle.

There is one point which this theory does not explain— that is, why a nephew or cross-cousin has to make an offering before he can help himself. On the other hand, this fact is not irreconcilable with the theory; it is neutral.

All things considered, we have every reason to be pleased with the theory, for it explains so much. The evidence is very scanty, for little attention has been given to kinship, at least to the religious character of the kinship customs, but I believe that nine-tenths of them are religious in origin, and that the key to them will be found in re-incarnation. Rivers has shown that kinship systems are all based on some form of marriage, but these marriages themselves are, I am certain, based on religious beliefs. It seems absurd at first sight that a man should marry his grandmother, as he does in the New Hebrides, or address his father as "my son" as he does in the hills of Fiji; but if a man is his grandfather *redivivus* it is perfectly logical, as all customs are when they are understood. It is a further merit of the theory here expounded that it suggests an explanation for so many other features of kinship systems.

CHAPTER XXVI

Why Study Savages?

THE reason why savages have been studied is that they are so different from ourselves and therefore excite our curiosity; also that our imagination in transporting us among them takes us away from the dull tameness of European life. The excuse for studying them has been that they are a living replica of primitive man, about whom we want to know since he is our ancestor. This excuse, however, is beginning to fail us: it is becoming more and more evident that savages are a long way removed from primitive man; they may be behind the times, but not to that extent; they have all been exposed to civilised influences. The Australians, so long held up as the pattern of primitive man, and the Melanesians, who have somewhat superseded them, are neither of them beyond the reach of Asiatic influences. We know that Buddhism, for instance, had reached Java in the seventh century of our era; there is no knowing how much further it may not have travelled in the next twelve centuries. Greek influence has been traced as far as Japan; that is far more than half-way to Hawaii, where helmets are found of Greek design. Mohammedanism is strong in the Malay Archipelago; may it not account for the vague ideas which Fijians and New Hebrideans uncertainly hold concerning the seventh day? Is it likely that all these mighty waves and many others before then, which have as yet no name, stopped short of New Guinea just to oblige us and preserve for our study examples of primitive man?

If savage cultures are largely made up of broken fragments of higher things, what can be the use of studying them? What interest can savage peoples have for us unless they teach us what our forefathers were like? Who but the local antiquary cares whether they marry their aunts or their cousins, what trivial deeds their grotesque gods may have performed? Who cares about their chiefs with pedigrees eight generations long, their Liliputian wars, their empires not fifty miles broad? These things set down in good English with an artist's touch, dwelling only on what is of universal human interest, may fascinate for an hour, but in themselves are they worth the drudgery of scientific research?

Savages may have been affected by various civilisations but they are always behind the times, just as the provinces take up London fashions when London is beginning to discard them. I heard "Daisy! Daisy! give me your answer do", sung in Aden in 1908 when it had long been forgotten in England. And so with big things: a religion or a custom becomes the craze in one part of the world when it is dying or dead in another. Buddhism now flourishes everywhere except in its original home in Northern India; and the birthplace of Judaism and Christianity is now in the hands of Mohammedans. If these famous creeds were the earliest, we should not go to savages to gather information about them, for we have quite enough original documents; but religions existed long before these comparatively modern ones, religions about which archæological evidence is so meagre that we have not been able to give them a name, still less to make out their main principles. Our information about them is so scanty that every bit of it is precious; even the corrupt forms that may be found amongst savages are worth studying for lack of first-hand evidence; they are the only living representatives; the originals exist only as dry bones, and only bits of them too. The evidence of modern savages may not be as good as that of ancient manuscripts, buildings, and images, as far as these are available; but such remains are so scrappy, so haphazard that we cannot even hope to understand without the aid of living examples. The archæologist is at the mercy of accidents: if the climate tends to preservation, and if durable material, such as stone and pottery, has been used abundantly, he can find out something; if inscriptions are full and many, that something may become a great deal. However, given a bad climate and a people who used only wood, and where is your archæologist? It is easy to conceive a people of no mean culture with a wooden technique, and without writing. The Aryans may have been such a people, creative of great, yet perishable things; they must have been great to spread their speech from the Ganges to the Atlantic; yet their contemporary remains will never be equal to their achievements; for our knowledge of them we shall always have to depend on survivals of much later date, on the speech and customs of later generations and other races.

Even where the material is abundant, as in Egypt, it is impossible to interpret without a knowledge of living forms; inscriptions assume in the reader of them a knowledge which we no longer possess; those things which men suck in with their mother's milk, which are fundamental and therefore most important to us, are left out, and only that which is not the common knowledge of their time is set down at length. To study them without a knowledge of modern forms is therefore like reconstructing extinct animals from a few bones without any knowledge of existing species. The archæologist and the scholar too often attempt this impossible task. It must be admitted that the efforts of anthropologists have been somewhat wild, and such as to frighten away those who are used to system and accuracy, but the subject should not be blamed for the errors of its votaries; every new study must trip and stumble a good deal before it can walk, and that consummation will the sooner be reached if those trained in the more orthodox branches of history contribute their disciplined minds to the task. But too often historians have no thorough and sympathetic acquaintance with any existing religion other than their own, not even with Roman Catholicism, which is so near at once to us and to the Ancient East. Without that sympathy ancient religions will only appear absurd and childish, as Egyptian religion does to Erman, who nevertheless has constituted himself its historian. The deification of Roman emperors is treated as mere flattery and exaggeration. I know a distinguished scholar who could not be made to see that Antiochus Epiphanes could perfectly well assert his own godhead without being a fool or a knave, but only an orthodox pagan who accepted a current dogma of his time. Did a scholar saturate himself with the beliefs of a people who still believe in the divinity of kings at the present day, he would end by thinking it the most natural belief in the world, not one which he would himself hold, but one for which a very good case might be made out. To take an example that touches more closely, the Kaiser's claim to be God's vicar on earth has usually been treated amongst us as a symptom of insanity; yet our own forefathers held that doctrine quite soberly not so very long ago. Could we so familiarise ourselves with their point of view as to enter into the spirit of it we should understand a great deal better both what has happened and what is likely to happen in Germany; on the other hand, if we could be permeated with the modern German notions, we could understand the history of the Stuarts thoroughly.

The more languages a man learns to speak and think in, the quicker he is to grasp the hang of any new one; even so, the more religions he saturates his mind with, the quicker he will be to see the logic of any other. It is not until that frame of mind is reached that we can hope to place the history of religions on the same footing as that of language or of art.

The study of savage races does more than merely induce such a spirit, it may supply the key to actual facts. When Dr A. M. Blackman was puzzled by an ornament on the head of an Egyptian birth-goddess, he found the explanation in modern Uganda [1]; in so doing he was only following the example of Dr Seligman and Miss Murray who had reached important conclusions by comparing ancient Egyptian inscriptions with modern Baganda practices.[2] Nothing at present forbids us to believe that the *kava* ceremonial of the South Seas comes from the same source as the *soma* ritual of India; if this could once be proved, each would throw light on the other.

The indebtedness is not all on the side of the scholar and the archæologist; the anthropologist cannot get on without either, for they alone can supply the decisive evidence. Savage customs are but imitations, often poor ones; ancient remains alone are the genuine article—unfortunately they exist only in fragments; but we must use margarine when we cannot get butter. Until recently, anthropologists have too often ignored ancient documents; the tendency is now happily to make more use of them, and in consequence a new point of view is gradually winning acceptance in anthropology. When the combined study of ancient remains and modern survivals has at last prevailed we shall have to reconsider many an article in the anthropologist's creed: that magic is earlier than religion, that animism and secret societies are primitive, and so forth. Much that is now thought to be early will appear to be late, and much that seems late will turn out to be early. The history of civilisation must ultimately be based on ancient records. We study savages as the

[1] "Some Remarks on an Emblem upon the Head of an Ancient Egyptian Birth-goddess", *Journal of Egyptian Archæology*, 1916, p. 199.

[2] *Man*, 1911, No. 97.

naturalist would study modern reptiles. Our lizards and snakes are not ancient saurians; they cannot tell us how ancient saurians were built or how they lived, but they can help us to interpret the fossils; in fact without them we could never understand the fossils.

CHAPTER XXVII

Are Savages Custom-bound?

SAVAGES are commonly supposed to be the slaves of custom to a far greater degree than the white man, who by contrast appears as the child of reason. This view has been so often repeated that it is mistaken for fact. It is high time that it were challenged, as it stands in the way of the quest for origins by placing the savage and the white man in watertight compartments, and thus forbidding us to make use of one in order to understand the other.

If there is one thing that a long residence in the Pacific and daily intercourse with the people, especially the children, has impressed upon me, it is the thinness of their customary life as compared with the extraordinary complexity and pervasiveness of ours. You could never describe all our customs in one volume, or even in two, but you can theirs. If we think that the savage is a greater slave of custom than we are, it is because we see the mote in the other man's eye, but not the beam in ours.

I once had an argument with a chief in Rotuma on the subject. I said to him: "You Rotumans think that we have little etiquette. On the contrary, we have far more than you, but you do not notice it. One reason is that we learn it at a much earlier age than you and so it comes quite natural and is hardly seen. Now I will give you a demonstration; I will make this boy eat in European style." I made the boy, aged about twelve, sit at a table with knife and fork. "No", I said, "don't stick out your elbows; don't fill your mouth" and so on, and in a very short time he was reduced to tears and declared that he had sooner not eat than eat like that.

It is a rooted idea among the Fijians that it is no use teaching children because they are watery-souled. I explained to my friend Salesi that we started as babies and the result was that our complicated customs came quite easy to us and involved no hardship. "I see," he said. "We see how quiet the white children keep, and we pity them. Now I understand."

The fact that savages begin to learn late makes it impossible for them to learn much. When I had to teach Fijian boys I soon discovered that the first thing to do was to teach them their own customs, of which their ignorance was phenomenal. In their natural state the less intelligent never learnt things which we should think it impossible not to learn. There actually were adults who did not know correctly the kava ceremonial, although it was an almost nightly occurrence. I was present once when a leading nobleman, aged about eighty, put all his side to shame at a potlatch by wording the acknowledgment of the gifts as if he were the giver, a mistake which was against common sense as well as against custom, and one which I should certainly not have made.

One result of learning late is that custom is not so much second nature as ours is. In Fiji it is certainly the creation of nature's gentlemen, but it lacks the subtlety of ours; it is very obvious and conscious. Ours is so elusive that Asiatics commonly fail to grasp it, and seldom rise above a caricature.

Another result of learning late is that they remember having learnt, and therefore when you ask them why they do a thing they say quite honestly, "Because our fathers taught us", or "Because it is the custom of our country". These answers are quoted as proof that they are ruled entirely by custom, and not like us by reason, but the truth is that they do not deceive themselves as much as we do. We learn so early that we forget having learnt, and think that reason is our prompter. Besides, our minds are more active and curious about causes, without always having the leisure or patience to go in search of them. If any one asks "Why have you got a second chamber?" we do not answer, "Because in the Parliament of our fathers the third estate sat separate from the other two", but "Because we need a check on the popularly elected chamber". A savage will probably tell you that he washes the bodies of the dead because it is the custom, but a white man will probably say, "Why, it is only common decency", and a white woman will reject with indignation Dr A. M. Blackman's suggestion that we do it because ancient man helped the deceased to be reborn by pouring over his body the vivifying waters.

Man is distinguished from the animals by his capacity for handing on to his posterity what he has himself acquired. The white man is distinguished above others by his greater development of that capacity, by the tremendous burden of custom he is able to bear almost without being aware of it. It is our blindness in trying to impose the same burden on other races that is everywhere stirring up revolt against the white man and his ways.

CHAPTER XXVIII

From Ancient to Modern Egypt

"EGYPT" says Lady Duff-Gordon "is a palimpsest in which the Bible is written over Herodotos and the Koran over that." Herodotus himself was written over the Pyramid Age which overlay the predynastic, and so on even perhaps to the Palæolithic and beyond. It is still the custom to make prints of hands with blood on doors and on saints' tombs. Red hand-prints are found in Europe in the Upper Palæolithic.

The new is not always written over the old, but often beside it. Thus the ancient Egyptian water-lift was supplemented, not superseded by the water-wheel, and in Hellenistic times by the water-screw. The reason is that the earlier can sometimes work where the new cannot. The water-screw, for instance, is only suitable for small differences of level. Even the water-wheel has its limits, and when the Nile is low has to be eked out with the lift. As for the latest comer, the engine pump, it requires a capital which the smallholder never possesses, or he would not be a smallholder. It is no doubt partly for the same reason that the adze which we can see in use on the reliefs of Saqqâra can still be watched at work in streets traversed by the latest type of car. It is an all-round tool, armed with which a competent carpenter can achieve much with next to no capital.

New conceptions are continually arising which form the kernel of new systems of thought. Backed by the enthusiasm of newness, these attack and break up the older cultures, as a small keen army strikes at the heart of a large inert host, destroys the links between the units, and disperses them into scattered bands. So the new dispensation destroys the central ideas of the old, and leaves only fragments which are eradicated, assimilated, or left alone, according as they resist, surrender, or remain indifferent. Take Islam, the latest comer; it is a system of conduct with a limited range; a great part of human activities, such as mechanics, buying and selling, and others, lie outside its interests, and so have not been attacked, but carry on much as of old. The rest was often, as we shall see, revolutionised more on the surface than in the depths.

Egypt is now a highly centralised State, so centralised that it may be said that politically Cairo is Egypt. We know, however, from ancient records that it once consisted of two rival kingdoms, the Upper and the Lower. It is to the Ancients we owe the fusion; yet thousands of years of union have not completely concealed the join. Upper and Lower Egypt still form a contrast: a Delta man penetrating beyond the no-man's-land that lies between Cairo and Minya feels himself in a foreign country. The differences of custom and character are sufficient to keep the populations of north and south apart when they meet in Cairo, leading them in different paths, the Delta folk into the more individualistic occupations of domestic service and shops, the more gregarious Upper Egyptians into labour gangs on the railway, docks, and in quarries.

The manner in which these two realms have been welded into the solid mass we now see has been preserved to us. It was carried out in accordance with the ancient theory of kingship. The king represented the god of the land; to acquire new lands he had to become the god of those lands. He had to annex the god in order to annex the country. The king of Upper Egypt took the red crown, the abode of the goddess Buto, and added it to his own white crown in which resided the goddess Nekhbet, and so became the lawful ruler of the two lands. Since then the two lands cannot long remain apart.

The two kingdoms were themselves composed of what had once been principalities, nomes with their gods, temples, standards, and processions. Their crowns could be and were fused, fusing the deities. In time the all-embracing divinity of the king swallowed up the local gods, reducing a host of principalities to two kingdoms.

Thanks to the protracted labours of those early unifiers, whoever now takes possession of Egypt receives a ready-made centralisation.

The king's divinity provided them with a theory for gathering all things into his hand. The land was tributary to him as to a god, and paid one-fifth of the produce. Like the gods he owned a considerable domain, so that the land was divided into royal domain, temple lands, and private tenures. This classification is still maintained by the Egyptian code. The proportions only have fluctuated. In the Pyramid Age it is estimated that the king owned the greater part of Northern Egypt. By about 1870 Ismail Pasha had built up once more this domain to include about one-fifth of the arable land; but his extravagance forced him to cede a great part to the State, thus introducing a new distinction between the public and the private domain. This latter has been built up again to a considerable size.

The temple lands are now represented by the religious *waqfs* or endowments. They have been estimated at one-twelfth of the cultivated land. The Minister of Waqfs represents the ancient "scribe who establishes the endowments of all the gods". The rest of the land, as land conquered from infidels, is considered to have been either distributed by the conqueror to Muslims as military fiefs subject to tithe or left to their owners on payment of tribute. Military fiefs were not an invention of the Arabs; they were well known to the ancient Egyptians.

As all divinity was concentrated in the king, so was all service, since godhead is there to be served—that is, to have such things done to it as will make it beneficiently efficacious to the people. Already in the Old Kingdom this concentration had reached such a pitch that much of the energies of the people was dedicated to the service of the king.

Having done its work the divinity of kings has become superfluous and has so far evaporated that traces of it are now very hard to find. As has often happened in the history of civilisations, it has all been concentrated in one last holder, a prophet, who continues to reign in the spirit for ever and so has no successor.[1] In Islam even that prophet does not enjoy full divinity, but only the nearest that Islam allows to it, proximity to God. That belongs so pre-eminently to the Prophet that it can only be enjoyed in a minor degree by anyone else. Much that was royal has thus passed to the Prophet. If Pharaoh's name was mentioned it was followed by some such prayer as "May he live, be hale and healthy". Now it is the Prophet who enjoys the addition, "God bless him and preserve him".

The gap between the god and the king had already begun to widen in very early times. Already in the Fifth Dynasty the king from being Horus and Great God had been lowered to Son of Rēʿ and Good God. Successive ages have widened it into that proximity which, as we shall see, is so characteristic of Islam.

This lowering of the king's status in relation to the deity has not always had such a disturbing effect on custom as might be expected. Thus the ancient Egyptians used to build temples in connection with the tombs of their kings, mortuary temples, as they are called. The modern Egyptians build domed tombs for their rulers and attach to them a mosque. These tombs form cities not unlike those of the Pyramid Age. The externals have changed:

---

[1] Hocart, *Kingship*, pp. 120 ff. (Clarendon Press, 1927); *Kings and Councillors*, pp. 168 ff. (Luzac & Co., 1936).

domes, rare in the Sixth Dynasty, are now inevitable; the Qur'ân provides the decoration instead of bas-reliefs forbidden by the religion; if the ceiling is still adorned with stars it is as an artistic motif, and no longer to make the temple a world in miniature; finally, this city of the dead need no longer be in the West. In spite of all these changes the main idea remains. It may not appear at first sight, because the tomb-mosque is not dedicated to the king but to the one and only God; but then the old mortuary temple was not really dedicated to the king either in the New Kingdom, but to Amūn, the real recipient of the cult, and the priests were priests of Amūn. It was the dead king's temple only in so far as he embodied the god, and when he died he returned to the gods, to the Sun, to Rēʿ, to Amūn. It is not, then, a change from the worship of man to worship of God, but in both cases the worship of the god is linked with a deceased sovereign. The difference lies in the exact nature of the link. Pharaoh was an impersonation of the god, and when he died "the limb of the god returned to its creator". The rigour of Islam forbids any such identity; the most that it allows is nearness to God.

Here we have the hard kernel of Islam to which all ancient customs must fit themselves or break. In this case the custom has fitted itself with ease. As of old, continuous worship goes on in the tombs of kings, and, as of old, endowments are made to pay for their worship; only it is no longer addressed to the deceased identified with the god, but on his behalf to Allah; there are no special texts to promote this identity with the deity, but the texts come from the one and only book that is read alike in mosque, tomb, house, or street, the Qur'ân, and it is read to ensure the nearness of God. The reciters are not priests specially affected to the cult of the dead, but generalised scholars selected and paid to do what every scholar does anywhere, to read the revelation. There has been a complete levelling out of all worship. Islam means standardisation, and standardisation becomes inevitable when everything is concentrated at the head.

Thus, after the king's divinity has been reduced to nothing the habits it has engendered remain. Centuries of vice-royalty have not weakened them. Everything still revolves round the king; he is still the master without whose consent nothing can be done. He can still defeat popular leaders, especially if he plays his ancient part of religious leader. To deserve the title of "the pious king" is to win over the masses, and to enjoy a reverence that is not adoration but readily suggests it. "The universal demonstrations of loyalty", writes an Egyptian, "prove beyond the least shadow of a doubt that King Fârûq is almost adored by his subjects. . . . In this connection it should be borne in mind that Ancient Egyptians actually worshipped their kings, who were looked upon as symbols of Egypt's greatness and glory." It remains the official doctrine that the monarchy is purified by God, and it is preached on Fridays that he who disobeys the king disobeys Allah.

As constantly happens in the history of man, a reasoned system has left behind a deposit of unreasoned (not necessarily unreasonable) behaviour.

One element in the glamour and power of kingship is the faith that distant greatness is ever more ready to help the oppressed than nearer and smaller greatness. The modern proletarian is just as convinced as his distant forebears that if he could only reach Pharaoh he would get redress, but the petty powers stand in the way.

These petty powers were in the nineteenth century recast on European lines; but Ancient Egypt had fully worked out the essential features of a bureaucracy. By the Eighteenth Dynasty it had completed an evolution which had been repeated elsewhere. Like the kings of

modern France the Pharaohs had drawn their vassals
into their orbit as mere satellites. The great lords became
officials. There has been no solution of continuity. The
nome lords went on under Christianity. "The Arab
conquest merely substitutes Moslem sheikhs or emirs for
pagan and Christian nobles." There have been fluctua-
tions between feudal independence and bureaucratic
dependence; there may yet be. "In the last century the
beys divided Egypt among themselves almost in the same
manner as the chiefs of the mercenaries in the eighteenth
century B.C." [1]

A highly centralised system requires a host of clerks,
men who can write letters and keep documents. In
Ancient Egypt to administer and to make a record are
synonymous: the official is a scribe. Then, as now,
government employment enjoyed the greatest prestige
and appeared to offer the most desirable career, because
it seemed an easy life compared with other occupations
and ensured a steady livelihood from the government, or,
as the ancients expressed it, "from the king's house".

Since the end of the New Empire at least the govern-
mental machinery could scarcely be said to function as it
was intended to do. Centuries of mismanagement have
schooled the village to withdraw into itself and to run
its own affairs, not by a cadre of officials, but by public
opinion. It has its code of loyalty and secrecy. Between
it and the administration stands the mayor, half official,
half squire, ready, if the central power should weaken, to
become a feudal lord, as has happened in the past. As
official he has to represent the government; as chief to
keep the secrets of the village.

Behind this invisible rampart of exclusiveness more
effective than walls of stone, the Egyptian village runs

[1] G. Maspero, "Un manuel d'hiérarchie égyptienne" (*Journ. Asiatique*, no. 4, 1888).

itself along grooves traced in ancient times, by habit rather than by system. There is no social theory, and so no crystalline pattern such as we find in countries to the south and to the east, but a somewhat amorphous, yet highly cohesive, crowd. Comparative evidence, however, aided by fragments from Ancient Egypt, convince us that this absence of system is the residue of a system as definite as the caste system of India and farther east, and akin to it.[1]

That system once gravitated round the king and the gods. The service of the court and temples required priests, sculptors, linen-workers, washermen, cobblers, butchers, bakers, carpenters, fly-whisk bearers, a whole panoply of occupations. We can see the divine counterpart of that organisation officiating round the god in the bas-reliefs; for "the divine court is organised on the model of the terrestrial", or rather the two are one, since the king of Egypt is king of the gods. There is Ptah, the artificer; Khnum, the potter; Thoth, the scribe; Hathor, the nurse; Heket the midwife; Anubis, the embalmer, each playing his part in the royal ritual.

With the breakdown of the old religion these courts dispersed, the craftsmen were set adrift. They no longer revolve round king, feudal lord, or temple. Having lost its old meaning, the old organisation has also lost its fullness: in a community struggling for bare existence there is no room for painters, sculptors, superintendents of stables, and such luxuries; the occupations have been pared down to the minimum requirements of the village. It is no longer a monarchic theory that prescribes the occupations, but the necessities of existence and of a simplified democratic religion.

The barber, for instance, is a village dignitary, but his status is not defined, as it is in India, by a theory of

---

[1] Hocart, *Kings and Councillors*, chap. ix, and *Caste*, pp. 144–9.

society. He is hereditary in practice, but not by rule; he is neither appointed nor paid by a lord or by the community jointly, but establishes himself where there is work and is paid by individuals a fee fixed by custom. However much his status may have changed, his purpose has changed but little: he is there because the modern peasant, like the ancient, has to have his head shaved and be circumcised. As for the reason why, it has got lost long ago; but the Egyptian barber still carries on the habits without the reason.

Even more attenuated is the washerman of the dead. He appears to be the last vestige of the embalmer. Mummification has been swept away by new systems of thought, but the washing of the corpse goes on. The original priestly character of this craftsman still survives in the prayers he has to speak, and the elaborate rules that complicate a simple operation.

It is commonly asserted that there are no priests in Islam. That is purely a matter of definition. What interests us here is not the definition of the man but his function. Now there is in Egypt a body of men who perform much the same functions as do priests elsewhere. If we will not call them priests because they are laymen as well, landowners perhaps or village shopkeepers, then Ancient Egypt had no priests either, for under the Old Kingdom "nearly every person of rank assumed besides their worldly profession one or more priesthoods".[1] Priesthoods were in fact often identical with State appointments.

The hereditary character of the priests is gone. Even in Roman times when it was most strict it was not absolute. Ability to read a hieratic book was then accepted as a substitute for descent. Now proficiency in the sacred books is the only basis. To be a sheikh it is necessary

[1] A. Erman, *Aegypten und aegyptisches Leben*, new ed. (Tübingen, 1923), p. 331.

to know the Scriptures and the law. The seminaries of El Azhar scatter over Egypt these clerics who, as preachers, teachers, registrars, bind the country together more effectively than the administration. A peasant speaks of "us Muslims", not of "us Egyptians". Even so, of old they were primarily worshippers of Rē' and Amūn with all the common customs that implies, and their wars were the wars of Amūn. The Arabs introduced no new principle when they warred in the name of Allah.

These clerics continue in the simplified and standardised form so characteristic of Islam the functions of the ancient priests. They read the Qur'ân as the ancient *kherheb* used to read the holy books of paganism; they are authorities in law like the priests of Ma'at, the goddess of justice; they teach reading and writing for sacred rather than for everyday purposes.

There is the *imâm* who is the authority on all those social relationships that come within the orbit of Islam.

The schoolmaster carries on the work of those who dictated the Instructions of Amenemhēt I, the Teaching of Duauf, the Story of Sinuhe, and all those texts that were copied by generations of schoolboys in antiquity. Only, he does not range so widely; he is confined to the Qur'ân.

This narrowing of scope is characteristic of Modern as contrasted with Ancient Egypt. There are those who complain that it is impoverishment; but sometimes, at least, it means a welcome simplification. Thus the writing which the schoolmaster now teaches is a great improvement on the old one. The hieroglyphs were a combination of several principles that had succeeded without superseding one another. The Arabic writing contains no new principle, but employs only one out of the several ancient ones. It should be noted, however, that some simplification had already been undertaken by the later ancients under Greek influence, producing demotic.

There were priestesses in Ancient Egypt. Islam will not have women in office; but, cast out of the official system, they have found a refuge in the popular religion, which, in Egypt as elsewhere, subsists in the basement of the intelligentsia's edifice of thought. They live on in reduced circumstances as the self-appointed vehicles of the spirits of the dead.

Besides clerics the village has craftsmen: potters, blacksmiths, wheelwrights, mat-makers, shearers, farriers, and others. They settle where there is work, and the father hands on his occupation to his son. This was noted by Herodotus as characteristic of Egypt, and he is confirmed by numerous inscriptions: we know of one headship of the painters of Amūn which was inherited by seven generations. There is no rule about it, as usual in Egypt. Unlike the Hindu jurists, the teachers of Islam are not interested in popular organisation; they leave that to the people themselves, and the people do not think, but simply carry on. So used are the people to the heredity of occupations that if a man does not succeed to his father's work he nevertheless retains the title and is known as the Carpenter, the Engineer even though he may be a clerk in government employ.

The village functionaries are paid not in cash but in kind. The barbers and the ferryman will turn up at the harvest to get their annual fee of maize or wheat. Even so, the Pharaohs paid their workers in fish, beans, corn, and firewood. A peasant will now engage a learned man to recite the Qur'ân weekly so that the Lord may have compassion on a deceased kinsman and be with him in the grave; at every harvest he will pay him his due in wheat or maize. Even so, an ancient Egyptian would make arrangements for paying in produce from his lands those who made periodic offerings of bread and beer at his tomb.

It was foreigners who brought coinage to Egypt, and coinage never has become acclimatised. In the big towns the economy is largely foreign; the village retains the primeval barter. Even the landowners who know and use coinage at the town end of their transactions still follow the ancient way at the village end. The tenant pays his rent by surrendering $\frac{1}{4}$, or $\frac{1}{2}$, or $\frac{10}{14}$ of his crop according to the degree of assistance he receives. There are estates where the labourer rarely handles money, save for the few piasters he makes on selling chickens and eggs. We have indeed the remarkable spectacle of a modern international bank owning an estate where the tenant-in-chief pays both labour and landlord with the beans he grows. I have seen an even later institution, the ice-cream vendor, come into contact with that primeval economy, surrender to it, and accept eggs in payment.

It may seem unaccountable that a people that has so often led the world, and was tutor to the Greeks, should have been so slow to profit by one of the greatest inventions of mankind. It is not that money is strange or unwelcome: everyone understands it and grasps at it; yet the same peasant who uses money in the town goes back to barter when on the land. Perhaps the best reason I have heard is that "they are accustomed to do so from ancient times". The real problem is not why customs persist, but why they ever change. Inertia has preserved barter, but not stupid inertia.

We are apt to ascribe to customs and institutions an absolute value. We believe money to be a boon everywhere under all conditions, and conclude that a people that cannot see those advantages must be dense indeed. The Egyptian peasant, however, has been trained for millennia in the hard school of experience and not of abstract economics. He prefers barter because it eliminates the middle man. An excellent reason for being paid in maize is that maize is food; but if food is to be had directly from the neighbour's field, why go a roundabout way to get it through a shop?

From the landowner's point of view it is submitted that to pay in money means keeping a reserve at the bank to be drawn on weekly or monthly, whereas under the sharing system, settlement takes place twice a year as the crops come in. The Egyptians have never taken kindly to finance. Greeks and Syrians were welcomed in antiquity because they supplied a missing sense. They still continue as grocers to fill a gap which the Egyptian is disinclined by temperament to fill.

The configuration of Egypt has never favoured the growth of such an ability in the countryside. Commercial genius finds most opportunity in long-distance trading. It is only through a narrow opening to the north that Egypt can export and import on a large scale. Internally each bit is so like every other that there cannot be much exchange of commodities. Overseas trade has therefore been undertaken mainly by maritime neighbours such as the Greeks, the Phoenicians, and the British. Now, as of old, Alexandria is essentially a foreign town.

Nature has allowed Egypt to become a land of large economy in one dimension only, north and south. Hence not only the exchange system of the countryside, but its transport also, remains much as it ever was. The donkey has continued to be the chief conveyance since before the Pyramid Age, because he is so well fitted to the conditions. The only change is that he is now ridden as well as driven, and that the camel has come in to share his task.

The distances east and west are small, the land thickly populated, the towns numerous, the holdings small. Imagine the dream of an enthusiastic modernist come true, and every peasant owning a car. To make all the little holdings, down to one acre and less, accessible to cars would sterilise so much land as would seriously affect the food supply, nor would the capital invested in carriage be proportionate to the loads carried. What produce is not consumed locally, perhaps within earshot of the field, has at most a few miles to go to the river or the nearest collecting centre. Within easy reach of most villages flows a great waterway which is blessed with a wind that blows one way and a current in the opposite direction. It is the great artery fed by innumerable capillaries, the banks of the canals and drains, and nothing has yet been found more suitable to run along these banks than the Egyptian donkey.

The slow and cheap transport is still provided by sailing barges. They have changed their shape and enlarged their capacity, but still convey the same kind of grain and the same kinds of pots, and load the same stone from the same quarries. The nineteenth century has added cotton, maize, coal, and other goods; it has supplemented sail with steam, and has duplicated the river with a railway for fast transport; but once more the new does not displace the old, but merely ekes it out.

The local circulation centres in the local market, which, like so much else, retains a great deal of its ancient character simplified. It has not quite the same range as on the reliefs at Saqqâra. That is an inevitable consequence of extreme centralisation which impoverishes country life, as we can see happening in Europe. In ancient reliefs the men dominate the market. Now in Lower Egypt it has passed almost entirely into the hands of the women, but south of Minya the men still retain it, because they disapprove of their women selling in public.

Where the sphere of trade is restricted the sphere of marriage tends to be restricted also. The peasant, and still more his wife, do not like their daughters to pass out of easy range. A girl who marries at what is for us a short distance is cut off from her family. In Upper Egypt it is even more a matter of kin than of distance: it is a shame to marry one who is not kin, even if he lives in the village. The proper marriage everywhere is that of agnatic first cousins. This is only a little less exclusive than the ancient custom. Kings used to marry their sisters. The wives of the common people are often described as sisters; but we do not know how far the term we so translate has the same meaning as our own word, or how far it does not include, besides sisters, other female agnates of the same generation. Many, if not all, the "sister marriages" recorded among the common people may be unions with cousins. In that case no change has occurred beyond condemning the closer union which was certainly encouraged in high circles, if not in lower ones.[1]

Islam has, unlike Christianity, absorbed very little of the marriage ceremony. The procession, the mock fights, the feasts and all those wedding episodes which are common in some form or other all the world over are completely ignored. They are customary, not part of Islamic law. The one episode which Islam has annexed is the marriage contract. Curiously enough, it is the very one about which the ancients have left us very detailed information. It has been taken over almost unchanged. In antiquity, as now, the husband paid a dowry and promised to pay a further amount on divorcing his wife. The proportion that now prevails in the Western Delta between the immediate and the deferred payments is 2 : 1, but 1 : 1 occurs as in ancient times. Note that this is now one of the few money transactions: payment is never in kind. The ancients had no coinage, but they paid the

[1] In technical parlance it all turns on the question whether the ancient kinship system of Egypt was classificatory or genealogical. There can be no doubt that it was derived from a classificatory system, if not itself classificatory. Kinship terms are still used at the present day in the same manner as in classificatory systems; *e.g.* paternal uncles may be addressed as fathers, at least among the peasantry. See Hocart, *The Progress of Man* (London, 1933), chap. xxi, and chap. xxii above.

dowry in weights of precious metal, not in corn. Coins later took the place of weights, but the principle remained the same: it was not, and still is not, a commercial transaction like barter. Then, as now, the bride brought various materials with her, then mainly garments, now furniture; but the ring which the bride presents to the bridegroom has not changed. Then, as now, all that she brought with her was hers, to be taken away at divorce. In the ancient contracts it was stated that the children inherited the property. The claim of the children to inherit seems to have been in the process of solidifying as law. The process is now complete, and so it is no longer necessary to specify their right in the marriage contract, since it follows marriage automatically.

Plurality of wives was not of course instituted, but only sanctioned by Islam, for it is world-wide. Cases of two wives occur from the Middle Kingdom on. Polygamy was undoubtedly royal in origin, a duty of kings rather than a privilege. It is this aristocratic character that has caused its spread, rather than any advantage, for not every man is capable of managing several wives. Polygamy is often a sacrifice of peace to prestige. Yet such is the force of snobbery that polygamy has spread right down to the peasantry. At the same time it is disappearing at the top. Europe is now the arbiter of *bon ton*, and Europe has decreed that polygamy is barbarous. Thus we are assisting at a complete reversal of the ancient institution: from being first royal, then aristocratic, polygamy is becoming plebeian, because the peasant is the last to be reached by the changes of fashion; besides, his wives and children work, and so are an asset instead of a burden, as they are in higher spheres.

Concubines, as distinct from wives, were an important part of Pharaoh's state. They were kept in a seclusion as strict as that which still prevails and has become associated with Islam. The Pharaoh's harem was known as the "House of the Isolated", and a foreign princess who entered it was lost to the world.

We have by now acquired some experience of the way in which a new dispensation establishes itself on the ruins of its forerunners. Of the pre-existing structure, parts lie completely outside the new plan, and so remain untouched; for instance marriage observances. Others, like the marriage contract, fit in so well that they are incorporated with scarcely a change. Yet others had to be remodelled to harmonise with the new theology. We have seen how kingship had to be reconciled with the new conception of God. So had all beliefs and customs which were associated with the old theology: they had to shed their paganism.

Thus the pig was so unclean to the Ancient Egyptians that it never figures in texts or pictures of the Old Kingdom, and in the days of Herodotus swineherds were not allowed to intermarry with the rest of the people. It was alleged that Set had taken the form of a black pig in order to attack Horus. The myth thus links the pig's uncleanness with a cosmological system in which it was the vehicle of the Adversary. When that Adversary became the Devil his vehicle perforce became evil. When the old gods became obnoxious this uncleanness was not abolished, for it was strongly held among the Semites, but its last tenuous links with its theoretical basis were cut, and it was set adrift as an isolated, inexplicable, but all the more tenacious observance.

The principle of ablutions before worship was known to the Egyptians as it was to many other nations. Pharaoh was purified by having water poured over him. This, and not bathing as in India, is still the prescribed technique. The people were also accustomed to wash before reading the holy books and before entering the temple. All that was necessary was to detach the observance from the temple and attach it to the mosque.

The attitudes of prayer, too, were not very different from what they are now. The two sets are merely variants. No great change of form was therefore needed. The main change was in the intention. Islam reserves them strictly for God. In the bas-reliefs they *appear* to be accorded to men, but it must be remembered that the king was a god, not a man. The true points of difference are whether there is one god or many, and whether a man can be identified with the god or not.

Some Arab customs came in the wake of the new system of ideas, not as an integral part of it. They could thus settle down in peace beside similar indigenous fragments. Thus the new shape of tomb was not obligatory. It acquired considerable popularity, for some reason or other, and is by far the commonest now; but it did not oust completely the old, stepped, *mastaba* form which is now known to be at least as old as the First Dynasty. Having come down to the masses it is naturally much reduced in size. So far from being antagonistic the two types can actually blend, as is usual in tombs of the Khedivial family: the simple Arabic tomb is superposed on two or three high plinths. The result is a *mastaba* with the high proportions of the Arab type.

There are cases, however, where compromise is impossible, because the old is irreconcilable with the new. The only course left is for the new to exterminate the old. But that is not easy when the mass of the people are attached to the old. The old custom can only be eradicated by eradicating the people, and it is obviously impossible to wipe out several million people. Persecution is ineffective, for it merely drives the old practices into concealment.

Men are very tenacious of their hopes of salvation and

health. Possession by the spirits of the dead promises relief from the ills of body and mind, and the sufferers will therefore defy bell, book, and candle in pursuit of this relief. Hence the unimpaired vitality of possession.

In antiquity many diseases were ascribed to it. It still holds its ground as a theory of hysterical disorders, a theory clear-cut and easy to grasp: the soul controls the body; let another soul get possession of the body, and the patient will become to all intents and purposes a new person. The theory does seem to work, as many wrong theories do. It appears to act as a mental cathartic, and while that is so the negative fulminations of the learned are in vain. Only a positive policy of better scientific treatment can hope to drive out this crude, but popular method.

It is the women who are the stronghold of possession. It is they who generally hold out longest against new notions, the more so in Egypt as Islam addresses itself especially to the males. So long as the men almost monopolise the mosques women feel its influence less. Thus they persist in wailing for the dead according to the ancient custom, although this is forbidden by the Islamic tradition. Worse still, they daub their faces with blue, the ancient colour of mourning. Among the men are some better acquainted with the law and they disapprove. Sometimes they are resolute enough to prevail, and Islam wrests another conquest from the ancient culture even now in the twentieth century; but the women can be very obstinate, and forestall opposition by hastily painting their faces and presenting their male folk with a *fait accompli*.

We speak of culture and ideas conflicting, but that is only a figure of speech. In fact, of course, it is the bearers of one set of ideas conflicting with the bearers of others. It may be men *versus* women, but the more important conflicts follow the lines, not of sex, but of social and intellectual status. The intelligentsia has one point of view and it is fond of imposing it upon the lower classes. It is much addicted to systems and apt to dislike anything that does not fit into the system, merely because it does not fit. The masses, on the contrary, often prefer the meaningless because it is meaningless.

When a practice becomes detached from the ideas that inspired it it becomes meaningless, like our fear of being thirteen at table. Ancient Egyptian medical treatises abound in formulæ, and recipes which had evidently lost their meaning at the time they were written down in the form in which we possess them. The systems to which they belonged had already decayed then and must belong to a much earlier stratum. In some cases the very words are a mere jumble of nonsense syllables.

Such charms being meaningless are apt to be unstable, since meaning helps to keep customs true to type. It is a thankless task therefore to try to identify ancient examples with modern ones. Nevertheless the industry of scholars has unearthed definite evidence that ancient Egyptian medicine survived into modern times. A treatise by Abu Sahl ʿIsa ibn Yahya contains prescriptions which can be termed translations of some of those found in the Ebers Papyrus, and the author constantly appeals to a work by Thoth, the old god of science. Another proof of continuity is that in modern, as in ancient magic formulæ, the patient is referred to as the son of his mother, not of his father as in everyday usage; Ahmed the son of Fatma, not of Mahmud. Erman has even produced an old Egyptian charm against any kind of witchcraft closely resembling a modern remedy for hæmorrhoids. In both cases a beetle is cooked in oil, the wings and head separately in fatty matter. It is the same remedy become more specialised in its application. This narrowing down of the purpose is also to be observed in tattooing. This world-wide custom is in origin part of a generalised rite for promoting life; in Modern Egypt it is used for specific diseases.

Modern opinion is not as favourable to ancient charms as Abu Sahl, and a continuous attack is being made on them, but they show considerable tenacity. Even more tenacious is the belief in the evil eye. It seems once to have belonged to a cosmological system in which the sun and moon were the eyes of the world. Special virtue was attributed to the eye of Horus, by which the moon was generally meant. Models of it were therefore used as amulets. The good eye abounds in our museums of antiquities; but of the evil eye we hear little beyond the mention of " a chapter on warding off the evil eye ". Nowadays, fear and jealousy, sentiments which seem to be the aftermath of great civilisations, have given exclusive prominence to the evil eye, while the good one has disappeared. What remains has, of course, been attuned to Islam by the masses, who are usually equally loyal to the new and to the old. It is Allah who is now invoked against the evil eye which is supposed to be inspired by the devil. They assimilate it to temptation which can be set aside with the aid of God. That is another characteristic of the change that has come over Egyptian culture: its tone is strongly moral. The old religion was a quest of prosperity; it has yielded its place to a rule of good conduct.

Light blue was much favoured by the ancients as a lucky colour, probably because it is the colour of the clear sky. Beads of that colour are still to be seen on the radiators of the latest in cars as a protection against the evil eye. The cosmic connection however, is gone.

The conflict between intelligentsia and the masses goes on over the fairs which are annually held in honour of the saints. These remain too obviously pagan to be left in peace by the purists of Islam. Whether any particular festival is the lineal descendant of an old heathen one is not of great importance; it is sufficient that the genus continues the ancient way with its processions, its visits to the shrines, and so on. Only, having lost the support of the great, these fairs are much simplified and amorphous. The celebrations have not the elaborate structure of the ancient rituals; the variety of episodes is gone with the variety of the pantheon, though the ship is still carried in procession at the mosque of Abu'l Haggag in Luxor. There is now only one God to glorify, and the ways of doing so are reduced to one or two. All the rest which cannot be reconciled with the severe simplicity of Islam is relegated to the secular. Juggling, games, dramatic performances which are incompatible with the austerity and single-mindedness of Islam are despised, and even persecuted, by the purists. If they cannot be abolished altogether they are segregated from the religious exercises. Thus a wedge has been driven between the religious and the profane which did not exist before. The profane is merely the religious that has been cut out by a new system, and left to sink into pure amusement, even fooling.

The low estimation in which these fairs are held reflects the diminished state of all the minor powers before the rise of one supreme God. Whether any of the modern saints are old local gods in disguise is doubtful; some are definitely known to be real men who lived in Arab times, perhaps all are; but that is as immaterial as the antiquity of their fairs. As a class they continue the functions of the ancient gods and of the ancient dead (the two run into one another in virtue of the fundamental principles of the religion). This is shown by such concrete cases as that of Imam Shafa'i, a famous jurist, to whom letters are still written for advice, just as they used in antiquity to be addressed to the dead. It is the continuity of idea that interests us, not of persons.

The saints are able to continue the ancient tradition,

though on a lower plane, because they fill a void which monotheism has left between the humble peasant and the Lord of the World. They are interested in individuals, not in the universe, and they specialise in different ailments. Already in antiquity the great gods seemed too remote to concern themselves with the wishes and troubles of the simple folk, and so, in private, magic recourse was had to the lesser gods.

These saints are no longer gods, but only near to God. Theoretically they have no power in themselves, but only as intercessors. The change of theory, however, makes little difference to the procedure among the common folk. Vows are made just as if the saint's power were his own. Tombs are visited, physical contact is sought by stroking or kissing. The devotees pass their hands over the rails which enclose the tomb, then stroke themselves and their children as if they were collecting and dispensing an emanation from the saint himself. In the same way the ancients are to be seen in the bas-reliefs transmitting with their hands the vital principle represented by the 'ankh symbol. Only their descendants do not transmit anything as concrete. They act as if *baraka*, blessing, streamed from their hands, but if asked to explain their action they say that *baraka* consists in having good children, money, much luck; there is no hint of any supernatural property that can be communicated like a fluid. The whole theory of the act has vanished leaving behind it only the act and its effects.

The act, however, is so concrete in its suggestion that it is only too easy to put back into it the concrete intention, to interpret it as what it seems to be, the gathering and dispensing of life as a kind of fluid. One feels it is only the vigilance of the teachers of religion that keeps the thought from being pulled by the action in the direction of frank heathendom.

The same suspicion attaches in some quarters to

sacrifices. These still take place on occasions such as funerals and the Great Feast. The interpretation, of course, has been revised: the ancient identity of god and victim and worshipper is gone. The sacrifice is only allowed to draw the worshipper nearer to God; hence it is called *qurban*, from *qirib*, to draw near. Yet even this concession does not reconcile the more extreme purists.

The process of narrowing down all worship and all life to the service of one God was completed, but not begun, by Islam. The seed of monotheism was inherent in the old religion. The gods had not such distinct individualities as we are accustomed to expect of gods. Two can be combined into one, like Amūn and Rē'. The king, the magician, or the dead man can be several deities at once. The process of fusion can be carried out systematically till one god absorbs all the others and becomes all in all. By the time of the Eighteenth Dynasty Amūn, fused with Rē', had outdistanced all the other gods. The heretic king Akhenaten made too sudden a jump towards monotheism, and there was a reaction; but at the end of the Nineteenth Dynasty the gods were being neglected; and by Roman times Egypt was prepared to take an active part in the spread of monotheistic religion. Mohammad carried the process still further by rejecting all compromise and focusing all thought on one indivisible god. He thus reduced all worship to a simple and uniform expression. As the god is a god of right conduct which has prosperity as a consequence, and no longer of prosperity which is to be obtained by right conduct, the ritual has been simplified in the extreme. A technique of prosperity is no longer needed, but only the observance of rules.

That indeed sums up the evolution of Egypt since antiquity: simplification and levelling, with a consequent loss of structure and a strong moral tone. The process

began before Islam. It would probably have continued
without the aid of Islam, since it has affected those depart-
ments of life which lie quite outside the interests of Islam,
such as the village organisation.

The ancient, more complex structure seems to have
served its purpose by fixing the relations of man to man;
then it dissolved away. We might compare Ancient
Egypt to a live coral full of animalcules building up with
admirable activity. As the building is completed they
die, leaving a solid mass to be battered by successive
storms and corroded by events till the clear and geometric
outlines are obliterated.

Every now and then there is renewed activity. We
are now witnessing such a revival. Modernism is the new
leaven that has succeeded to Islam. Its core is so different
from that of Islam that the two seem in no danger of
conflicting. A mechanical gospel seems too remote from
one centred on the unity of God ever to cross its path.
But you cannot drop mechanism into the waters of life
without its sending out eddies that expand and expand till
they must collide with the older eddies of Islam.

The outcome we cannot foretell, but we must note that
the new movement tends more and more to seek its
inspiration from ancient rather than medieval Egypt, in
accordance with a general rule that the more "advanced"
a movement is, the farther back it goes to find its golden
age. It is significant that the statue of the awakening
of Egypt in Cairo reverts to ancient motives. Even more
so does the mausoleum of Sa'ad Zaghlul, the apostle of
Egyptian independence. The Ophthalmological Congress
was honoured with a stamp bearing the Horus eye. When
the Khedivial Mail line registered in Egypt it did so under
the more ancient style of Pharaonic Mail Line.

No revivalist movement has ever brought back the past,
nor will this one; but it can take and adapt old ideas
from the past. That is not, however, the chief benefit

that can be expected of a renewed interest in Ancient Egypt. It may not contribute a single artistic motif, or mechanical device, or scientific concept, but it must inevitably break down much narrowness, enlarge the sympathies, and fire ambitions by bringing into contact with greatness that is not less great for not being modern.

CHAPTER XXIX

India and the Pacific

ORIGINS cannot be reached through the study of any single culture. We could never have reconstituted the speech from which are descended all Indo-European languages by the aid of Latin alone, and what is true of language, which is part of culture, is true of the whole. We cannot follow the course of Indian thought further back than the Vedas without the help of indications from connected cultures; indeed we can scarcely hope to understand the Vedas themselves without using living beliefs as a commentary. We must therefore seek out all the collateral relations of Indian civilisation if we are to infer their common ancestor, and must piece together the information supplied by each of them.

I shall start by giving my reasons for believing that in the Pacific Ocean we find a culture which is closely connected with the archaic culture of India. In order to meet the objection that might be made to a composite picture made up of elements from all over the Pacific, I shall limit my comparison to Fiji, and notice other parts only when they have points in common with Fiji.

I should myself require nothing more in the way of evidence than the identity of the kinship system used by the South Indians and the Koro Sea tribes of Fiji. Both use the standard cross-cousin system—that is, a system deducible from cross-cousin marriage, unmodified by any other principle; the maternal uncle is the same as the father-in-law, the paternal aunt as the mother-in-law, and so on. This system is not now found in Northern India, but it can be shown to have prevailed there in Brahmanical times. The Buddha's genealogy is decisive;

it shows cross-cousin marriage in every generation. Mr
K. Mitra has collected examples from the older literature,
and reports that the *srutis* uphold this form of marriage;
in fact a verse of the *Rigveda* was appointed for such
unions, and was quoted in support of the practice. This
verse, addressed to Indra, says: "Joyfully they offer the
caul (it is the portion even as the maternal uncle's daughter
and the paternal aunt's daughter)". It seems probable
that the supporters of cross-cousin marriage were the
more conservative, and adhered to a custom which was
usual in the Vedic age, but which, like so much else, was
gradually pushed south. It is interesting to note that a
Fijian addresses his female cross-cousin as "my portion".

No doubt the usual objection will be made that because
of the uniformity of human nature the same ideas may
occur independently to different peoples. This proposition
is all very well in the abstract, but unfortunately it is
invoked in the most unreasoning manner to obstruct
every attempt at linking up the cultures of different
peoples. Those who apply it to kinship should pause
to reflect on all that is involved, firstly, in inventing a
kinship system, and secondly, in getting it adopted.
What they imply, consciously or unconsciously, is that
man has a predisposition to classify his relatives in certain
ways, but they never show what this predisposition
consists in, nor what they suppose to be the innate mental
processes involved. It requires very little acquaintance
with kinship systems to satisfy one that there is no such
predisposition; for there are no relationships distinguished
by one people which are not confounded by another, not
even the relation of father and son. A man of a certain
Fijian hill tribe may address his father as "my son", not
from any innate tendency but because he is carrying his
system of alternate generations to its logical conclusion.
We class all our brothers together, and can see nothing
in common between them and our grandfather, but the

same hill tribe classes elder brothers with grandfathers, and younger brothers with grandsons. Some see no difference between the father's sister and the mother's sister; others see no resemblance. It soon becomes evident that, beyond the vague direction given by procreation, there is no predisposition to classify relatives in any particular way; what determines people to develop one system rather than another is not their mental structure, but some theory to which they have subscribed. Rivers and Kohler have shown that certain classificatory systems flow logically from marriage rules. Had they pursued the subject further they would have realised that those rules are based on wider-reaching principles. These we are only beginning to descry; we can see that they are there, but cannot define them with scientific certainty. We must be content with *supposing* that the cross-cousin kinship was the consequence of a division of the aristocracy into two groups, sky people and earth people, who intermarry and by intermarriage secure the proper fertilisation of the earth by the sky. The doctrine of reincarnation also appears to play a great part in these systems. It is probably owing to a form of this doctrine that both Fijians and Tamils of Ceylon prefer to name a boy after his grandfather.

If the cross-cousin system had been invented independently in India, Fiji and America, is it likely that all three should have had the same idea of prescribing opprobrious language between cross-cousins? In Fiji a man makes a point of calling his cross-cousin a cad and such like. In Tamil this is so much the custom that the word *maccan*, cross-cousin, is itself a term of abuse. Mr E. W. Gifford writes to me: "What we know about cross-cousins in California is exceedingly scant, but in two tribes at least there is familiarity between cross-cousins. . . . A recent investigator has found that a joking relationship exists between cross-cousins among the

Serrano in Southern California." The Fijian practice makes it quite clear that there are religious implications at the back of this curious custom.

The religious background is further indicated by the rule that maternal relatives eat the sacrifice. It was once observed in India, where it may go back to the Vedic age. It is still observed by the Mekeo of New Guinea; Seligman does not give their kinship system, but says that their "young men may only marry the girls of their allied village". The Fijians have carried it to great lengths in ceremonies which they share with the Mekeo. The custom and the theory appear very clearly among the Thonga of South Africa, though their kinship system differs somewhat from the standard cross-cousin system.

I think I have adduced enough facts to satisfy anyone that there is much more involved in the cross-cousin system than the classification of relatives; there is a whole theology, which we shall be able to reconstitute if we collect every example of the system and examine it carefully. We shall, however, never succeed if we listen to the soporific dictum: "Similar customs may arise independently in various parts of the world."

I have dealt elsewhere at length with social organisation, and will only say here that every important feature of the Indian caste system finds its parallel in Fiji.

Divine chieftainship is the religion of Eastern Fiji. As this formed the greater part, if not the whole, of religion in archaic times, it may be said that Ancient India and Fiji had the same religion; but the study of religion has too often confined itself to the nature, attributes and activities of supernatural beings, a limitation which is purely arbitrary and precludes any understanding of the origin and function of religion. In this narrow sense the religions of India and Fiji have little in common. Fijian religion is highly simplified; it has but one word for god, demon or spirit of the dead. The Fijians can

16*

indeed distinguish between a ghost and what we should call a god by adding a qualifying term to the word, but it seems that their gods are conceived of as departed spirits, those of the divine ancestors who are reincarnated in the chiefs. The cult of the dead has overspread their theology and assimilated all supernatural beings to one type. Such a religion has little in common with the Vedic religion, which possesses a great variety of gods, demons and spirits; yet close to Fiji, in Polynesia, we find sky gods, sun gods and earth goddesses, and the legends told of them are similar to the Indian myths, so similar for example in the cosmic egg or the separation of heaven and earth that it is impossible to doubt their common origin. There seems little doubt that this religion once occupied at least the coast of Fiji, and was expelled thence by ghost-worshipping negroids, leaving behind most of its accompanying social organisation. It has also left traces in the shape of vague mythical beings called in some parts by the Polynesian name *tupua*, to whose actions the peculiarities of the islands were ascribed. Of these legends I have elsewhere in this volume given examples. Near Lakemba was an island whose god used the reefs as his path; in Ceylon they say the west coast reef is Ravena's path.

Fire-walking is widely practised in India. In Fiji it is confined to a single clan; it is also known in Tahiti. The performance has excited the wonder of all beholders, and in spite of much ingenious speculation no satisfactory explanation is yet forthcoming. Will anyone venture to say that this is the sort of thing that might have occurred independently to different peoples? Is this not swallowing the camel of coincidence while straining at the gnat of migration? No one can deny that the Fijian and Tahitian rites have a common origin; is it then more difficult to coast, as it were, from India to Fiji than to cross the ocean from Fiji to Tahiti? The Fijians do not trace its origin to some hypothetical but unspecified mental process; they say that it was taught them by a goddess, and is an heirloom of the clan.

The death ceremonies differ considerably; India often cremates, but Fiji always buries. Both, however, share the custom of suttee, and in both the devoted widow could be rescued by a kinsman of the deceased to be his wife.

These are some of the resemblances I have picked up while following other paths of research; they are sufficient to establish a common origin for the two cultures. The argument has made it pretty plain that, on the whole, Fijian culture is the more archaic. I say "on the whole", because in the South Seas all culture is simplified. This is partly due to the character of the people, but chiefly because it is impossible to maintain a complicated civilisation in small islands scattered in a vast ocean and destitute of metals. We must expect to find much of the original civilisation lost or atrophied. Even so, however, we cannot derive Fijian culture from that which is mirrored in the Vedic literature, but rather both from a common original which has in India been much battered by the storms of successive invasions, but which has been better preserved in the isolation of the Pacific.

CHAPTER XXX

Decadence in India

LIKE the archaic art of Greece, and the work of the
mediæval primitives, the Indian art of the era before
Christ is distinguished by good and leisurely craftsmanship
but faulty technique. It has not yet mastered its
materials, its ambitions are not high, and it is easily
contented. It is interested in things and not ideas, and
loves to tell a story. The gates of Sanchi, one of which
has been copied for the Indian section of the Victoria and
Albert Museum, are covered with Buddhist legends
simply told. So are the somewhat later monuments at
Amaravati, the spoils of which adorn the staircase of the
British Museum.

Narrative gradually fades out, and sculpture devotes
itself increasingly to the portrayal of ideal figures. It
enters on what we may call the classical phase, which
culminates in the fourth and fifth centuries of our era,
the period known as the Gupta era. It has all the
characteristics which mark classical art elsewhere—
mastery of technique, perfection of form, aspirations that
do not transcend the means of expression, self-restraint,
the complete adaptation of the means to the end. Among
its finest productions is the Sanchi torso at the Victoria
and Albert Museum.

Gupta art, like all art, passes its zenith and declines
into a florid and elegant but nerveless accomplishment,
Then comes the revolt against form without content,
against the excessive restraint imposed by classical
standards of perfection. It is the romantic period of
Indian art. The emotions rise up against the tyranny
of intellect, and in the pursuit of intensity destroy form.

The revolt is in full swing in the seventh century. Even those who do not like its violence and defiance, its exaggeration and cult of the monstrous, must allow a certain greatness to that art. At all events it is better than the inanities of late Gupta, just as the art of our romantics, with all its faults, is better than the artificial and hackneyed work of their predecessors. It may be unhealthy, but it is powerful. Being a revolt against the period immediately preceding it, it harks back to archaic models. Decadence is always archaistic, so old types and old subjects are revived, but no expert will ever mistake an archaistic for an archaic piece of work. The spirit is entirely different, and the spirit always peeps through the surface of imitation. The romantic art of India delights in the presentation of old myths which had suffered the eclipse of Buddhism, but it is not the story that really interests the artist but the opportunity for emotional expression and for flaunting an aggressive creed. The moral bias is typical of decadence.

The revolt wears itself out; the energy departs; the monstrous ceases to be vigorous and is merely tame, and nothing is left but that standardised and uninspired art which is the only Indian art known to most Europeans.

It is the final phase of Indian art which Professor C. G. Seligman had in view when he classed the Indians as an introvert people. He was thinking of the classical period of the Greeks when he put them down as extroverts. The characteristics which he has ranged under those two psychological terms are not so much the mark of race as of phase. To speak in less technical language, we might say that to take an interest in things and rejoice in activity for its own sake is archaic; to be interested in ideas and act from ulterior motives is decadent.

Concerning the progress of art in India, we have abundant evidence. Much of the art is recorded in durable materials such as stone and bronze, and so has survived. Students also abound, for the study of art is a pleasant hobby. But art is not the most important activity of man, and we cannot hope to diagnose the malady of decadence unless we study its symptoms in man's other activities. This is not easy because the materials are scanty and the students few. I will not venture, therefore, to study them in the vastness of India, but will draw on the evidence, meagre as it is, which has come to my notice during my archæological researches in Ceylon.

Ceylon is linked to Northern India from the first century B.C. to the sixth A.D. Then something, we do not know what, happened, and we find Ceylon switched off from Northern to Southern India. Its normal progress is arrested and there seems to have been a drop in artistic achievement; then the ascent is renewed. The peak is reached when India is well advanced in decline; the classical period is in the ninth or tenth century. This shows that the phases are less regular than they appear in Sir Flinders Petrie's *Revolutions of Civilisation.* No doubt there are laws, but their operations are disguised by disturbing factors. The disturbing factor here seems to have been a wave from Dravidian India.

As usual, archaising tendencies appear with the beginning of the decline—that is, in the tenth century. Types of sculpture are revived which had gone out of fashion in the fourth. This archaising appears in religion. The Buddha had been cremated, and his remains deposited in topes, which are hemispherical structures, brick or stone versions of our round barrows. The tope had thus become the chief Buddhist shrine, and up to the fourth century A.D. it was the centre of worship. Kings vied with each other who should build the largest, as the Pyramid builders had to surpass one another, and the dimensions reached vied with those of the Pyramids. The maximum was reached in the fourth century. Then it dropped to smaller dimensions, and became an appendage to a monastery containing other shrines on an equal footing. In the twelfth century the colossal tope reappeared, and the largest ever built belongs to that century. It was a last flicker before the extinction, which seems to have taken place in the next century.

We know from the Pali chronicle that the history of the tope reflects the history of doctrine. Ceylon was converted to Buddhism when it was still in that fairly pure form known as the Little Vehicle. Ritual and mystical tendencies, however, soon spread from India to Ceylon under the name of the Great Vehicle, the form of Buddhism which still prevails from Tibet to Japan. By the fourth century it was disputing the ascendancy and may have won it. In the twelfth the Church was purged of heresy, and Ceylon returned to the Little Vehicle, in which it has remained to the present day.

Travellers in Ceylon have been impressed by the multitude of monasteries found the ancient capitals, and have commented on the rampant parasitism they imply. It is not quite fair, however, to regard these swarms of monks as consisting entirely of drones. A great many were doubtless nothing more, but many others took the place of our schoolmasters, professors, parsons, hospital staffs and charitable organisations. But there is a limit to the number of such persons which society can usefully employ, and if that limit is exceeded the surplus differ from drones only in that they are busy. A country which maintains as many intellectuals as Ceylon had to in the tenth century is top-heavy. The excess of intellectuals is not only superfluous but mischievous, for men whose brains have been trained to activity but are given no useful outlet are sure to find one in pure destructiveness. Further, the multiplication must result in the decline of intellectual achievement, for with the larger intake of recruits the average is lowered, and those born to think are swamped by those for whom thinking is merely a claim to be exempted from the rough work of life. The later history of Sinhalese literature is one of mechanical copying. The monastic order sank lower and lower, so that when it was reorganised in the eighteenth century the king had to send to Burma and Siam in order to renew the apostolic succession.

I have outlined the rise and decadence of India and Ceylon from the first century B.C., but the history of India does not begin then. What came before that? Was India steadily rising from about 1000 B.C., the time of our first records, the Vedas? Does the first century represent a beginning or a continuation? As we go backwards in time from the earliest art we meet with facts that are at first disconcerting. In the third century B.C. arose the most extensive empire that existed in India before the British, and empires are symptomatic of endings rather than beginnings. Before that, in the sixth century, we assist at the birth of a religion which is a characteristic product of decadence. Buddhism is pessimism; existence it says, is pain and sorrow; escape from these evils lies only in extinction. These are not the sentiments of a people with a future, but of one that has lived. There are pessimists in every age, but it is only in periods of decline that they catch the popular ear. We are living in such a period, and so we are in a position to understand Buddhism. The author of Ecclesiastes represents the same phase among the Jews. This disgust with life would have been unintelligible to the early Greeks and Romans, but it was a favourite theme of the Fathers of the Church. It seems clear that in the sixth century B.C. India was in a state of decadence.

Let us analyse the Buddhist doctrine to see if we can discover the cause of its pessimism. Contact, it says, causes sensation, sensation desire, and desire pain. It would seem, then, that the people to whom the Buddha addressed himself so successfully were suffering from an excess of desire; moderate desires, if they can be satisfied, are not painful but pleasurable.   They must have wanted more than they could win or enjoy, and so they suffered. We are familiar with that state of mind in spoilt children, and for that matter in spoilt adults; they have their own way so often that they get no satisfaction from it, whereas to be thwarted causes them intense annoyance.   When life has been made too easy it is apt to become painful. The legend of the Buddha shows that the Indians had made this psychological discovery.   It depicts him as living in luxury, never allowed to come into contact with the ugly side of life.   He becomes satiated with pleasures and over-sensitive to the unpleasant.   The crisis comes one night after the usual pleasures; his wife and his dancing-girls are asleep, and the sight fills him with disgust.   He escapes from the palace and wanders forth into solitude.   At first he goes to the other extreme, and almost starves himself to death, but finding no balm in extreme asceticism he seeks a middle way, a life of renunciation without severity.   He suppresses all desire, and retires from the world of the senses into a world of ideas.   He seeks internal peace.

It matters little whether the legend is true or not. Fiction is often truer than history, for fiction tells us what the people feel, and evidently they felt that the need of their times was not the conqueror of empires but the man who, having conquered the tyranny of desire, showed others how this could be done.

Posidonius, a late Stoic, declared, like the Buddha, that "pain arose out of passion and desire"; in his time, towards the end of the republic, Rome was beginning to suffer the pains of decadence.

Men at the present day are merely restating in more modern, and sometimes in more scientific terms, the discovery which had been made by the Buddhists and contemporary sects some two thousand four hundred years ago, and remade later by Stoics and Christians.

It would lead us too far afield to make an exhaustive catalogue of the characteristics that mark Buddhism as a reaction to decadent conditions. Only one more need be mentioned. No religion has ever carried pacifism to such extremes as Buddhism. Non-resistance is one of its keynotes. To take the life, even of an animal, is sinful, and this sin must be avoided at the cost, if necessary, of one's own life.

If Buddhism is the product of a decadent age, it must have been preceded by a classical period, and the classical by an archaic one. Our earliest records are the Vedas, of about 1000 B.C. It is no longer possible to regard them, with the earlier Vedic scholars, as the spontaneous effusions of primitive man just awakening to the beauties of the world and bursting into song like birds at a spring dawn. Mankind was already very old in 1000 B.C., and the Vedas had centuries of poetic technique and ritual behind them. The error of the discoverers of the Vedas does, however, bear witness to the freshness and manly vigour which marks those hymns, and which contrasts with the weariness and soft prolixity of the Buddhist writings. The moral contrast is equally remarkable. Buddhist hymns and prose subordinate everything to morality and idealism. Morality in the sense of being saintly does not worry the Vedic singer; his interest is in the increase of progeny, cattle, health, wealth and security. He has no wish to proselytise, for that would mean sharing with others, even enemies, the secret of material prosperity. He is innocent of pacifism; it is part of his religion to smite the heathen.

The next stage is represented, about 800 B.C., by a voluminous prose literature on the ritual. There is no longer the same freshness; cold reasoning prevails. There is as yet, however, no sign of idealism; the end is still purely practical, and the ritual aims at nothing more than material prosperity. We hear much of evil, but it is not moral evil or sin, but only the hostile powers which blight man and his cattle, and abet his enemies.

In the later ritual books a kind of mysticism begins to make its appearance. An increasing stress is laid upon knowledge as a substitute for ritual. Asceticism comes more and more to the front. From an early time it was prescribed as a preparation for the sacraments, but by degrees it overspread the whole lives of religious men. As world weariness increased, it became a favourite means of escape from the world. And thus we come down again to Buddhism.

Thus between 1000 B.C. and the present day India has passed through two cycles of rise and decadence. There is nothing surprising in this. Minoan Greece declined, and then emerged again as the Greece we know. On the ruins of the Roman Empire a new civilisation was built. Sir Flinders Petrie thinks Egypt was revived several times.

We can now understand what has seemed a paradox to students of Indian art. Buddhism is pessimistic and not for the happy; it scorns the senses and seeks to escape from them. Yet early Buddhist art is happy and softly sensual; it delights in alluring female figures and worldly pleasures. The paradox is only apparent; early Buddhist art belongs to an entirely different phase from the original Buddhist gospel. The art has inherited the doctrines of the gospel, but the spirit has passed away. The bas-reliefs of Barhut and Sanchi stand in the same relation to the Buddhist canon as the art of mediæval Europe to the New Testament and the Fathers. Primitive Buddhist artists, like the Italian and Flemish primitives, took their subjects from the preceding decadence, but not their outlook; the pious legends were merely good stories to tell in pictures.

Just as our Renaissance dropped Christian for Pagan subjects, so the Indian Renaissance, which began in the fourth century, harked back from Buddhist hagiology to the old Vedic gods. There was this difference, however, that whereas the Pagan gods were revived merely as a poetic fiction, the Vedic gods who had never died out were revived in earnest.

I have dwelt on Buddhism because it reveals the nature of decadence better than anything else in Indian history or perhaps in any history. The gospels may grapple with the same disease, but it is by way of exhortation; they offer no diagnosis. Buddhism is more methodical and comes nearer to our modern psychology, not in its conclusions but in its manner of proceeding. It marks an important stage in the history of mental pathology. The Greek philosophers may have far surpassed the Indians in their analysis of mental processes, but India has made considerable contributions to the study of functional disorders. This it has done not as the Greeks would have done, as a matter of purely speculative interest, but in a manner typically Indian, for the practical purpose of removing suffering. One reason why the Indians have been so interested in the disease is that they have suffered from it so acutely. For decadence is a functional disease of society made up of all the functional troubles of the individuals who compose it.

ACKNOWLEDGEMENTS

These chapters were originally published in the places listed below. We thank the publishers for their permission to reprint them.

Ch. I. "The Life-giving Myth", in *The Labyrinth*, ed. by S. H. Hooke (London: S.P.C.K., 1935), 261–81.

Ch. II. "Flying Through the Air", *Indian Antiquary*, LII (1923), 80–2.

Ch. III. "Turning into Stone", *Folklore*, LIX (1942), 84–8.

Ch. IV. "The Common Sense of Myth", *American Anthropologist*, XVIII (1916), 307–18.

Ch. V. "The Purpose of Ritual", *Folklore*, XLVI (1935), 343–9.

Ch. VI. "Ritual and Emotion", *Character and Personality*, VII (1939), 201–10.

Ch. VII. "The Origin of Monotheism", *Folklore*, XXXIII (1922), 282–93.

Ch. VIII. "The Divinity of the Guest", *Ceylon Journal of Science*, Section G, I, Part 3 (1927), 125–31.

Ch. IX. "Yakshas and Väddas", in *Studia Indo-Iranica: Essays presented to Professor W. Geiger*, ed. by Walther Wüst (Leipzig, 1931), 3–10.

Ch. X. "Money", *Ceylon Journal of Science*, Section G, I, Part 2 (1925), 85–90.

Ch. XI. "Modern Critique", *Man*, XXIX (1929), 138–43, art. 102.

Ch. XII. "In the Grip of Tradition", *Folklore*, XLIX (1938), 258–69.

Ch. XIII. "Snobbery", in *Custom is King: Essays presented to R. R. Marett*, ed. by L. H. Dudley Buxton (London: Hutchinson, 1946), 157–65.

Ch. XIV. "Chastity", *Folklore*, L (1939), 288–91.

Ch. XV. "Saviours", *Folklore*, XLVII (1936), 183–9.

Ch. XVI. "The Age-Limit", *Folklore*, XLVIII (1937), 260–3.

Ch. XVII. "Childhood Ceremonies", *Folklore*, XLVI (1935), 281–3.

Ch. XVIII. "Baptism by Fire", *Man*, XXXVII (1937), 87–8, art. 109.

Ch. XIX. "Initiation and Manhood", *Man*, XXXV (1935), 20–2, art. 23.

Ch. XX. "Initiation and Healing", *Man*, XXXVII (1937), 41–3, art. 54.

Ch. XXI. "Tattooing and Healing", *Man*, XXXVII (1937), 167–8, art. 196.

Ch. XXII. "Kinship Systems", *Anthropos*, XXII (1937), 345–51.

Ch. XXIII. "Blood-Brotherhood", *Man*, XXXV (1935), 113–15, art. 127.

Ch. XXIV. "Covenants", *Man*, XXXV (1935), 149–51, art. 164.

Ch. XXV. "The Uterine Nephew", *Man*, XXIII (1923), 11–13, art. 4.

Ch. XXVI. "Why Study Savages?"

Ch. XXVII. "Are Savages Custom-bound?" *Man*, XXVII (1927), 220–1, art. 150.

Ch. XXVIII. "From Ancient to Modern Egypt", in *The Legacy of Egypt*, ed. by S. R. K. Glanville (Oxford: Clarendon Press, 1942), 369–93 [original title: "The Legacy to Egypt"].

Ch. XXIX. "India and the Pacific", *Ceylon Journal of Science*, Section G, I, Part 2 (1925), 61–84.

Ch. XXX. "Decadence in India", in *Essays presented to C. G. Seligman*, ed. by E. E. Evans-Pritchard (London: Kegan Paul, Trench, Trubner, 1934), pp. 85–96.

INDEX

Agni, 99, 103
Albigenses, 156
Antigone, 150
Aristotle, 25

Baptism, 47, 144
Bezpopovtchina, 156
Birth ceremonies, 153–4
Blackman, Dr A. M., 203, 207
Bloch, M., 149
Blood-brotherhood, 185 ff.
Borough English, 132
Brahman, 11
Bride, West African, 120
Buddhism, 17, 18, 56, 76, 243

Canney, Prof. M. A., 158, 165
Caste, 237
Charlemagne, 124
Chieftainship, divine, 237
Child-marriage, 135, 150
Church, Christian, 76, 144
Circumcision, 165–6
Clothing, 131–2
Colonies, 136
Comans, 187
Coronation, 121
Covenants, 190 ff.
Cremation rites, 154
Cross-cousin marriage, 234–6
Currency, shell, 98

Death rites, 145
Demon, 87
Dionysius, 105, 108 ff.
Duff-Gordon, Lady, 208

Eddystone, 48, 51
Egypt and Uganda, 203
Eskimo, 45
Etiquette, 205

Evans-Pritchard, Prof. E. E., 57, 131, 183, 185
Evil eye, 228
Exchange, Fijian, 101–3

Fairs, Egyptian, 229
Fire-walking, 157, 238
Fletcher, Miss, 48, 154, 162, 189
Forde, Prof. C. D., 24

Gifts, Fijian, 99
Gnostics, 156
Gold, 99 ff.
Grote, G., 112
Guest, 78 ff.
Gupta, 240–1

Hako ceremony, 48–9, 189 ff.
Heaven and earth, 31
Hero pattern, 146
Homer, 9–10
Horse-sacrifice, Vedic, 145, 191
Horus, 72
Hymns, Vedic, 50

Igalas, 191
Igbo, 48
Inca, 50
Incantation, Assyrian, 19
Indra, 14–16
Initiation, Australian, 160, 164; Eddystone, 162; Fijian, 160; Indian, 145; Omaha, 161–2; Shawnee, 168; Maya, 164
Islam, 222–3

Jukun, 192
Junod, H. A., 197

251

Kalevala, 19
King of Ceylon, 145–6, 242; divinity of, 67–9; of Egypt, 67–8, 209 ff.; of England, 69, 72, 119; Homeric, 67–8; Indian, 69; of Israel, 75; Siamese, 144; Sumerian, 67; of Tahiti, 29–30; Vedic, 125
Kinship, 174 ff.
Kiwai Papuans, 154
Koryak, 50

Livy, 105
Loritja, 160, 191
Lot's wife, 33

Mahāvamsa, 88 ff.
Mair, Dr L. P., 173
Marriage, Indian, 143; royal, 119 ff.
Mead, Dr Margaret, 183
Medicine, Egyptian, 227
Middletown, 129–30
Mikado, 31
Mint, 100
Miracles, Buddhist, 28
Missionaries, Christian, 134
Mommsen, 111
Money, 97 ff., 219
Morte d'Arthur, 10, 26
Muhasena, legend of, 34–5
Muir, J., 115
Myth, Aranda, 21–2; Christian, 26; Fijian, 20, 33, 40; German, 27; Malay, 19; Rotuman, 41, 43; Sinhalese, 33; theories of, 39; Vedic, 14, 15; Winnebago, 23, 49; Yuma, 24

Nala, story of, 28
Napoleon, 124–5

Odysseus, 78–9
Oedipus, 147–8
Origen, 157

Pacifism, Buddhist, 246
Pessimism, 244
Petrie, Sir Flinders, 113, 242, 247
Pigs, 224

Plutarch, 109, 116
Polygamy, 133
Popul Vuh, 146
Porphyrogenitus, 143
Posidonius, 245
Prayer, Winnebago, 52
Priests, Egyptian, 216; Fijian, 87

Quakers, 55
Queen, 119–123

Raglan, Lord, 146–8
Renaissance, 9
Retirement, Indian, 151
Ritual, Aranda, 51; Buddhist, 50, 56; Fijian, 48, 56, 60; Indian, 60
Romulus, 108
Rose, Prof. H. J., 105

Sacred marriage, 145
Sacred Prostitution, 140
Sacrificial victim, 151
St Catherine, 150
St Chrysostom, 52
Saints, 229–30; Egyptian, 60
Sanskrit, 10, 11, 328
Seligman, Prof. C. G., 203, 241; and Mrs B. Z., 93, 188
Simon Magus, 156
Sister's son, 195–8
Soma, 12, 13, 16
Sona, story of, 81
Sophocles, 113–4
Stones worshipped, 37
Strabo, 151
Sun-god, 72
Suttee, 239

Tattooing, 169–70
Temple, Kandyan, 107
Topes, 242

Water-wheel, 208
Wheel of life, 155
Witchcraft, Zande, 57, 61

Zeus, 78, 80
Zionism, 126

DATE DUE

DEC 11 2009	

GAYLORD   PRINTED IN U.S.A.